Sam

Sam

The Autobiography of Sam Torrance

BBC BOOKS

Acknowledgements

To all the managers who helped me: Derek Pillage, Sandra Greenslade at IMG, David Barlow at IMG, Katrina Johnson at IMG, and last but not least my current manager who helped us so much through the Ryder Cup, Vicky Cuming, and her able assistant, Helen Wilson.

To all my sponsors: thanks for the faith.

To my coaches: there's only one – my dad.

The European Tour: Ken Schofield and thanks to Gordon Simpson for making sure my memory is accurate – too many others to mention, but thanks for everything.

The caddies: Willy Aitcheson, Matty, Tiny, Billy Rutherford, Brian Dunlop, Malcolm Mason and John Wilkie.

To the players who made my journey so special – you all know who you are but there are three I have to mention: John O'Leary, David Feherty and Michael King.

To all the Ryder Cup teams I played in, the one I vice-captained and the one I captained – thank you for so many special memories.

To my dear friend Alan Fraser, without whose help I could never have written this book.

And finally, to all my fans who have supported me for over 30 years – you did make a difference. Thank you.

Published by BBC Books, BBC Worldwide Limited,
Woodlands, 80 Wood Lane, London W12 0TT

First published 2003. This paperback edition published 2004.
Copyright © Sam Torrance 2003 and 2004
The moral right of the author has been asserted.

ISBN 9780563521440

Commisioning Editor: Ben Dunn. Project Editor: Helena Caldon
Copy Editor: Tim Glynne-Jones. Designer: Linda Blakemore
Picture Researcher: David Cottingham
Production Controller: Arlene Alexander

Printed and bound in Great Britain by
Clays Ltd, St Ives plc

Picture credits

*BBC Books would like to thank the following for providing photographs
and for permission to reproduce copyright material. While every effort
has been made to trace and acknowledge all copyright holders, we
would like to apologize should there have been any errors or omissions.*

Photographs copyright © of the author except for:
Section 1: p.2 (top) Courtesy Teignmouth Golf Club; *Section 2:* p.3
(bottom) Steve Munday/Getty Images; *Section 3:* pp1&2 Dave
Cannon/Getty Images; p.3 (bottom) Stephen Munday/Getty Images;
p.5 Getty Images; p.6 Ross Kinnaird/Getty Images; p.7 Andrew
Redington/Getty Images; p.8 Ross Kinnaird/Getty Images; *Section 4:*
p.2 (bottom) Ian Stewart/Phil Sheldon/The Golf Picture Library; p.5
Stephen Munday/Getty Images; p.7 Matthew Harris/The Golf Picture
Library; p.8 Jamie Squire/Getty Images.

The Random House Group Limited supports The Forest Stewardship
Council (FSC®), the leading international forest certification organisation.
Our books carrying the FSC label are printed on FSC® certified paper.
FSC is the only forest certification scheme endorsed by the leading
environmental organisations, including Greenpeace. Our
paper procurement policy can be found at
www.randomhouse.co.uk/environment

Contents

1 My proudest moment · 9

2 From Largs to Sunningdale · 11

3 'Have you got a game?' · 25

4 On tour · 39

5 To boldly go... · 57

6 Yankees and presses · 74

7 Ryder Cup at last · 86

8 The putt that changed my life · 103

9 Suzanne · 120

10 The broomhandle · 132

11 Flying rugby tackle · 151

12 The wedding · 162

13 'Guid drink' · 178

14 Man of God · 187

15 Jesse resigns · 202

16 September 11 · 218

17 Langer's neck · 235

18 One Tiger and 12 lions · 255

19 Out of the shadows · 273

20 'Your captain here' · 293

Career statistics · 322

Index · 326

To my mum and dad who gave me everything;
to my wife, Suzanne, who means everything;
and to my children, Daniel, Phoebe and Anouska,
who are everything.

1

My proudest moment

'What has been the hardest part of the week for you?' the American television reporter asked.

'Not watching my dad play,' my then 14-year-old son Daniel replied without the slightest hesitation as we stood on the practice putting green at the De Vere Belfry at the start of the Sunday singles.

I cried.

Yet it had been precisely the not playing that made captaining Europe to Ryder Cup victory the greatest achievement of my life, greater by far than holing the winning Ryder Cup putt on the same green 17 years earlier. I have always been a player: 685 tournaments on the European Tour in 32 years between 1971 and 2003, more than any other golfer. I play golf. It is what I do. Being a captain, being responsible for others and for myself, is not what I did. Making selections, making decisions and making speeches – these were all alien to me.

That is why I am more proud of what I did as Ryder Cup captain than anything I have ever achieved in golf. It was the most important thing I had ever done by a mile, and to have done it successfully was as special as anything will ever be to me. Even if by some freak I were to win the Open Championship – and players in their 50s tend not to – it would not match the Ryder Cup.

You've got to realise that I'm no saint. I would say that I am a good person, but I can have a drink or two and I can party with the best. I am not a rebel and I don't think badly of myself, but it was a hell of a job for someone like me to take on. Very different than it would have been for someone like my old friend and fellow Scot Bernard Gallacher. Bernard has always been right down the line, straight as a die.

It is not really for me to say that I am a character. But I am a character, given to the occasional bout of extreme behaviour. So taking on the captaincy was huge for me. I had to toe the line. It was special to me that I could do that. Many thought I could not. Some within golf believed I was very much the wrong man for the job.

'You can do it,' my wife Suzanne said. 'I believe you can do anything if you put your mind to it. You just have to want it enough.'

That was not in question. My whole life has been the Ryder Cup. My career has been about trying to get into the team, eventually making the team and then staying in the team. The world knew how important the Ryder Cup was to me, even before the life-changing event of holing the winning putt in 1985. To be captain – and, moreover, a winning captain – has been an experience second to none.

I have been on a tremendous high ever since. Everywhere I go, complete strangers, even people who don't play golf, stop to congratulate me. Eighteen months later, as I have embarked on a second career in Senior golf in the USA, it still has not stopped. It will never stop for me. It will never leave me, ever. I will be dead before it leaves me. It was really that special.

But people react to the moment of victory in different ways. Bernard did a funny little jump before running to lift Philip Walton in the air. I looked down at the ground and my whole life flashed in front of my eyes.

Starting in a town called Largs.

2

From Largs to Sunningdale

From the stone wall to the right of the 18th tee at Routenburn Golf Club you get a panoramic view of Largs, the Firth of Clyde – the sea to us – and across to Millport.

I used to sit there as a ten-year-old, waiting for the priests and their money. My life-long love of golf and gambling began with the shillings that I pocketed from Brother Nicholas and his holy fourball, continuing to the money matches for which the Sunningdale Club is renowned and on to the betting games that the professionals play.

Largs to Sunningdale, perched at each end of the golfing and social spectrum, is the journey of my life. I made it twice – as a 17-year-old, side-burned, wide-eyed Scot who became an assistant to Arthur Lees at the Surrey club and again 15 years later when I set up home with Suzanne. I was by then 'the man who holed the putt to win the Ryder Cup'.

We bought a house in Virginia Water, just three miles from Sunningdale, though half that distance if only they would reopen a back gate at the top of the practice ground. The level crossing can be a nightmare. I used to drop off the kids before heading to the clubhouse for breakfast with the guys. 'Queenie', as Michael King is known in the game, my great friend and fellow professional, would be there. So, too, the likes of Huge Bum, Dickie, Dodge and Cashmere.

We would sit round a big table, chewing the fat, telling stories, enjoying a blether, taking the piss out of each other. Having fun. I think my whole life has been based on having fun. What could be better?

It is a bit of a myth about Sunningdale being snooty. There's money around all right, and no shortage of tradition. Rollers in the car park and high-rollers in the comfortable leather chairs of the clubhouse. Captains of industry everywhere, Queenie knows them all, but there is precious little snobbery.

Sunningdale is full of eccentrics, like the Hon. Paddy Packenham, the late Lord Longford's son. Paddy would always be turning up wearing different coloured socks or different shoes or even no socks at all. His trousers would be held up by a tie instead of a belt. Paddy is still around and I still play a lot with his son, Harry. Paddy once told me I would never make it on tour unless I improved my short irons. He was dead right.

I love Sunningdale. Sunningdale Old, as the name suggests, the more senior of two wonderful courses, is absolutely magnificent. The debate continues to rage about the merits of the Old, designed in 1901 by Willie Park, and the New, the 1922 creation of Harry Colt. Basically, the New is tougher, the Old more majestic, more acclaimed and more popular with the members. *Golf World* has regularly ranked it the best heathland course in Britain and always in the top 20 overall. If I had one round to play before I died, it would be there rather than at St Andrews or Augusta or wherever. It is just sublime. A great setting, great ambience, great halfway hut, great clubhouse, great everything. Great food, provided by Chris Osborne, the chef, who weaved his culinary magic when I was an assistant more than 30 years ago and still does to this day.

So, you can imagine my delight – not to mention disbelief – when I received a letter from Myles Elliott, the captain, inviting me to become an honorary member.

I was so proud to be asked to join under the system of the captain's prerogative. When I went there as an assistant in 1971, I wondered if I would ever make it into the clubhouse. Now I was being made an honorary member. Imagine, the wee boy from Largs an honorary member of Sunningdale.

Largs and other such Ayrshire coastal towns are the destinations in mind when Glaswegians talk about going 'doon the water', either at weekends or for the two-week summer holiday known as the 'Glasgow Fair'. More so before the advent of the cheap package holiday made the search for sun, or rather escape from rain, affordable. They would walk along what we called the 'prom' or what the sign declared as The Esplanade. Then it would be into Nardini's for an ice cream. Wherever you go in the world, from Helensburgh to Hong Kong, from St Andrews to St Kitts, mention of Largs usually brings the reflex response, 'Nardini's'. Daniela Nardini, the sharp-tongued Scottish temptress in *This Life*, is one of the more exciting flavours to have come out of that ice cream factory.

Lou Macari, of Celtic, Manchester United and Scotland, emerged from the opposition. A list of famous people from Largs would not be the longest. There was Sir Thomas Makdougall Brisbane, an astronomer among many other things. He served under the Duke of Wellington at the Battle of Waterloo before he became Governor General of New South Wales in Australia, and eventually gave his name to a crater on the moon, as well as to the Queensland capital. Lord William Thomas Kelvin, the 19th-century physicist and inventor, was born in Belfast but lived in Largs. The fact that he is buried next to Sir Isaac Newton in Westminster Abbey suggests he conjured up much more than the electrical theory for submarine telegraph cables, whatever that may be.

Of more modern vintage are Gallagher and Lyle, not my fellow golfers and good friends but the musical double act, Benny and Graham, whose tapes and CDs I have listened to over the years – and not just out of hometown loyalty.

Largs is perhaps most celebrated as the place where the Vikings landed. In 1263 King Alexander III defeated Hakon of Norway at the Battle of Largs, a brutal two-day contest fought on land and sea. Seven centuries later, the battles between me and my dad were just beginning. They were to prove almost as fierce.

I was born in Largs on 24 August 1953, a son for 16-year-old local beauty June and Bob, or Robert, as she still insists on calling him. I turned out to be an only child, despite determined efforts to provide me with a brother or a sister. For the one and only time in my life, I was early, more than a month so. I was born with no fingernails and one ear to the side, though it was my size which caused much hilarity. My mother says my grandmothers could not stop laughing. 'How,' they wondered, 'could two big people like us produce such a tiny thing? Not even five pounds.' My paternal grandmother, Marion, took it upon herself to bathe me in oil every morning.

I feel the irony in every calorie I now count. A lifetime weight problem has seen me have more diets than hot dinners, even if some of the more blown-up photographs in this book suggest otherwise. But at the start of 2003, by way of preparation for turning 50 and becoming a Senior golfer, I was giving a wide berth to potatoes and bread as part of my non-carbohydrate diet. Some people might be surprised to discover just how disciplined I am about it. For all my apparent reckless behaviour and indiscipline, when I put my mind to something, I carry it through.

Just getting food on the table was a problem for the Torrances in the 1950s and 1960s. Life was so hard and money so short that twice a day, during a dawn-to-dusk shift as greenkeeper at Kelburne (the private golf club in Largs), Dad would carry a bag of logs a couple of miles to our council house in Alexander Avenue so that the fire could be kept going.

Lee Trevino, who became a friend, was always going on about his poor upbringing, with enough one-liners to feed several hilarious stand-up routines. 'My family was so poor they couldn't afford kids. The lady next door had me,' he would say. 'I was 21 years old before I knew Manuel Labour wasn't a Mexican,' was another of my favourites.

If Manuel Labour was a Mexican, manual labour came from the west of Scotland. Dad was a bricklayer before becoming a greenkeeper and a professional golfer, though not the kind of professional we recognise today, with their cashmere sweaters and Rolex watches. He wore overalls and drove tractors and cut greens and sold tees and, when all that was done, gave lessons. He played golf in his spare time, i.e. before light in the morning and in the twilight hours before darkness fell on those long summer nights.

His dad was a bus driver and a boxing-booth fighter, the guy you had to go three rounds with to win a quid or a fiver. Sammy, after whom I was named, according to the old Scottish tradition applicable to the first born, was as broad as he was tall, 'the wrong shape for golf', according to my father.

Still, Sammy liked to play and was as proud of Bob's golfing ability as Dad became of mine. My only memory of Grandad was of a face looking into my pram in the back garden. He died tragically on a golf course, having run three miles across town and up the steep hill to

Routenburn after a shift on the buses in order to caddie for my dad in an exhibition. His exertions – and perhaps a few whiskies for fortification from a gallery well stocked with half-bottles – proved too much for his heart.

Marion, his wife, was a French polisher. She worked on the *Queen Mary* and the *Queen Elizabeth*, two of the great ocean-going liners built in the famous Clydeside shipyards. Apart from the office girls, French polishers were the only women among the tens of thousands of shipyard workers. They dressed in men's overalls but wore headscarves instead of cloth caps. Her hardest ever task, it is said, was stripping down the white driver from my father's first clubs, a hickory set of Donaldson's New Yorkers. It took her months.

My mother's father was a baker. She was the youngest of six children and the only girl. She had five older brothers and got hell when she started going out with my father. 'I was his lush brush. The whispering was just horrendous. It was so different then. I was not quite 17 when I had Sam. I had never washed a dish, never cleaned any clothing. My mother had done everything; I thought the end of the world had come.'

But she says I was a very good baby, very happy, never one to demand a dummy. 'Just a good wee boy.' Dad was working all day, every day and playing golf at night, often until as late as 11pm. My mother used to take me to the pictures. It was about all we could afford. She would grip my hand to keep me quiet. I remember us seeing Yul Bryner in *The King and I*. I've loved the cinema ever since and became quite a film buff.

I worship my father, though he can be very hard and we have not always seen eye to eye on things. There is a strong-willed streak in both of us which, judging by an incident at St Andrews a couple of years ago, has been passed down to the next generation of golfing Torrances.

I was caddieing for my son, Daniel, when he topped his drive into the rough.

'A 2-iron please, Dad,' he said.

I gave him what could be described as an old-fashioned look. 'You cannae hit a 2-iron from there,' I said.

'I want my 2-iron.'

Dad was close by, sporting a grin as wide as the River Clyde. 'Sam,' he said, 'I had 40 years of that; it's your turn now.'

I deliberately use the word 'strong-willed' instead of 'stubborn' because I always think the latter has negative connotations. I see my strong will as a big positive. I am right until proved wrong and perfectly open to reason in between.

Dad was the hardest-working man you could ever know. You just could not tire him. Even now, though in his seventies, he stands for hour after hour on the practice range at tournaments, or in one of the bays at the sportscotland National Centre Inverclyde, high above Largs, coaching some of Europe's finest golfers. He has always been my one and only teacher, though nowadays I willingly share him with the likes of Ryder Cup players Padraig Harrington, Thomas Bjorn and Paul McGinley, and dozens of others. Later life has rewarded him with the status of being one of the greatest coaches in the world.

Considering his obsession with golf, Dad was a late starter. He never hit a ball until he was 16 and that, by his own reckoning, was more by accident than design. Sammy was playing his usual Sunday fourball. Dad walked up the hill to meet him and got there just as they were driving off at the 17th. His brother-in-law took out a new ball and hit it into the right rough. Panic stations. Nobody could afford to lose a new ball like that. But Dad walked straight to it.

Someone said that he had a great eye for golf and that he should try a shot. So he was given a hickory clique, a 2-iron, and had a go. He nailed it. 'It gave me such a great feeling,' he told me. 'I have been practising for more than 50 years and I have never had the same feeling since!' Even into his 70s, he hits hundreds of balls every day, many more than me. He's still searching for that feeling, still looking for 'The Secret'. I keep telling him: there isn't one.

It was not until after the family moved to Rossendale in Lancashire that I began to play golf. But I was not so keen that the Ryder Cup represented a more attractive proposition than playing with my pals. I refused to go to the match at Royal Lytham in 1961. Dad never lets me forget it.

But my friendship with Stephen Bury, a policeman's son, was cemented on the nine-hole course where my dad was professional and a greenkeeper, too. No rest for the wicked. No rest for Mum either, as she worked in the pie factory, the pro shop and, as if that were not enough, served lunches in the clubhouse to earn extra money.

Stephen and Sam: we were inseparable. If I did not stay the night at his house, he stayed at mine. We began to play golf together all the time. I was eight years old and just starting to become a 'wild bugger', according to 'faither's' strict interpretation of behaviour. It was really no more than childish pranks. For example, we would lie in hiding in the deep valley that separated tee from green at one of Rossendale's short holes ready to pinch the members' balls that fell short and were sucked back into the undergrowth. Dad found himself in front of the committee for that.

The first indication that I might have some talent for golf came at Rossendale, though I remember nothing of the occasion. According to Dad, I ran into the house one day claiming that I had shot 39 for the nine holes. I was nine years old.

'You lying git,' was apparently Dad's encouraging reaction and he took me straight out onto the course, where I shot 39 again.

That year, after five blissfully happy ones at Rossendale, we moved back to Largs and to the tied house overlooking the bay which went with the job of professional. It is there to this day, virtually unchanged, though a 2-ft larch tree from the Scottish Highlands, planted in the garden on our arrival, now towers above the chimney pots.

Golf began to take over my life. Within a year I was on that wall, anxiously looking down the 17th for a sight of the priests. Brother Nicholas knew what I wanted. The bet was quickly struck and we would play down the last for a shilling – 5p to the post-decimalisation generations. A shilling was worth something then. If the 18th was halved, we would play up the 1st. I always won, whether it took one or two holes. It never took more. When I was older, I would play full rounds with the Brothers.

I played for money all the time, whether single holes, full rounds or just on and around the 18th green and practice putting area. We chipped and putted or just putted for hour after hour after hour for pennies, tanners and shillings.

Golf has always been a gambling game, from the five-bob a corner Saturday morning fourball to the complicated mixtures of presses, double presses and whatever played by professionals.

I firmly believe that playing golf for money at such a tender age gave me an edge in later life. It became a habit that I could not break. Not that I wanted to. I have hardly ever played a non-tournament round without what I call a 'wee bet'. It made practice rounds more like tournament rounds. It sharpened my concentration and meant I worked on every shot as opposed to just hitting the ball. If there was something on it, I would try all the harder. That was always my attitude.

That was as true on the green baize as on the green. If I had not become a professional golfer, I might have tried to make a living playing snooker. Who knows how good I might have become had I channelled all my energies into snooker rather than golf?

To my great disappointment, I have never managed a century break, my best being a couple of 98s and three 96s in practice or friendly matches. Before the children came along I would practice as much as seven hours a day in the winter. There were a few of us on the European Tour who could pot black, and the rest of the colours; Ian Woosnam and D. J. Russell, to mention just a couple. John Hawksworth was my opponent for an 11-hour marathon session in Belgium once.

Who could ever forget that final at the Crucible in 1987 when Dennis Taylor defeated Steve Davis on the final black in the final frame to win the world title? Well, Dennis went straight from Sheffield to a pro-am at Woburn, followed by eight hours of snooker with Sam Torrance and a few friends.

I did not need to be asked twice to take part in a televised professional/celebrity event. My partner was Cliff Thorburn. I made the highest amateur break of 35, not bad but I was desperate for the century. Another made-for-television special saw me play golf and snooker with Stephen Hendry and Alan McManus.

Snooker has been my second sport since boyhood. From the age of 11, all my spare time was split between Routenburn golf course and the Stevenson Institute, the archetypal smoke-filled snooker hall with its contrasting shadowy figures and bright-coloured clicking balls.

To breathe in the intoxicating atmosphere was to risk nasal congestion from a potent mixture of Woodbine and chalk dust. I loved it. It was where the big boys gathered.

The Stevenson Institute, tucked away in one of the back streets in the centre of Largs, was run with a cue of tungsten by Mary Beck, a tyrant who stood 4ft nothing in her high heels. Great lumbering 6ft-plus giants with a drink in them would meekly do her bidding. What she said went. No question.

You had to be 13 or 14 to get in. I was a regular, straight from school every winter's day. No one ever asked my age. Then one day I had a hole in one and the local paper printed a story under the headline: '11-year-old son of Routenburn pro gets hole in one.'

On my next visit I was taken into the office. I was petrified. I thought I would be banned for life. But she smiled, told me I was a well-behaved boy and said I could keep coming.

Of course, I was playing for money. The Stevenson Institute was the kind of place where guys would appear … and disappear just as suddenly. A bloke from Glasgow turned up one day. He was playing by himself on table 4, generally regarded as the best of the eight. I was in my early teens, but I could really play by then.

'Do you want a game?' I asked.

'I only play for money,' he grunted in reply.

I put my hand in my pocket and pulled out my only coin. 'I've got half a crown.'

'All right.'

I beat him. If he was a hustler, he was not a very good one. I had watched his game and I thought, 'I can take him.'

The compulsion was to make money. There was no sense of embarrassment at reducing everything to such a basic capitalist instinct. We were not the poorest in the town by any means but cash was tight and old traditions died hard. We lived in a working-class community where the men worked their bollocks off, gave their wives the housekeeping at the end of the week and drank all their 'pocket money' – all of it – on a Friday night. The cycle was repeated every week, every month and every year. That was my dad's routine, his dad's and probably his dad's before that.

I always wanted to make money. If I saw a way to make money, I would grab it. That's what life was. You needed money.

Occasionally, this desire took me across a line. My love of gambling even at such a young age made me a bit of an addict on the one-armed bandit in the Routenburn clubhouse. The more so since I found a way of winning all the time. The old Bally machine, as it was called, with Bally's wild, allowed you to hold a reel only once. I discovered a way to hold again and again until you got the jackpot. Wow, the jackpot! And not just one jackpot. I emptied the machine every day for a while. Then suddenly, mysteriously, without anything ever being said, the machine was removed.

Life was hectic. There was certainly no time for homework. But I never bunked off. I never played truant. My parents would not have permitted it. Every day I walked down the hill from Routenburn, across town and up the hill on the other side to Largs High, a bloody long way. The school bus stopped near my house on Red Road but it would not pick me up because I lived inside the town area. Had our house been a few hundred yards further away, I could have caught that damned bus.

Every weekday I repeated that tortuous journey, though not for that many years. I left school at the age of 13. All I wanted to do was play golf.

I was scratch within a year, albeit only scratch at

junior level and, therefore, not recognised outside my own club. About this time I remember a professional coming to visit: his name was Eric Lester and he was a friend of my father, supposedly. My proud dad asked him to run the rule over me but could not have expected his verdict. 'That's the worst swing I have ever seen,' Lester said.

Dad was furious. 'That's what you know about the swing,' he growled. Anyone who has heard Dad's gruff accent would appreciate just how scary he could sound.

'Never mind, son,' he said to me. 'Harry Bannerman thinks you are something special.' Not always, as it happened.

There was no full-time amateur circuit in the 1960s, as there is now. Not that my folks could have afforded to send me around the country to tackle the best in Scotland. My occasional sorties out of the area – to the Scottish Boys or the British Boys championships – had to be fitted in around work. My amateur record was not that much to write home about, not least because I turned pro at 17. Good enough, though, to be selected for the Scottish Boys team, a moment of great pride for all the Torrance family. I remember David Chillas beating me in the Scottish Boys Strokeplay Championship at Carnoustie; Russell Weir dumping me out of the Scottish Boys when I lost a lead over the last few holes due to diabolical putting; and Ewen Murray, now the Sky Sports golf commentator, stealing victory from me in the semi-final of the British Boys at Hillside.

He must have chipped and putted 13 times against me, and at the 18th he thinned a chip that struck the pin and stopped stone dead instead of going through the green. I have never forgiven the bugger and he knows it. I have told him often enough.

My first job – like the first part-time job of so many school teenagers these days – was stacking shelves in the local supermarket. But my work at Templeton's in Largs, and subsequently at the Co-op, was full-time. It was not long before I crossed that line again, though I do not really consider selling three pounds of potatoes to my granny for the knock-down price of threepence a hanging offence. I had worked my way up to be in charge of the fruit counter, from stocking it up to serving. Ah well, it was back to stacking shelves.

I installed television relay systems, and worked as a van boy for a big guy called Ian Fairlie who used to delight in never switching on the heating in the vehicle, even in the depths of a Scottish winter. Then I drove an open-sided whisky van for Jimmy Wham, whose bottles were imaginatively labelled 'Wham's Dram'. This was a dangerous job on several levels. Imagine the security aspect of a naive 17-year-old driving crates of whisky in an open-sided lorry into outlaw territory. As for the van itself, there was more tread on a blank piece of paper than used to be on the tyres.

For those reasons, my mother was as happy as I was when Dad fixed up through Jimmy Letters, the owner of John Letters golf club manufacturers, for me to be interviewed by Arthur Lees for an assistant's job at Sunningdale. Jimmy was a big friend of the family and Arthur had played Letters clubs throughout his career.

Mum took me down south. Neither of us had been on an aeroplane before. We were picked up in a car, driven to Sunningdale and taken into the clubhouse. It was like entering another world. Nervously, we had smoked salmon for lunch and neither of us had the faintest idea how to tackle the dish.

It would be untrue to suggest that life became a plate of smoked salmon. But I had been given a taste for it...

3

'Have you got a game?'

'Good morning, sir, have you got a game?'

Every day, the question was the same. It always came first from the smiling, tousled-haired Scottish teenager who made sure he was ahead of the other Sunningdale assistants in greeting members from pole position at the door of the professional shop. 'Good morning, Mr King, have you got a game?'

'Queenie' King, along with Peter Oosterhuis and Peter Townsend a 'Gerald Micklem lad', was a young English amateur of ability invited by the former Walker Cup player and Royal & Ancient captain to become a member at Sunningdale.

Michael became 'Queenie' to his fellow professionals right after the stock market crash of 1974 forced him to trade his gentleman tag for that of a player. He became a great friend, my closest since we came to live in Virginia Water. We speak at least once every day on the telephone.

As a prominent member of the self-styled 'Bad Boys' at Sunningdale – including the likes of Mike Hughesden, Martin Devetta, Richard Upton, Blaise Craven, John Fitzpatrick, Rodger Sturgeon and Tony Biggins – he featured strongly in the banter that surrounded our morning chats, money matches and afternoon games of backgammon.

'Excuse me, Torrance, this is the members' bar,' he would say in the days when I was afforded courtesy at the club but had no other membership privileges. 'Have you signed the book?' Of course, he knew I had not.

'Good morning, ordinary member,' I would say

after being made an honorary member, something I regard almost as highly as meeting Suzanne, the birth of my children and captaining the winning European Ryder Cup team.

It is important to show no mercy in these exchanges. A Sunningdale dictionary would place 'sympathy' between 'shit' and 'syphilis'.

Nowadays, Queenie and I argue about who gave whom shots in the year when I was an assistant and he was already a Walker Cup player. Whatever, young Mr King, a teasing rather than respectful appellation, represented a way into the money matches that would supplement my meagre income and stir my competitive juices.

I was at the front of the queue of assistants every morning like the keenest of the litter, panting for walkies with his master. A walk was the last thing on my mind. I wanted out of that shop and onto the golf course. I was not there to be the kind of assistant who would be content to sell balls, give a few lessons, learn how to regrip clubs and fit in nine holes with his mates at the end of a long day. I was there to improve my golf and get on tour. Fast.

As it happened, I was to learn all about club-making, regripping, teaching and running a shop, all the requirements to be a club professional. I spent a week at Lilleshall during my early years as a professional and passed a PGA exam that allowed me to become a club pro should my tournament career fail to develop. It was a kind of insurance. I shared a room that week with the late, great Ronnie Shade, who was to become a big friend and a bigger influence on both my life and my golf.

The vice in my golf shed at home – by no means my only vice, it has to be said – is not there for show. Many of the hundreds, if not thousands, of clubs neatly stacked or just lying around have been tinkered with or regripped. I used to love sanding down and varnishing the old wooden clubs, having perhaps inherited a taste for French polishing from my grandmother.

Apart from being a way to improve my golf, games with the members amounted to an opportunity to make a few bob. More than a few bob, actually. Sunningdale members, especially wonderfully generous ladies, such as Mrs Fortune and Trish Leatham, became the equivalent of my Largs priests as a source of much-needed pocket money. Mrs Fortune would take the assistants for tea; Trish would take us for a game of cards.

It was not really possible to live on the wages alone. If memory serves me right, assistants received £5 per week, £5 a lesson and £5 for playing with a member. Half of the latter two fivers went to Arthur Lees, the professional.

We played for my fee and whatever else the member suggested. The aim was to be invited into one of the money matches, which were proportionately bigger in those days than now.

Trish, a substantial woman in full sail, loved to gamble, from the tables at Monte Carlo to the gin rummy sessions in the upstairs room at Sunningdale. Trish, who is related by family to Highclere, has always been one of the genuine characters at the club. I was thrilled that she made it along as one of the special guests for the dinner held when I became an honorary member.

What a night that was. A perfect opportunity for my fabled emotions to run riot. I even managed to squeeze a tear out of Queenie's eyes and, as he always insists, he 'doesn't go there'. An astonishing 145 people crammed into the two dining rooms for an evening of haggis, bagpipes and speech-making. A few clips of the Ryder Cup were shown, courtesy of the European Tour. Ken

Schofield, the executive director, a dear old ally and friend, said a few words. Paul McGinley and Darren Clarke, two of my Ryder Cup players and two of the pros who are afforded courtesy at Sunningdale, also spoke supremely well and with great kindness towards me. I was completely overwhelmed.

For a professional to be made an honorary member at Sunningdale was a very big deal, something for which Queenie and the 'Bad Boys' had campaigned hard. Arthur Lees had been made one but I do not know of another. I felt very humble.

My winnings during that summer of 1971 provided me with enough of an income to open my first bank account. It may seem strange now but I remember feeling tremendous pride when receiving my first cheque book from the Sunningdale branch of Barclays Bank. I thought about Mum and Dad and Largs and, very probably, shed a tear.

There was no need for me to put on the charm. The twinkle in my eye was natural, neither forced nor phoney. I was genuinely enthusiastic, genuinely friendly and genuinely keen to play.

I certainly appreciated the good fortune of landing at an idyllic place like Sunningdale. The old oak tree behind the 18th green looked much the same then as it does now, Sunningdale's signature feature long before golf course architects came up with the notion. What drama those spreading branches have witnessed in almost a century of golf.

Sunningdale Old was where legendary American amateur Bobby Jones compiled what in 1926 was perceived to be the 'perfect' round of golf – a 66 made up with the classic symmetry of 33 shots and 33 putts. Jones, who had stopped by on his way to victory in the Open Championship at Royal Lytham & St Anne's, never scored more than a four at any hole. At 10 of the 18, he needed either a 2-iron or a wood for his second shot.

That story illustrates three of the dramatic changes in golf over the decades: a 66, while still pretty good, would be considered nothing spectacular these days, with Nick Faldo averaging 65.5 over four rounds when he won the European Open at the Old in 1992; if a professional had 33 putts on a Thursday and Friday of any event nowadays, he would have every weekend off; and modern technology has transformed the distances a golf ball travels. I can reach all the Old par 5s in two shots and can just about drive the green at two of the par 4s. I doubt if I would require more than a 4-iron – and often much less than that – for my approaches to any of the par 4s.

Sunningdale New, less bunkered and less tree-lined than its more distinguished older brother, tighter from the tee, longer and with less receptive greens, has had its share of moments. How many people, for example, know that Gary Player won his first tournament as a professional there in 1956? Most members prefer to play the Old, with its individually sculpted fairways so redolent of Pine Valley. As I said, given one round before I die, it would be there.

You can imagine, therefore, the crushing disappointment I experienced in 1982 when I allowed the European Open to slip from my grasp on the course I knew so well and held in such affection. Only a Dunhill Cup failure within weeks of my Ryder Cup triumph in 1985 and, perhaps, being pipped by Colin Montgomerie in the race to win the Order of Merit in 1995 rank higher in the let-down charts.

To win at Sunningdale would have been unbelievable and maybe that was ultimately the problem. Queenie told me he felt crushed under the pressure when faced with the opportunity of winning on his home turf.

I went out in 30 in the last round and, although Manuel Pinero, the eventual winner, came home in 30, I lost it rather than his winning it. I was leading going into the last round, playing with Greg Norman and Sandy Lyle, if I recall. I eagled the 1st hole, which was obviously the best start possible, made a three at the 2nd, another birdie three at the 3rd and yet another three at the short 4th. I missed a very makeable putt for what would have been a fifth three in a row at the 5th, having hit the perfect tee shot. I parred the 6th and 7th, three putted the 8th, after my nearest challenger Lyle hit a glorious tee shot onto the green at the par four 9th, and drove to within 16 inches of the cup for my second eagle of the outward half.

I had parred the 10th and the 11th and was about to par the 12th when Norman said something to me about 'laying up'. I had pulled my tee shot slightly at the short hole, not deliberately played safe. It seemed a very strange thing for him to say. He was about 10 shots behind, not a threat. My tee shot at the short 13th down the hill was a good one but the ball trickled off the green and into a fluffy lie. I took three to get down for my second bogey of the round. I was still one ahead with the reachable and birdieable 14th ahead.

Cue my old snap hook drive under pressure. John Jacobs, my Ryder Cup captain the previous year, was there as I walked off the tee.

'Come on, Sam, you can still make par here,' he said.

Which I did, having hit a great recovery shot back to the fairway and a good up and down from the greenside bunker. But everyone else was birdieing that hole and I had lost ground on Pinero. I was on the 17th fairway when Huge Bum, as we call Mike Hughesden, a Sunningdale member, one of the 'Bad Boys' and then a

BBC roving reporter, came up and said to me, 'Greg says you're playing away from the pins.'

'Absolute rubbish,' I replied. 'Trust me, I'm going for the pins, I'm just not good enough to hit them at present.'

Afterwards, people remarked about the timing and content of the question. But I did not really notice or make much of it. I never bring it up with Huge Bum. Did I mention about irony at Sunningdale?

I three putted the 17th and that was pretty much that. Home in 37 for a closing 67. Not bad for a closing round, you might think, but I knew that back nine so well I should have been scoring 32 or 33 with my eyes closed. That hooked drive on the 14th did for me, as it did on several occasions.

When Arthur Lees took me on as an assistant, he did not see much in my game. Indeed, he would have preferred it had I spent more time in the shop and less on the course. He remains something of a legend at Sunningdale, a huge character, fondly remembered by the members. He participated in all the big games, whether on the course or in the card room. Arthur had been a Ryder Cup player and I considered it an honour working for him.

Although I was to become closely associated with Sunningdale and many members were to become my friends, my spare time as a 17-year-old was spent with the other assistants and the caddies. Fraternisation with the members was limited to a drink in the clubhouse after a game. What little time I had to myself would more often than not mean a game of darts in a local pub which, despite changing its name from The Exchequer to Chequers, has always been known as The Marriage Wreckers. A lively place, as you can imagine.

Suddenly, though, I had no place to live. When the daughter of the family with whom I lodged separated from her husband and returned home, I needed to make alternative arrangements. Easier said than done. Sunningdale was not Largs with its numerous seaside bed and breakfast establishments. Affordable rental accommodation was at a premium.

Jimmy Watt came to the rescue. Jimmy was Arthur's main man, an honest, fantastically hard-working bloke who had lost his arm in a car accident. He was the kind of tough Scot you always wanted on your side. Arthur may have been head professional but Jimmy ran the place. He did everything, including trying to balance the fact that Arthur was occasionally prone to giving new clubs away rather than selling them.

Unbeknown to Arthur, Jimmy arranged for me to stay in the shop on a camp bed. There was a shower upstairs and a huge television. Everything I needed, really, since women had not become part of the equation. I couldn't pull the skin off a rice pudding in those days.

Arthur, never the first to arrive in the morning, remained oblivious to the set-up. Until one night I was sound asleep on the camp bed in the middle of the floor when just before midnight I heard a key in the door.

'Jesus Christ,' I muttered.

I sat bolt upright to see the door opening, the light switch being turned on and the figure of Arthur appearing in the doorway. He was not alone.

'Right, lass,' he says, quick as a flash, 'this is the shop.' The 'guided tour' came to a halt there and then, as did my nocturnal occupancy of the pro shop. I spent the next day trying to find another place to live. Eventually, I ended up sleeping in the staff quarters inside the clubhouse, a happy placement that allowed me to play cards with the chef.

The most important event during my year at Sunningdale was the beginning of a lifetime friendship with the McKenzie family, my first and only benefactors. Angus and his two sons, Norman and Gerald, were Canadian oil men from Calgary who owned offices and flats all over London as well as N. Peal, the famous gents' and ladies' outfitter in London's Burlington Arcade. Norman, the younger brother, was closer to my age and very quickly became a close friend. We played a lot of golf together. Mostly, though, we had a lot of fun.

When we played, I would always seem to birdie the last three holes to take the money. A gambler knows the importance of the final holes. You can be six down but come out ahead financially by taking the presses and buys. Norman thought I did it on purpose, that I could turn it on when I wanted. That's not how it was; it just seemed to happen that way. Whatever, they were impressed enough to sponsor me when I went on Tour the following year.

'All we had to do was give him a tenner, enter him in his first tournament and he was away,' Gerald would always say.

It was not quite like that. Angus, who must be the most travelled person that ever lived, made all the arrangements, from providing me with my first car, a silver Volkswagen Beetle, to arranging for me to go shopping. That meant a trip to N. Peal where a delightful man called Sidney Levene, who sounded and looked like a film star, kitted me out with cashmere sweaters.

Gerald accompanied me to a tailor's shop in Savile Row for a jacket and a pair of trousers. 'You can't go on Tour without a pair of Oxford bags,' Gerald said. They cost what seemed like a fortune.

There was never a contract and they never took a percentage of my winnings, at the start or later. They were just the most incredible, generous people who wanted to see me get on Tour.

They took me to Las Vegas to try to prequalify for a tournament and they gave me money to play the tables in the casinos. I am almost embarrassed to say I remember losing it all and hanging around looking for more. The old Torrance luck stepped onto the tee when I put my last couple of dollars in a one-armed bandit machine, only to yelp with glee as it spewed out 500 dollars. It seemed like a million dollars and I felt like a million dollars.

That was a common state of mind for a young Scot who, when golf took me to the London area, stayed in a beautiful apartment in Franklins Road, Chelsea, opposite the Chelsea Flower Show and just off the King's Road. Again, courtesy of the McKenzies. The swinging '60s had not stopped swinging by the time Torrance and the '70s met head on.

The McKenzies owned their own course in Calgary called Gallagher's Canyon, where Arnold Palmer once played an exhibition. I was so pleased that Angus, Gerald and Norman were able to be present when Michael Aspel opened his red book for the *This Is Your Life* television programme.

I had a taste of what was to follow during my year as an assistant when Arthur allowed me to play in the Agfa-Gevaert Tournament. I survived the halfway cut and, by doing so, gained entry into the Daks. Somewhat reluctantly, Arthur gave me another week off. 'That one's no good,' Arthur was to say to Jimmy the day I left Sunningdale to go on tour. 'All he wants to do is play golf.'

He could not have been more right. Some at Sunningdale were more encouraging. Peter Francis, a member whose family owned a little concern called Standard Oil, later to become Esso, gave me £100 in cash to help me on my way. It was a lot of money in those days.

It had been a great year, made special by the members, the McKenzies and my parents, for whom no sacrifice was too great. Mum and Dad even sent down their own car so that I could get about – a Vanden Plas Princess 1100. I remember collecting it at Hounslow from my uncle Billy's and driving back along the A30, petrified, at about 10 mph. Everyone was tooting their horns at me. The rabbits in the headlights were a lot less startled than me.

The Vanden Plas took over from the Vespa which I used to ride everywhere. God, I thought I was cool on my heavily mirrored scooter. One evening it got me to London and a recording of *Top of the Pops*. The tickets came from a BBC television producer whom I had been teaching at Sunningdale. Carnaby Street still ruled teenage fashion, with skirts hovering between mini and micro length. Years later Sir Michael Grade tried to get me a copy of the tape but the BBC library had to confess a gap in their archives.

There was always one on *TOTP* in those days – not so much now. You know the type, the 'look-at-me-mum' dancer who tries to get into every shot. That was Sam Torrance, I'm almost embarrassed to admit. Everywhere the camera pointed, there was me bopping about in demented fashion. I had promised Mum and Dad they would see me on television and I made certain they did. Guess who volunteered to fill one of the seats in the background as Perry Como sat on a stool singing 'It's Impossible'? Yes, the gallus hunk of Ayrshire bacon with the dodgy hair. Mind you, the whole experience was worth it for seeing Olivia Newton John walk out of the studios in the tightest of hot pants. Wow!

It was time to go home, time to return to Largs, my base, and the kind of globetrotting that private jets make light of but that 30 years ago was something of an exhausting ordeal.

Then it was time to go on Tour, a Tour very different then from now, a fledgling Tour that did not begin until April and lasted only until the autumn. The European Tour was just as it said on the tin – a tour confined to Europe and, therefore, to the months in which the weather was favourable.

Although I had enjoyed a fantastic year at Sunningdale, full of fun and laughter, going back to Largs was no wrench. I was a Scottish boy going home to embark upon a career that I had always dreamed of.

I was 18 and I was ready, so ready. I thought so, Dad thought so. Coaching was much less technical then than it is now, but my father's principles have not changed too much over the years. Initially he told me to hit the ball as hard and as far as I could with a big shoulder turn, placing the emphasis on distance rather than accuracy.

'We will straighten it up sooner or later,' he would say. I'm still waiting.

His insistence on a player having power is very much what he and I are telling my son Daniel, who, to the great pride of his watching father, reached the last 16 of the Scottish Boys Championship in 2003 at his first attempt. At the age of 15 he had beaten opponents two years older than him. Daniel is golf mad and with enough talent to suggest to both his dad and grandad that he has a big future in the game.

'Teach the person, not the method' has always been one of my father's mantras. But obviously my 'natural swing' was a natural reflection of my father's basic beliefs. I swung how he told me to swing. Videos comparing then and now and my peak would show essentially the same swing with the rough edges smoothed out over the years. Dad always thought my strong grip a 'bit dodgy', certainly alongside someone like Ian Woosnam, who possesses the most wonderful grip. Woosie was born to hold a club in his hands.

My father has always been a leg man. 'The legs are the generator,' he says. 'Have you ever heard of someone coming off the course saying his arms and hands are tired? He complains about his legs and back. If the legs go, you've had it.'

Curiously, the straightening of my legs at impact brought me my length yet was the cause of the hook that plagued me all my career. My biggest early fault was shutting the face of my club at the top of the swing.

Dad used to say I swung the club better than Snead, at the time when my swing was recognised as about the smoothest on tour. The early 'violent attack' attributed to me by my friend John O'Leary, had gone, to be replaced by something a bit more silky.

But 'faither' was not always so complimentary and our sessions on the practice range would generate a lot of electricity.

'I can't do that. I can't do that,' I would scream.

A few weeks later I would be on the telephone saying, 'It's working, it's terrific.' A lot of our discussions were done by phone. He knew my swing so well that he could teach me from thousands of miles away, long before e-mails, web cams and faxes.

I have always drawn the ball right to left, the way a right-hander should play. I will argue until the day I die that it is more of a natural movement for a right hander to swing in to out like a shot in tennis or the action of throwing the discus. If you are playing a fade – the left to right trajectory that many pros adopt for greater control – you are cutting against yourself. A professional must be able to hit a fade but I think the draw is the more natural shot.

There was precious little subtlety in the method of

the Ayrshire teenager who went on Tour in 1972. My method was to hit the ball as hard as I could and use a pretty hot short game to make a score.

Within a few months, one excitable reporter was comparing me to Arnold Palmer for my 'up and at 'em' approach to the game. I was certainly up for it, and when I set off for Spain I was thinking, 'Let me at them.'

4

On Tour

My first full year on Tour was 1972, my first event was in Spain. The McKenzies, who were covering my expenses, booked the flight and the accommodation.

'Right,' I asked at reception after checking into my hotel in the centre of Gerona, 'where's the golf course?' I could hardly wait.

I would have to. The golf course turned out to be two hours away, but this simple geographical mistake did not even tug at my galloping enthusiasm. Nor did boldly walking forward in the clubhouse and introducing myself to what turned out to be the quietest golfer on the circuit. Mild-mannered 'Gooey' Guy Hunt, never an extrovert, became a tournament administrator for the European Seniors Tour.

I had won the princely sum of £35 for making the cut in the Agfa-Gevaert Tournament at Stoke Poges the previous year while an assistant at Sunningdale. Then, as now, you had to survive the 36-hole guillotine in order to be paid. But there was another, even more vital, reason for avoiding the dreaded blade. Anyone who completed all four rounds – we played 36 holes on Saturday in those days – avoided Monday prequalifying for the following tournament. The top 60 in the Order of Merit at the end of one year were also excluded from the rigours of prequalification for the following year. Happily, after finishing 37th in 1972, I was never again required to go through that ordeal.

For the first few months, however, the missed cuts mounted up. I failed at the Spanish Open and again the following week at the Madrid Open, which was won by Irishman Jimmy Kinsella, the only European Tour victory of his career, as it transpired. In the kind of delicious irony that sits easily with the Irish, Jimmy played in Madrid only because he was unable to get a flight home after the Spanish Open.

When I eventually made a cut at the John Player Trophy at Bognor Regis, I led with nine holes to play. But the pressure and the howling gales overcame me and I finished 9th in a tournament won by Ross Whitehead. My first year was to prove a great success, however. Two victories – in the Under-25 Match-play Championship and the Radici Open, an unofficial 72-hole strokeplay tournament in Italy – earned me the 'Rookie of the Year' award and a working holiday with the great Henry Cotton at his Penina home in Portugal.

If the strokeplay victory was bigger in terms of the number of people I beat over four rounds, the Under-25 success has stayed longer in my memory. And not just because you always remember your first anything – first kiss, first drink, first – ! A comment from my opponent at lunchtime prior to the final angered me so much that I performed as if a man possessed. I suppose I was what came to be known in sport as 'in the zone'. I had defeated my fellow Scot Bernard Gallacher in the semi-final, a source of great pride to me at the time. Bernard, who was to become a good friend and my captain at three Ryder Cups, had won the PGA Championship and the Order of Merit in 1969, at the age of just 20.

My winner's cheque was for £370. But there was another, potentially greater, reward for victory that week. The champion would gain entry to the forthcoming Dunlop Masters, one of the biggest events in the golfing calendar. Doug McLelland, the other finalist, was already in the field for the Masters, a fact he made known to me in rather bumptious fashion as we lunched in the Royal Birkdale clubhouse prior to our match.

'Don't worry, Sam,' McLelland said pointedly as he sat with his friends. 'You will get into the Masters as runner-up because I am already in.'

This, to a west of Scotland man, was not so much a red rag to a bull as a blue scarf to a Celtic supporter or, indeed, a green scarf to a Rangers fan. I could not believe that someone would say that. Why would anyone want to antagonise me?

'Fuck you,' I thought, as I left my lunch on the plate, stood up and walked briskly out of the door. 'I am going to have you.'

No matter where I hit the ball on the green that afternoon, I holed the putt. From 5 yards, from 10 yards, from 30 yards. I beat McLelland 5 and 4.

I was on the telephone to home before I had removed my spikes. I probably phone my parents more than any other son because what I have done I have done for them, and what I have achieved I have achieved for them. They gave me everything and they made everything possible. Another highlight of my year was making it through qualifying into the Open Championship at Muirfield, my first of 27 consecutive appearances in the greatest golf tournament in the world. The run was broken in 1999 when I was forced to pull out of the Open at Carnoustie because of injury. A very bad day.

I finished tied for 46th as Lee Trevino lifted his second Claret Jug in a row, though my memories are less of how I played, more who I saw and what I experienced. I remember Arnold Palmer walking onto the practice putting green, swathed in cashmere and with the deep suntan of the rich and successful. He looked like a bull. I had goose bumps the size of golf balls all over my arms. I could not take my eyes off him.

Jack Nicklaus was always my hero, though. I may not have rushed to Royal Lytham for the Ryder Cup in 1961, but I was up that lamppost at St Andrews in 1964, straining for a sight of Nicklaus the year Tony Lema won the Open. There was a photograph from the 1972 Open of Nicklaus on the practice range, watched by a throng of enthusiastic golf fans. I was right in the middle, just as I had been when Perry Como was performing on *Top of the Pops*.

Nicklaus was using a club with a brown casing, which made it look older than it was. I don't know what came over me when, without any warning, I shouted out one of the dumbest questions of my life. 'Is that a hickory shaft?' I asked. I realised my mistake almost before the words were out and my face turned bright red with embarrassment. Thank God he did not know I was a player about to compete in his first Open.

Nicklaus was to hit a shot that week that taught me a great deal and led to a significant improvement in my game. I remember him being maybe 140 yards from the green at Muirfield's 17th hole and hitting a shot with no more than a half to three-quarter swing. I had never seen that before. It looked so majestic. I wanted to swing like that. I could hit cuts and hooks and low runny shots but I never really thought about anything other than a full-blooded shot until that day. It was to become a key to my game.

There was another episode that stuck in my mind from that year's Open, a shot that was to haunt me 15 years later as my putting deteriorated to the point of jeopardising my career. As I was walking from a green to a tee, I saw pork pie-hatted Mr Lu, the eventual runner-up to Trevino, on another green twitching extravagantly on a putt. 'What the hell was that?' I thought. It was like a wriggling snake. I had never seen anything like it in my life. And I did not want to see it again. I had witnessed my first yip. I was to see many more over the years before experiencing my own, the first step on a path that led to my employing the strange-looking, but strangely effective, broomhandle putter.

I have always believed that comparisons between different eras are invidious and not as revealing as you might imagine. It would be extraordinary if prize money failed to grow, a dereliction of duty if facilities did not improve as the years went by and if lessons were not learned. But the European Tour that I joined in 1972 was a very different animal from the one that now roars virtually 12 months of the year, moving with the seasons from one continent to the next and one hemisphere to the other. I was in at the start of European golf in that the appointment of John Jacobs as tournament director-general of the PGA on 1 October 1971 is recognised as the official birth of the European Tour.

The season did not begin until after the Masters at Augusta. And it ended as the autumn leaves were decaying on the ground. The haphazard organisation had led to oddities like a matchplay championship in which a 36-hole semi-final was followed by an 18-hole final. It had not been that long since David Snell stopped travelling to tournaments on his motorbike with his golf clubs slung across the tank and a holdall strapped to the pillion.

There were no courtesy cars, no practice facilities to speak of, no player lounges, no crèches, no mobile physiotherapy unit, no corporate hospitality, no platoon of volunteers recruited, for example, for the specific job of raking bunkers.

The wonderfully named Jimmy Bagge, who worked for Dunlop, used to come up to you on the first tee with a present. 'I'll gie you three balls now and another three on Friday if you make the cut,' he would say.

But it was not as simple as that. There were not enough balls to go round. Jimmy, who should have looked like the spivish George Cole in the St Trinian's films but sadly did not, used to hide behind hedges with his little gifts, dishing them out to the younger players with a future and missing out those he considered past their prime.

Last time I heard, the Tour was providing 4,000 new balls a week for practice at tournaments.

But it would be a big mistake to infer from the comparison of then with now that we felt hardship. We enjoyed a wonderful camaraderie in those pathfinder days, sharing rooms, sharing bottles of wine and sharing a love of life as well as golf. We met in the pub or at a restaurant, not at adjacent exercise bikes or running machines. There was often a sense of occasion in a simple dinner, as golfers and golf reporters sat round the table eating, drinking and trading stories. Renton Laidlaw, aka Henry Currie, then of the *Evening Standard*, among other publications, and now of the Golf Channel, is still alive and circumnavigating the globe with seemingly unlimited enthusiasm. Sadly, legends such as Jack Statter and Peter Dobereiner, two of the best to crack a red and a joke, are no longer with us.

I used to say to my close friend and touring companion John O'Leary, 'It was great to be around before the popular press became popular.' O'Leary would nod and smile in that gentle Irish manner of his. He would point out how our impromptu get-togethers could never happen now because of pressure of time, prying eyes and even laws governing public safety.

Robert Sangster, the millionaire racehorse owner, has been a friend of ours for a long time. After his Derby winner Golden Fleece died of cancer he decided to stage a pro-am tournament to raise money to combat the disease.

A ridiculous amount of money was collected for the time. Anyone who was anyone participated. By 3am the next morning Jimmy White and Alex Higgins were playing snooker in Kingswood Golf Club with me and Geoff Lewis, the jockey. There were hundreds of people in the room, enough to shatter every health and safety regulation ever written.

Pro-ams were huge in the 1970s, staged not on the eve of the tournament as now, but on the Sunday, the day after, at a course near to the event. Crowds often as big as 20,000 would come along to see all – and I mean all – the top professionals, from No. 1 Peter Oosterhuis down, playing with celebrities such as Sean Connery, Bruce Forsyth, Ronnie Corbett and Stanley Baker. And very often you would stay there on the Sunday night for what could turn into quite a session.

At the end of '72, though, all that glamour lay ahead. I had my 'silver machine', as the song goes, the Beetle provided for me by the McKenzies, which I drove all over the country. It had a wire basket running underneath the length of the dashboard, home for all my eight-track cassettes. I have never been a gig-goer but I loved to speed across the countryside singing along with the Beatles or Rod Stewart or Largs' own Gallagher and Lyle.

By then I had learned to fill the tank with the right fuel. I tried diesel on the day I picked the car up at the Benson & Hedges at Fulford and found myself spending an unscheduled extra night in a motel.

The accommodation was somewhat more luxurious at Penina, where I spent a fortnight as the prize for being named 'Rookie of the Year'. To be so young and to spend time with a legend such as Henry Cotton was both a joy and an education. And not just in matters of golf. He introduced me to a perfume that he promised would become a big seller. It was called Paco Rabanne. He tried to get me to eat squid in a black gunge. He failed. He taught me how to avoid stating the bleeding obvious with a system of fines. Any time I said something that did not need saying it cost me several escudos in fines.

Of course, he was a great teacher and, as with any golfer who visited him, he had me bashing away at a tyre with a club. This was very much his trademark. In return for receiving all manner of wisdom, we had to clean golf balls – barrels and barrels of golf balls. There was no complaint.

I was always a strong right-handed player, susceptible to the odd destructive hook. 'Try this,' he said. 'Put your right forefinger against the side of the shaft and don't grip with it all. Now, hit the ball.' I holed it. My first shot with a 6-iron flew straight into the hole from a distance of maybe 160 yards. It was unbelievable, just a magical moment. Not that this represented any wonder cure. I would battle against a hook for many years before my 'vicious attack' on the ball, as O'Leary called it, disappeared to be replaced by a much more rhythmical swing.

I was already receiving a good press; on occasions a great press. I was 'the next Arnie', according to one commentator, and 'the greatest British prospect since Tony Jacklin', according to another. It was all very flattering, though, fortunately, my solid Scottish upbringing ensured I did not become too big-headed.

There were to be no more tournament victories until 1975. The reason was simple, but my father would not have understood had he known at the time. I doubt if he understands now. I was just enjoying myself too much. If I won, I won, and if I missed the cut, so what? I was having a ball. My aim was not much more than winning enough to retain my exemption each year and having a good time. Back in Largs, under the close and critical eye of my father, I at least offered the illusion of working hard on my game.

Mimicry is not the least of the gifted David Feherty's talents. Feherty became one of my best friends and remains so, despite the fact that his job as one of the most respected – and highest paid – golf commentators for CBS in the United States keeps us apart much longer than both of us would like. He is always urging me to follow him there and pick up the microphone.

'Mair balls, hit mair balls,' Feherty would say in a gruff voice, copying Dad in word and philosophy. It was his solution for everything.

Dad says I was never a hard worker. He just doesn't think there is any other way. He played a bit with Christy O'Connor, who, he says, was a genius with very little effort, and Bobby Locke said that practice was a waste of good shots. But he points out that they were unorthodox swingers and that to some extent Colin Montgomerie falls into that category. The more he practises, the worse he gets. He is as good as anyone in the world, at one time the best. A natural.

Sam Snead practised every day of his life. Ben Hogan, Dad's hero, worked incessantly. Then there were Gary Player, Peter Thomson and, of course, Jack Nicklaus – all the greats practised hard. 'You could have gone right to the top,' Dad tells me. 'You had an orthodox swing and hit the ball miles, as long as anyone. You could have been as good as Nick Faldo, as good as anyone. You could have won majors. If Gary Player had the talents that you had, he would have been unbeatable.'

Mum – as mums do – took my side, recognising the type of person I was rather than the type of person Dad wanted me to be.

I have no regrets. I have never looked back and thought what might have been. Having fun is what life was, or rather is, about. You are what you are. I have never been the hardest-working man on this planet. It is not in my bones. I love the game of golf. I love playing it and I will continue doing so until the day I drop. If I had been one of those obsessive practisers – like Nick Faldo or Vijay Singh – I would not have enjoyed it as much and maybe not have achieved what I did. We will never know.

Henry Cotton recognised my situation when he wrote in 1976: 'Like Billy Casper, Torrance will probably hold his form with the minimum of practice.' There was always the maximum amount of tournament play, however. I missed only two events during my first ten years on Tour – and that was because I broke my toe tripping over my luggage. Accidents can happen, and in my case they often did.

I was to base myself in my home town of Largs for the best part of the next 20 years, combining a full European Tour schedule with early year and post-season globetrotting and a healthy dollop of Scottish tournaments. Inevitably, Scottish events became less and less frequent, though I remained a strong supporter of the Scottish PGA Championship, which I won five times.

But in the 1970s I still played a lot in Scotland – rarely in the same event as my dad, who now had to combine his professional and greenkeeping job at Routenburn with coaching his son, either in person or via long, daily telephone calls.

There was one occasion, however, when we competed in the same pro-am. My dad was out later in the day than me and when the time came, I ventured back down the 18th to watch him finish.

'What's your score?' I asked as we met at his ball after a spanking drive down the middle of the fairway.

'One under,' he replied.

'You need a birdie to tie,' I said.

'Who shot that?'

Nothing was said. I was not going to tell him it was me in case I put him off. He parred the last, leaving me victorious. The headline in the local newspaper read: 'Father Follows in Son's Footsteps'.

He gave me his car that night to celebrate. I crashed it and wrote it off. '£300 in the front door and £400 oot the back,' was his somewhat mercenary view of the day's profit-to-loss ratio.

If I denied Dad on that occasion, I gave him a little something to enjoy in 1975. That year the Piccadilly Medal was, for the last time, decided on the basis of medal matchplay, i.e. the traditional one-against-one but counting in strokes not holes. I never made it to the final but I did beat the great Christy O'Connor Senior, who was one of my father's heroes. That was another moment when I thought I had a future.

My love of team golf pre-dated any involvement in the Ryder Cup. The attraction lies in the camaraderie and in the rare opportunity in such an individual sport to perform for team-mates and friends as well as for yourself. Some golfers get it, some don't. Some are suited to it, some are not. Although golf is built on solid virtues like trust and honesty, by its very nature it encourages a certain selfishness and self-obsession, not exactly ideal for the team ethos.

I loved being part of a team from the moment I was capped by Scotland at boys' international level in 1970. There followed a seam of professional team golf running through my career as rich as that of anyone in any era. I played in eight Ryder Cups, nine Alfred Dunhill Cups, 11 World Cups, all five Hennessy Cognac Cups, two Four Tours World Championships, three Double Diamond events and, most recently, two UBS Cups.

It began with the Double Diamond of 1973, memorable not just for the fact that Scotland won. I had not qualified for the team but was called up when Harry Bannerman injured himself and was forced to withdraw. I remember he himself telephoned me asking if I would like to take his place.

'Are you kidding?' was my reaction.

'My car is at Heathrow,' he said. 'So fly down to Heathrow and pick up my car.'

That led to my driving a gorgeous Rover down to Prince's at Sandwich on the Kent coast. The great Eric Brown was captain. Eric ruled the roost over the Scots boys. Everyone looked up to him, everyone obeyed him. He was a rough, tough character, a great man who put the fear of God into everyone he met. I am glad to say he became a good friend.

Eric's main piece of advice that week had been pretty unambiguous. 'If I ever see any of you leave a putt short I will boot your arse,' he said.

I had already enjoyed wins over Bob Dickson of the United States and Craig DeFoy of Wales when I faced Spain's Manuel Ballesteros, Seve's big brother, in the final match. I was 1-up playing the last, facing two putts from 25ft to win my tie and the match for Scotland. I crouched over my putt, looked up at the hole for the last time and saw Eric in the gallery. Don't be short, I thought. True to Eric's threat, I wasn't. I knocked it 4ft past and missed the one back. Fortunately, Ronnie Shade came from behind to win his match and give us the trophy.

What a night that was. I was barely 20 and celebrating a famous Scottish victory. I drove back to London the next day with a hangover that required several hairs of several dogs. So I headed for the West End, leaving Harry's pride and joy in a multi-storey car park with his clubs in the boot and mine in the back seat.

I never saw my clubs again as I returned to find a smashed rear window. Although Harry's remained safe in the boot, he did not think me so special that day.

There was quite a Scottish mafia in those days. Harry, of course, David Ingram, David Chillas, Norman Wood, Bill Murray, Alistair Thomson, Andrew Brooks, to mention just a few. I also became a member of British Caledonian Golfing Lions, who were flown by their sponsor during the winter to tournaments in South Africa, the rest of the African continent and South America.

We were a large squad, varying in number, with people coming in and out all the time. It proved quite a task trying to remember them all, but here goes: David Chillas, Ronnie Shade, Simon Cox, Norman Wood, Carl Mason, Tommy Horton, Brian Barnes, Dai Rees, Malcolm Gregson, Ewen Murray, Guy Hunt, David Ingram, Bill Reid, Sandy Lyle, Peter Tupling, Stuart Brown, Dougie McLelland, John Garner, Nick Job, Eric Brown and, of course, Sam Torrance. If I have forgotten anyone or included someone who was not a member, I apologise.

Derek Pillage, my first and most enduring manager, had the unenviable task of controlling us all. Pillage was one of the original golf managers who, at the height of his powers, looked after the interests of the likes of Lee Trevino, Johnny Miller, Billy Casper, Gay Brewer, Charles Coody and Julius Boros from the States and a whole host of Britain's finest players. But I suppose he was most closely associated with Brian Barnes.

Pillage was a friend and associate of the actor Stanley Baker, a relationship that earned him several scenes in *Zulu*, a favourite film for many people to this day. Once various editing departments had finished plastering the cutting-room floor with his face, though, all that remained was his considerable rear appearing through a window and descending a ladder.

'Saw yer arse last night,' I would say to him when we met.

What I did not know until recently was that Barnsie had been lined up to star, if that's the right word, in the follow-up, *Zulu Dawn*. Pillage even arranged for him to have acting lessons on the basis that Baker was going to forge a movie career for him. Sadly, Baker, a great friend of golf and golfers, died before the project got off the ground. I will leave it up to the reader to decide whether Barnsie would have been right for the role played by Burt Lancaster or Peter O'Toole!

Brian Barnes was instrumental in persuading Pillage to sign me up and it was a victory over Barnsie in Zambia at the end of 1975 that gave me the belief to move up a level. He was the biggest, most colourful character in golf at a time when there were a few more than now. He was a great player, probably better than he ever knew, a long, straight hitter with a good touch around the greens. As much as I always loved the description 'the man who sank the winning putt in the Ryder Cup', he grew to resent being introduced as 'the man who beat Jack Nicklaus twice in a day'. It remains a great feat illustrative of a temperament and talent that could have taken him to the very top, but for his well-documented drinking problem. It is great to see him looking so well and sounding so wise when providing expert analysis for Sky Sports' American golf coverage.

We both tell stories about each other at my first World Cup at Palm Springs, California, in 1976. To a Scot, the World Cup is football and just the biggest event in the world. As a Scot, playing for Scotland, I regarded golf's equivalent in a similar vein. Well, according to Barnsie, I could not get my kilt off after the gala dinner, so I walked into the cupboard, undid it and let it drop. Barnes was intent on not spilling a drop. He had been drinking a few cold beers during the first round and I don't mean surreptitiously. Then he began to mark his ball on the green with a can of beer. Finally, he tucked a can in his shirt pocket when he was putting, swigging the liquid down to a level so that it would not pour out as he bent over. By the third round Michelob, the sponsors, sent out a buggy with a fridge full of beer on the back. They loved it. The crowd loved it. Tommy Horton, a friend of Brian and mine (I call him 'faither'), was less pleased. He gave us a real bollocking. Anyway, Barnsie played brilliantly all week, finishing second in the individual event. Spain, with Manuel Piñero partnering a 19-year-old Seve Ballesteros, won the team competition.

It had been more than three years since my last victory when I beat Brian Barnes in a four-hole play-off to win the 1975 Zambian Open. I was sitting in the locker room with tears streaming down my face when he walked in.

'What's wrong with you?' he asked.

'I don't know,' I replied. 'I'm happy.'

That might even have been the start of my crying, though I suspect a lot of water had already flown under the bridge of my nose. But I was happy. I had just beaten the great Brian Barnes. Almost in that instant I began to believe in myself. And the following year I knuckled down, becoming a lot more serious about my golf.

Serious, but still up for a giggle when the time was right. Even when it was not. Some were less than amused when I returned to Zambia as defending champion the next year and, with tongue firmly in cheek, told a press conference: 'The truly great players of the world rank this event alongside the British and American Opens as the big titles to win.' The sponsors were delighted.

By the strict rules of tournament golf, I might have been denied that career-turning victory 12 months earlier. Before knocking in a 4-footer for the title, I conceded Barnsie's 1-footer by picking the ball up and handing it to him. The rules stated that both players had to hole out. The matter was raised among officials, only for Brian himself to stamp on it and effectively rule out any further discussion. That was a measure of the man.

The following day I was required to play with Kenneth Kaunda, the Zambian president. Not a great golfer but, you know, he never lost a ball! He was, however, an enthusiastic patron of golf and a big friend of Barnes. He referred to Barnes as his 'son' and Barnes called him 'Dad'. Imagine calling an African president 'Dad'. That was Brian Barnes.

Scots do not always stand on ceremony, if they judge the occasion right. There was the time that Frank Rennie, the long-time pro at Old Prestwick, was asked to join our group in Zambia, as an invitee rather than member of the sponsorship team.

'Are you a Golfing Lion, too?' Kaunda asked. 'No, I'm a dandelion,' Rennie replied. And, in certain circles, the name has stuck.

After my late success in 1975, I was bursting for 1976 to begin. What a year it turned out to be, with two European Tour victories and third place in the Order of Merit behind Ballesteros and Irishman Eamonn Darcy. My official prize money soared from £3,481 to £20,917 and my stroke average plummeted from 74.60 to 72.14. I felt much more focused, much more composed than the fresh-faced kid let loose on the world of tournament golf four years earlier. I had clipped my own wings. The time for fun was not over but the time to be serious had begun.

Another reason for the change was that I started travelling with Ronnie Shade. He was east coast and I was west coast, a distinction probably only Scots can appreciate. But we became the best of friends. He totally changed my life and my lifestyle. I was now rooming with an older man who went for naps in the afternoon, for heaven's sake. You tend to do what your room-mate does.

He was a great amateur, five times Scottish champion, who turned pro at a fairly advanced age and established himself as a really good tournament player before, tragically in 1986, cancer took him at the age of just 48. Ronnie was a terrific money match player who had the most infuriating habit of always keeping his head down, long after the ball had gone. When you saw the head down and heard the words 'No, Ronnie' you knew the ball was 3ft from the flag and you were in real trouble. Unless he was your partner.

The Piccadilly Medal at Finham Park, Coventry, brought me my first European Tour 72-hole strokeplay title and, incidentally, the biggest ever cheque won by a Scottish golfer. My two-stroke victory over Australian Bob Shearer was completed on a wild day and only after a little good fortune. My approaches to the 71st and 72nd holes were both misjudged and on each occasion I benefited from lucky bounces off the back of bunkers.

I telephoned home and then celebrated. That was always the routine. Colin Montgomerie says now that he regrets not celebrating his victories. Well, he might. I really cannot understand anyone – whether a drinker or not – failing to get together with friends and raising a glass to success.

Within a month – in the subsequent 72-hole strokeplay event – I had won again. Victory in the Martini International at Ashburnham in Wales was again achieved only after a wobble at the death. I knew on the tee at the last that I could afford a double bogey six and still win. I hit a perfect drive down the middle of the fairway, leaving just a 9-iron approach. From nowhere in my repertoire then or since I produced golf's unmentionable, a shank. The ball flew straight right into 3-ft-high hay. I would be lucky to find it.

But Brian Huggett, bless him, the little Welsh terrier, who had been spectating, saw where the ball landed. He ran across the green and down the hill and went straight to the spot. It took the biggest swipe just to move the ball but somehow I got it on the green and two regulation putts gave me the title.

It might be the only shank I have ever hit in my career.

Twice now I had faltered in the run-in, only to prevail. But I was beginning to live for the last nine holes of a tournament. Jack Nicklaus always said that about the home stretch on the final day. I felt that if I got into contention, I swung better. It stands to reason you have to be swinging well to get into that position. My focus then was on tempo, nothing but tempo.

The champagne could wait.

5

To boldly go...

I have played all over the world and yet I have never really left Largs; I live in England's stockbroker belt and yet my heart remains in Scotland, more specifically, in Ayrshire. I see no contradiction in either of those statements.

I have travelled the five continents playing golf, from China to Colombia, Austria to Australia and to that powerful little autonomous nation called Augusta. But I have always done so in the knowledge that I would soon be returning home, whether to the west of Scotland or to my beloved family in the south of England.

It is because I have always been a confirmed home bird – a homing pigeon with the wings of an eagle – that I never tried my luck on the United States PGA Tour. Not because 'these guys are good', as the advertisement goes, though they are (and were), but because I wanted to be back in my own home by Sunday night, or Monday morning at the latest.

There was one occasion when I might have switched my career to the other side of the Atlantic. I played in the Southern Open during the week preceding the 1983 Ryder Cup. I had been having a good year and it came as no surprise that I forced my way into contention. In fact, I finished tied for first at the end of 72 holes and only lost at the fifth hole of a play-off against Ronnie Black. It was close, very close. At the first extra hole, his ball plugged in a greenside bunker and he had to hole a 25-ft putt to avoid defeat. Victory would have granted me a three-year exemption in the USA, which I would have taken up. The money and opportunity were simply too great to ignore.

I would have packed my bags and moved to the States.

But it was not to be. And I was never keen enough on the idea to try to gain my US card at their qualifying school. I have always believed in life that you perform best when happiest and I didn't think I could ever be happy in that environment, week in, week out. However, I loved playing in the States and I regard many of the American players as my friends.

As it happened, that same year saw the publication of Greg Norman's book *My Story* and the so-called 'gutless poms' furore, which rumbled on for years and years, leaving a legacy to this day. My great friend Michael King – who remains big mates with Norman – and I can still wind each other up over the events of 20 years ago.

Norman wrote in 1983: 'So many talented golfers on the British Tour have not got the drive, have not got the guts or that inner power that is needed to go on and win when victory is in sight. The desire is there, but the raw courage required to turn that desire into a reality is sadly missing. There are too many good-time players on the British Tour who would be better off spending their spare time on the practice fairway, honing their skills to the point where they can stand up under the pressures that winning a golf tournament demands. Nobody can do it for them. They have to do it themselves.'

Those remarks were set against his general argument that British and European players needed to test themselves in America in order to become world beaters. It was a point of view surely disproved by Seve Ballesteros, Ian Woosnam and Nick Faldo, who all reached World No. 1 without committing full-time to the US Tour. All the Brits and the Continental players needed were the opportunities. The invitations have been more forthcoming in recent years, and the World Golf

Championship events have opened doors. It never used to be the case. By the beginning of 1985, when I received my first invitation to the Masters, I had played in only the Open Championship of the four major championships. My first of six USPGA Championship appearances did not come until 1991, and I only ever played in US Opens, in 1994, 1996 and 1999.

I had won too much of Greg Norman's own money in our pre-tournament matches over the years to think for a moment that he could possibly consider me lacking in guts. I was, however, outraged on behalf of my peers and on behalf of the European Tour. Greg got to hear my reaction before I had the chance to say it to his face.

'I have been known to be very indiscreet at times and there is every chance I might have dropped you in it,' was Queenie's delightful method of confession.

Not fancying life on the US Tour has not prevented my flying all over the globe in search of competition. It began in the 1970s with winter trips to South Africa, East and West Africa, South America and, eventually, Australia. I have played the Asian Tour and, on one occasion, competed (but not completed) in India. I have taken part in tournaments in the USA and in Canada and represented Scotland in the World Cup in China.

We were a bit like the crew of the starship *Enterprise* in those days, boldly going where few had been before. Jet travel was beyond its infancy but it was neither comfortable not particularly quick. I remember flying for 24 hours on one trip and being further away from my destination than at the outset. Work that one out. We flew – gratis with British Caledonian, of course – from London to Zambia, only to discover all flights from Zambia to Kenya were cancelled. So we hopped on a plane to take us from Zambia to Johannesburg in South Africa, seeking a connection to Kenya. All of that took a full day and yet in Jo'burg we were further away from Kenya than we had been in London.

These were exciting – and dangerous – times, when everything was new and life was to be embraced. But there was death and tragedy too. I was in Zambia the year gifted young professional David Moore was shot and killed by a drunken copper-mine worker who clearly became unbalanced. These were the days when players would stay in the homes of expatriates and very often participate in the lively social life of the expat.

Moore, who played football for Ipswich and was capable of a century break at snooker, had been to a disco with fellow pro Gary Smith, now the club professional at Wokefield Park in Berkshire. Both were sound but distinctly unsafe, as it transpired, in their beds when a screaming and roaring host burst in with all manner of wild accusations. He took Moore outside and shot him in the head while Smith dived into the bath-room, locking the door in a desperate attempt to avoid the same fate. The man broke down the door and held a gun to the head of an understandably terrified Smith for a full hour before being persuaded to stop. Poor Smith invented an imminent marriage in order to make the man think twice about his actions. Later that night the deranged man found a way to shoot himself after he had been taken to hospital.

Looking back on it now, I cannot fathom how and why the tournament continued the next morning as if nothing had happened.

There was another occasion in Nigeria when our visit coincided with a military coup. The practice was for the field to be split into three or four to play in pro-ams at different courses prior to coming together for the tournament itself. Three of the courses were all within an hour's drive from the capital Lagos. David Chillas and myself were among the unlucky ones who found ourselves up country in the middle of nowhere with the airports closed and a 6pm curfew instituted.

Three of us, including a Swedish reporter, hired a taxi, a big Mercedes, for a trip that was going to take two days. We planned ahead, booking a hotel we could reach prior to the 6pm cut-off point. We did not fancy being shot. However, we could not have planned for our driver brushing against a boy on a bike as we drove through a typical mud-hut village. Suddenly, we were surrounded by locals brandishing spears. They were not looking for a game of darts. Our laughter quickly disappeared when we saw the ash-coloured face of the driver and a speedometer rising dramatically.

We arrived in Lagos ten minutes after the first aircraft carrying golfers had landed from our point of departure. The coup had been put down and Nigeria's brand of normal service was resumed. It had been a futile, if dramatic, journey.

There were other near misses. Given the choice on arrival between a party at the clubhouse or an early night, suprise, surprise, I opted for the latter. So the wife of the ex-pat family with whom we were staying drove us to her home and the husband took his car full of our clubs to the course. On the way he was held up at gunpoint. He never saw his car again and I never saw my clubs. I remember once being driven to a farm and seeing a dead man with an arrow in his back lying at the side of the road.

I have suffered from malaria in Africa and, without a drink passing my lips, seen spiders and snakes on the ceiling. I was not hallucinating, however, when, pulling back the blanket of my bed in the house of an ex-pat, I saw a sheet covered in so many ants that not a centimetre of white was visible. But those were isolated incidents. I loved the golf, I loved the socialising and, of course, I loved the chance to win money at a time of the year when there was nothing doing in Scotland or, indeed, throughout Europe.

Only once did I abandon ship before the end of a tournament on these distant travels. I found India very difficult and not, as happened at one meal with President Kaunda, because I was required to eat with my fingers instead of cutlery. I have consumed enough fish suppers (fish and chips, as they say in England) in my time not to be fazed by trying to eat a curry with my hands. Gaylord Burrows, with whom I enjoyed some terrific money matches, had persuaded me to move from the Philippines to India. He said I would love it. He said the golf course was out of this world.

Royal Calcutta was truly one of the finest courses I had ever played. I shot 65 in the first round. But I found India an uncomfortable place and, again, nothing to do with the house of my Indian hosts, though it could have been the mansion from The Addams Family. It was huge and creepy and no one spoke English.

I started well enough in the second round to lead the tournament before just picking up my ball and leaving. I was not proud of myself for bailing out. I just couldn't take it any more. I had never seen poverty like it, people washing themselves in the open sewers that passed for streets. It was the most depressing sight of my whole life. So I boarded the first plane and flew home.

But it was not all sickness and diarrhoea. We had a lot of laughs. Dai Rees, the ageing Ryder Cup player with the column in *Golf Monthly* and the reputation to protect, was the boss man. I remember one birthday when he received an unexpected present. He removed his head cover on the first tee in front of the respectful gallery to discover a condom over his driver.

David Jaeger was the Tour's master practical joker. Some of his pranks were on a grand scale. We played at La Manga in southern Spain one year and were all frustrated that we could not get out on the Sunday night. Once a tournament was over, everyone was desperate to get home as soon as possible. The first available flight was not until Monday afternoon, a disaster for people on the road who valued their days at home. When the buzz started going round that a jumbo jet was coming in from Florida and would depart for London at 4am, this was regarded as the most welcome of news.

By 2.30am, it seemed that the whole hotel was assembled in the foyer, packed and eager to board non-existent buses for a fictitious aeroplane. Jaeger had started the false rumour.

He was also responsible for an evening of chaos at the Calatrava Hotel in Madrid, a gorgeous little place in the centre of the city where I regularly stayed over 20 years. The informality extended to guests taking their own keys from a board behind the little reception desk. Jaeger took all the keys, 30 or 40 or whatever, and jumbled them around so that not one single guest had the right key for the right room.

The only other hotel jape I heard to surpass that was when some Scottish rugby internationals removed every fixture and fitting from a team-mate's room – from bed to bathroom mirror – leaving the player to enter an empty shell and temporary insanity.

The combination of long flights, alcohol and the unfamiliar surroundings of hotels can bring their own difficulties, like the occasion when I became locked out of my room in Disneyland. John O'Leary and I were playing in a better ball tournament there, though I was sharing with Billy Longmuir. We stayed in the Polynesian Village, in a standard block of rooms with which many

British families will be familiar.

We had had a few on the plane. In truth, we were both drunk and by 2 o'clock in the afternoon both asleep on our beds. I got up to go to the toilet, a source of great danger for me over the years. I found my way not into the bathroom but into the corridor with the door back into the room locked. No amount of banging on the door could stir Billy from his drink-induced nap. Fortunately, I was wearing swimming trunks, the result of going for a dip on our arrival, but I was in considerable discomfort. I looked up and down the corridor and spied an alcove which I prayed was a toilet. I ran to the end of the corridor to find only an ice-making machine. But outside a door on the floor lay a tray with a coffee pot and mugs on it. There was no alternative in my mind. I picked up the coffee pot and was starting to relieve myself when the door handle turned and the door began to open. I dropped the pot, ran out the door, sped across the lawn and dived into the swimming pool, where I hid to the puzzlement of the sunbathers.

After the euphoria of 1976, I found myself again somewhat becalmed on the European Tour. I was still winning tournaments, for example, the Scottish Professional Championship in both 1978 and 1980. I even won the Colombian Open in 1979. But I did not win in Europe. It drove me mad. I felt I was good enough but the harder I tried the more frustrating my failure became.

Colombia was terrific because I beat my old friend Lee Trevino at a marvellous location high in the mountains above Bogotá. This was drug-running country, so our journey from a palatial farm hotel to the course usually involved being stopped by the army.

Trevino and I go way back to 1972, the year he successfully defended the Open at Muirfield, when I was just 18. Jimmy Letters, the club manufacturer and friend of my dad, fixed up a fourball at Dalmahoy, on the out-skirts of Edinburgh, for me and Ewen Murray with Trevino and Gary Player, no less. Imagine the thrill for a couple of young Scots lads to play with two such legendary figures.

We were firm friends by the time I holed the winning putt at the Ryder Cup in 1985, and Trevino, the US captain, approached me with the kindest words. 'I am glad it fell to you, Sammy,' he said.

I remember one Benson & Hedges at Fulford when Trevino came straight off a plane, a bit tired and emotional and somewhat jet-lagged, and onto the first tee for a practice round.

'Can I join you?' he asked.

I tried to explain to him that I had promised Steve the Doc, the tournament doctor, a game and that he was a pretty bad 24 handicapper who could give Spiro Agnew a run for his money in a scatter-the-gallery competition.

'Not a problem,' Trevino replied. Unlike some stars, he was perfectly prepared to go out with a rabbit.

Trevino was brilliant, Steve a little less so. We eventually made him tee up 40 yards down the fairway because he was killing spectators. As you might imagine, a huge crowd had gathered to see Trevino in action. He was terrific. He had the crowd in stitches with a masterclass in wise-cracking and shot-making. He even caught a ball in his hat, catcher-style, which Steve had nailed with his 3-wood and that was heading straight towards me, in his hat, catcher style.

Joking apart, he taught me how to play a plugged lie in a bunker so well that I reckon I am as good as anyone in the world at that shot. I am not sure that I should even reveal the secret. Well, all right, here goes: it concerns putting all your weight on the left side of your body. Then you pick up the club like an axe and drop it behind the ball. It just pops up so softly and slowly that you can actually see the name on the ball. The first time I tried the shot, it worked. It has worked ever since. Thank you, Lee.

1980 saw a rise in prize money, an upward move in my Order of Merit position (from 19th to 15th) and a 1.17 improvement in my stroke average. All good signs. Still no win on the European Tour, though. But when the big victory came by the end of the year it was to prove another of those seminal moments when my self-belief increased a notch.

In fact, looking back almost 23 years to that week in Melbourne and reviewing all of my 31 victories world-wide, I still consider my win in the Australian PGA Championship my best ever. I played the final two rounds with Seve Ballesteros, already an Open Champion and just six months after winning the first of his two green jackets. I also went down the stretch that year with Greg Norman, who had been taking Europe by storm and was just about to turn his shark teeth towards the USA.

I remember with some pride the compliment Ballesteros paid me after our 36 holes head to head, 'You are very tough, San, you are very tough.' Seve has always called me 'San', not Sam.

The week had begun with a practice round on the Monday and further practice early on Tuesday morning. 'Right,' I said to O'Leary, by now my travelling companion, 'I'm off.' I was not going to miss my first opportunity to attend the Melbourne Cup, which had been sold to me as one of the great sporting experiences. It was all of that, though I never saw a horse run a yard.

I had never been at an event like it in my life. Every square inch of this huge strip of grass was covered in blankets and people partying as if there was no tomorrow. It is fair to say I let myself go, as O'Leary discovered. He was watching the Cup on television and there was

Torrance on the screen, dancing away with his shirt off. But it did not seem to harm my golf.

I was leading going into the last round, with the combined might of Ballesteros and Norman in close pursuit. I remember I knocked it stiff from a bunker at the 16th to stay one stroke ahead and birdied the 17th to double my advantage. That was the breathing space I needed to secure what for me was a very important victory. I don't think it made much more than a paragraph in the British newspapers.

Defeating Seve in his pomp and Norman in front of his own folk gave me the confidence for the year ahead, the odd-numbered year of 1981 and, therefore, a Ryder Cup year. I was determined to gain selection at long last. In truth, I should have already made the team. Maybe I had wanted it too much; maybe I had not been sufficiently disciplined.

I had already represented Scotland in two World Cups and three Double Diamond events. I had played for Great Britain in three Hennessy Cognac Cups. The Ryder Cup had eluded me. Buoyed by my success in Australia, I embarked upon 1981 with my usual enthusiasm and a renewed self-belief. Reward came in Ireland, a country that has much in common with my native Scotland. The Irish are not unlike the Scots – good workers, golf-mad and lovers of life. It is the country, too, that makes my favourite drink, though, sadly, Guinness is forbidden on my periodic non-carbohydrate diets.

Two of my best friends and tour travelling companions in what I should not really regard as the good old days – though I do – were Irish: John O'Leary from Dublin and David Feherty from Bangor in the north. 'Brothers in arms' Feherty called John and me. When John quit playing, Feherty says I was a lost soul. He became a surrogate John, a replacement.

John and I began tournament golf at exactly the same time. John called me 'the hairy one'. David did not get on tour until 1980. He was not as young as some starting out but he received the same treatment from me as all the other youngsters, sharing what I knew, giving them encouragement. 'Don't be such a fairy,' I would say. 'Don't be such a Jessie.'

I certainly called Feherty a 'big Jessie' many a time. Once, memorably, when he was bitten by a snake in deepest...Surrey. We were playing in a money match, of course, ahead of the PGA Championship at Wentworth in 1992. Me and David against Wayne Riley and Roger Chapman. I was on my way to the 12th tee when I spotted a wee snake at the bottom of a tree. I poked it with my driver so much that it must have been well pissed off by the time Feherty arrived. He couldn't resist it. He went up there and did his David Attenborough bit. 'I'll identify this creature, no problem.'

He took a look at it, turned it over and saw it was an adder. 'That's the only poisonous snake in Britain,' he declared. He tried to flick it away but hit it fat and it wriggled up the shaft and bit him at the end of the index finger. I wasn't going to miss such an opportunity. 'You've just been bitten by the only poisonous snake in Britain,' I grinned.

'You bastard,' he snapped. 'Maybe I should go in.'

'We're £200 up,' I reminded him. 'Don't be such a fucking Jessie.'

So he sucked the poison and spat it out and we carried on. By the next hole, he couldn't feel his finger tip. It was stiff and absolutely numb. We played another couple of holes and it got worse. His finger was now straight out and swollen like a bee sting. 'I can't feel a thing,' he moaned. 'Not even if you hit it with a hammer.'

'Put the finger on this bench,' I said and I whacked

it with my driver. 'Did you feel that? No? Right, you can play.' We won the money, finished the round and headed for the St John's Ambulance people.

When he finally told them that he had been bitten by a snake – 90 minutes earlier – he was suddenly transported into the world of blue flashing lights, Chertsey Hospital and cortisone injections. He was admitted for the night. I bought him grapes but ate them all before I got there. And I made some comment to the waiting press along the lines of: 'It does not look good. Oh, you mean Feherty. I thought you meant the snake.'

David read all this the next day under the headline they must have delighted in writing: 'Irishman Bitten by Snake'. What they did not know was that we played on for an hour and a half. And, bizarrely, that might have been beneficial to him. The doctor told him that the centrifugal effect of swinging a golf club may have kept the poison at arm's reach, as it were. If he had been asthmatic or suffering from a heart problem, the poison could have killed him stone dead.

That's the way David tells it anyway.

O'Leary and I shared the same attitude towards life. We both delighted in finding the best place to stay at a tournament, never the five-star hotel but a residential hotel or a guest house or an apartment that drew us right into what the place was about. Nowadays, a professional's life is golf course, practice range, courtesy car, impersonal business hotel. It probably has to be. The money is so huge and the competition so fierce that there is little time or opportunity to experience the location.

Our *modus operandi* ensured us lasting friendships all over the world. John would pick me up at Heathrow, meeting my flight from Scotland, and we would then discuss where we were going and who we would meet on the way to the tournament. There were a lot of repeat venues in those days, so it was often a case of thinking 'What was the name of the bar lady?' and 'What was the guy in the locker room called?' People were delighted to be remembered and would do anything to make your stay enjoyable. Look after them and they would look after you.

One of John's favourite stories of our days together concerned a meal with Gerard Pangaud, a famous Michelin-starred French chef. We were playing in the French Open near Paris, some time during the 1980s. They had eight rooms at the golf club. We decided to take one and have a quiet week with some practice in the evenings.

I came into the clubhouse after the pro-am to find myself surrounded by the most elegantly dressed French women you could imagine. Actually, they were all over one of my playing partners, who turned out to be such a celebrated chef that Mark McCormack managed him.

The upshot of the day's golf and a few drinks in the bar was that we received a dinner invitation that evening to a new restaurant that was apparently all the rage in Paris. We got dressed up and stepped excitedly into the chauffeur-driven Rolls-Royce that had been sent to pick us up from the clubhouse. The guy was just fantastic. We were allowed in half an hour before the restaurant opened and were given the most exquisite pink champagne. While he enthused about his day's golf, we were ready to rave about his cuisine.

He disappeared into the kitchen, later to appear with a starter. It was purple. John looked at me and I looked at John and we both looked at this purple thing. We tried a taste but neither of us could eat it. The same applied to the next ten courses, all varying colours. We were so embarrassed and totally apologetic. For two hours we wriggled in some discomfort. But we all got on famously and the next day we sent over some golf equipment as a thank you.

John and I have always been enthusiastic social drinkers. People would see us with glass in hand and hear laughter and make certain assumptions. But it did not impinge on our golf. Everything was built around our star-ting times. We would not drink after Tuesday, though we might have a bottle of wine and stay up fairly late if we had a late tee-off time the next day. There was nothing worse than waking up early and having hours to kill before playing. If we had just made the cut or had a bad third round, we might occasionally let ourselves go a bit.

That was not the case at the Coral Welsh Open at Royal Porthcawl in 1980, when John enjoyed a comfortable lead going into the last round and I was in perhaps fourth position. John was, of course, out last, two groups behind me. We had been staying on the first floor of a three-storey residential hotel that satisfied our needs perfectly.

Since neither of us was off until lunchtime, we stayed out late, slept in and had breakfast mid-morning. We were both ready for the challenge ahead. The decision was to pack, put the luggage in the car and go straight to John's flat in Richmond after the tournament. The only problem was that we could not find the keys. No panic, we had plenty of time. We would break into the boot if necessary, retrieve our clubs and get a lift. However, I was driving a big British Car Auction vehicle on a sponsorship deal, which offered no way of penetrating the boot. One specialist and a frantic taxi ride later and I made my tee-off time by less than ten minutes. Neither of us enjoyed a good day on the golf course.

But I had to laugh when I reached the 9th to see the proprietor of the hotel standing behind the green dangling the car keys in his hand. They had been found in the third-floor bathroom. We were staying on the first floor, a lovely room with its own bathroom. I had been wandering again. Of which, more later.

My mood was much more upbeat at Portmarnock in 1981. So happy was I with my form that I backed myself with a local bookmaker to win the Carroll's Irish Open. Something like £150 at 22 to 1, if memory serves me right. Despite my passion for gambling, I have rarely bet on myself to win tournaments.

Portmarnock, like Royal Melbourne, is a true championship golf course. I don't know why but I have won on some great tracks. Having been brought up on the west coast of Scotland and, having played a lot of links golf, I am, not surprisingly, a very good wind player. I hit the ball pretty low and I love the dinky little imaginative shots required by seaside golf. There was, too, the half shot I learned from Nicklaus.

I was leading by five strokes going into the final round. The weather was perfect. My only moment of concern came at the 13th where that old snap hook fault of mine took my tee shot into a ditch. But I was able to hack the ball back to the fairway and from there I struck a 3-wood shot into the front left bunker. I upped and downed it for a par, which completely settled me.

I was still five ahead on the last tee, it was the kind of advantage anyone would relish. I fired a huge drive over the hill, leaving only a wedge to the green. There seemed like a million people around me, certainly the biggest gallery I had ever played in front of. It is Ireland's Open, after all. One of the Irish television commentators asked me how I felt standing there in the middle of the fairway. I told him it was very special. I don't think I swore!

We went back to Peter Townsend's house to celebrate. The bookie came round on Sunday evening to give me my winnings, more than £3,000 in cash. But, most importantly, I had clinched my place in the Ryder Cup team for Walton Heath later that year.

I remember sitting on a swing in Peter's garden, swinging away like a little boy lost in his dreams, looking up at the stars on a perfect summer's evening. I was ridiculously happy. Moments like those never leave you.

6

Yankees and presses

Gambling is evil and life destroying, even life threatening. And I love it. I love it with a passion. I love the thrill, the anticipation, the expectancy and the climax, whether winning or losing. It has been a big part of my life and it still is.

I first tasted the excitement as a boy taking shillings from priests at golf. I was not much bigger than an urchin when playing snooker for half-crowns in the Stevenson Institute in Largs. I was just a teenager when becoming involved in money matches while an assistant at Sunningdale, and by the time I returned to Largs to embark on my tournament career I was betting on anything that moved, a lot of it pretty slowly. Two flies crawling up a wall – it was a case of picking a winner.

Horse racing, greyhounds, cards – I did it all. I did it so much that in my early 20s it was taking over my life and affecting my golf. I would wake up in the morning and go straight to the racing pages. I did not think so at the time but with the benefit of hindsight and reflection it was probably detrimental to my golf. My mind was not totally focused where it should have been. It was on other things, like what horses were running today, what had run yesterday and what was likely to run well tomorrow.

Eventually it sank in. I realised it was taking over a part of my life that I didn't need to be busy on. I needed to concentrate on my golf. I needed to stop gambling. So I did. I didn't have a bet for 12 years, from my mid-20s to my late 30s.

Ironically, it had taken ten years of constant urging by a bookmaker, of all people, to persuade me of my folly. Bunny Wilkie, a small Largs bookie, who in a previous existence had been the top dog man in Scotland and very much a second father to me, nagged incessantly on the necessity of giving up betting. I listened wide-eyed in the back of his shop to amazing tales of fixed races and gambling coups, set against the underlying message that he had seen too many sportsmen ruined by their addiction. He never went on a golf course in his life but he liked me and I worshipped him. We had a great relationship. Bunny passed away but I like to think he is looking down with the same smile that I see in his son, John, a friend who used to caddie for me.

When I say I stopped gambling, I mean that I stopped betting on anyone else or anything else, two-legged or four-legged. I quit punting on racing and other sports. But I would still have 100 quid or so on a game of golf, or 50 or more on a frame of snooker. That was different. That was me backing my skill against the skill of someone else. The true test of that elusive combination of ability and nerve.

Trevino hit the proverbial nail on the head: 'You don't know what pressure is until you play for five bucks with only two in your pocket.' There is a clear distinction in my mind between playing golf for money and a betting habit that can lose people jobs and tear families apart.

Golf has always been a gambling game, from the 50p a corner OAP fourball on a Wednesday afternoon to the great money matches that were so prevalent in the United States in the 1930s, when wagers exceeded prize money. I love to read about the antics of the calamitously named Titanic Thompson, who was reputed to have taken $500 off Al Capone and lived to tell the tale. A card shark and a pool player, he could golf equally well right- or left-handed. Then there was the wonderful story when Raymond Floyd was snared into taking on the unknown Lee Trevino at Horizon Hills in El Paso in 1965, a tale told by betting expert and golf writer Jeremy Chapman.

'Have you heard of Lee Trevino?' Alvin Clarence Thomas, a financial backer, asked Floyd.

'No,' Floyd replied, knowing a match was in the offing, 'but I'll play anyone anywhere that I've never heard of.'

Lee Trevino, writing in his book *Super Mex*, described their first meeting: 'I'd never met Raymond, so when he drove up I got a cart and went out to pick up his golf bag. I carried his clubs into the locker room, put them in a locker, brushed his shoes, cleaned them and polished them. Raymond asked me, "Who am I supposed to play?" and I said, "Me." He looked at me and said, "You? What do you do?" So I told him, "I'm a combination of everything. I'm the cart man, the shoe man, clubhouse man and pro."'

Trevino won the first two matches with 65s, Floyd the third to win some of his pride and money back. He departed muttering something about finding easier ways to make a living. I loved Floyd, he was one of my favourite Americans and yet there is no man on this earth that I would rather not face. I just would not want to play him. At his height, he never backed down and he never knew when he was beaten.

Floyd and Trevino were the great American money pairing. Lanny Wadkins was another known to get especially animated when the money at stake was his own. Tom Callahan's fine book *In Search of Tiger* confirmed what I know of Phil Mickelson. He is one of their most eager practice-round gamblers, partial to a scary wager called a 'hammer', in which each hole is a match and the original bet can be multiplied over and over on each shot. A bit like our equally frightening afternoon games of backgammon upstairs in the Sunningdale clubhouse. Queenie taught me how to play backgammon; one day I'll teach him how to gamble! According to Callahan's book, Mickelson and John Huston once relieved Tim Herron and John Daly of $27,000 on a single shot.

The American author talks about Tiger Woods' enthusiasm for a wager and relates a story about the young golfer that takes me back to my boyhood in Largs. When Tiger returned from the course with his pockets jingling, his father Earl ordered him to stop hustling grown men for quarters. So, according to the writer, Tiger came home the next day with a wad of dollar bills.

My 'hustling' began with the priests and continued with a collection of Routenburn members who seemed quite happy to spend hours at twilight and often into darkness chipping and putting for cash with a young teenager on the 18th green. 'Bring 'em on' was my attitude. You could not bring them on fast enough.

There was an occasion when I, too, returned 'home' with a wad of notes that, years later, I regretted bringing out of my pocket and flashing about like the immature teenager I was. 'Home' at this time was my first digs at Sunningdale, when I stayed with a lovely artisan member by the name of Vic Reeves and his family. Vic was a decent, hard-working plumber, if I recall, and as nice as you could be. I came back one day, took him aside and showed him a bunch of £50 notes I had won on the golf course. I was just 17. I did not see any hurt in the eyes of a man who might have toiled for months for money like that. Years later, though, I felt it had been disrespectful, boastful and not very diplomatic. I regretted what I had done and I regretted not having the chance to tell him so.

As an assistant at Sunningdale you would play a member for your fee. If you won you received double and if you lost, more often than not you still got your fee. The members were very kind. We would play singles or fourballs. The big matches were the goal. Everyone knew they were going on and everyone was desperate to get into them. If a member wanted to play for a grand or two in those days, he didn't need a young assistant not carrying. But some would choose an assistant as a partner, take all the bets and give the assistant a percentage. That happened many times. I became a bit of a favourite because I was keen, polite and, crucially, did not lose very often.

Apart from my love of a golf bet, there was a certain imperative to play in these matches since it was impossible to cover my living expenses out of my wages. I didn't know anything about horses or any other form of betting in those days, though I did get involved in a few scary games of cards with my fellow assistants, the caddies and the club master.

John 'Badger' Davies, the former Walker Cup player and a bit of a money-match legend at Sunningdale, was probably the member who helped me most. He would bring me into games that would prove very rewarding more often than not. One day I lost £240 to him, a considerable amount of money for a 17-year-old whose official wages amounted to £5 per week. John would not take the money.

'No, leave it till the next time,' he said, disappearing into the clubhouse.

I didn't understand his attitude and thought it completely wrong. I went straight into the pro shop, looked out my precious cheque book, and wrote out a cheque for £240. I took it into Ollie – Oliver Lucas – the caddie master, whom the McKenzies were later to pluck

from Sunningdale in order to run their farm beside the
Queen's Course at Gleneagles. I think he retired in 2003.
I gave the cheque to Ollie because I was not allowed in
the clubhouse, asking him to hand it to Mr Davies. I sat
in Ollie's office, which offered an excellent view of the
members' bar. The transaction was completed amid
much laughter and hilarity on the part of John and the
other members.

The episode was important to me and not just in
gaining respect. I had made my point and shown my
position: if you beat me, I pay you. I did not want charity.
If I lose, I pay and, what is more, I pay right away. I hate
it when someone says leave it to the next day. I'd rather
pay double than wait 24 hours or even 24 minutes.

I used to love the money matches we would have on
Tour, usually on a Tuesday. To me, the most fun you can
have on a golf course is two pros against two pros for a
couple of hundred quid. Just go for your life. I think that
is fantastic. It is something that definitely improved me
as a golfer and improved my tournament capability.
A practice round on my own, me and the golf course, just
hitting balls, would be a form of slow torture. I would
play six holes and walk off. Give me a £200 match and I
might be 'two down, flat, flat, one up' on the presses and
I am in heaven. The amount does not really matter.
I have always believed that you practise more sharply if
you have got something on the game. You are playing for
pride not pounds.

That philosophy was adopted during my Ryder Cup
captaincy. I made sure my team played practice matches
for money. They had to play for a minimum of a hundred
quid or whatever. I wanted to know who beat whom and
who lost to whom. I wanted to know if Darren Clarke
and Paul McGinley could take money off Philip Price and
Pierre Fulke, for example. I wanted everyone in the team

room to know who was beating whom. And the players loved it.

I bemoan the passing of the exhibition match. I used to urge Derek Pillage, my manager, to arrange exhibition matches if he could. Now it is all company days. To me the ultimate company day would be four professionals playing against each other for money, talking about the game, having a laugh, trying to beat each other's butts. What entertainment, for the players and for the spectators. They would love the banter, since the wind-up, the heckling, the mickey-taking are all very much part of the contest. You could bring that back now and I am sure there would be a market.

Tuesday was always the day for the money match. Wednesday became pro-am day and tournaments would start on Thursday. In later years on the European Tour I valued my time with Suzanne and the family so much that I didn't travel to tournaments until Tuesday evening or early Wednesday morning in time to take part in the pro-am. That became my practice round. Occasionally, when we were away for a fortnight, like Dubai followed by Qatar, a match was arranged for the Monday between or the Tuesday or both.

If Floyd and Trevino were America's most legendary combination, then Lionel Platts and Hedley Muscroft were Britain's most lethal pairing. Neither ever established as fearsome a reputation in tournament golf as they enjoyed in money matches. Their golden period had really come and gone when John O'Leary and I began to take them on and beat them. There was a time when we thought ourselves invincible, ready to take on the world, a partnership just as feared as Platts and Muscroft at their peak.

We certainly had the sign on Greg Norman and any partner he cared to choose. Never more so than at

Portmarnock in 1980, when John and I absolutely murdered Greg and fellow Aussie Stewart Ginn. It was two days before the start of the Irish Open, towards the end of Greg's finest season to date in Europe. He had won the French Open by ten strokes and the Scandinavian Open and would subsequently win the World Matchplay Championship at Wentworth. He was to finish just £278 behind Sandy Lyle in the Order of Merit. It was pretty obvious at that stage that he was on his way to becoming the best player in the world.

This day, however, I was on song. And when I was on song I was pretty damn good. I was, I'm afraid, taking the mickey out of Greg, doing as much as I could to put him off. You would try to get under the skin of your opponent and it was not too difficult to irritate Greg. I loved all that – what fun! O'Leary and Torrance v Norman and Ginn was a match made in heaven for me. It might well have been the biggest money match I was ever involved in.

As John says, I always seemed to play fantastically against Greg. I was hitting it past him from the tee and hitting it closer to the flag. The more Greg got annoyed, the more birdies I had. We had won the match, the first press, the second press and the third press before playing for a double press at the last. If you win the double press, it is not such a bad day. But, glory be, having done nothing throughout the round, John holed a 50-ft putt on the final green to take the lot. We won every bet. Norman went ballistic. The next thing we knew Jackie Lee, Norman's caddie, told us he'd been sacked. 'Geez!' said John. 'This has got out of control.'

Another game we played against Norman at Southport illustrated how I could get him going. It was a similar scene to Portmarnock. We were demolishing them to such an extent that when Greg eventually birdied a hole, the 17th I think, I whispered to John, 'Thank God'. I had been driving the ball past Greg most of the day, something that always irritated a player who took great pride in his length. But I was always capable of a bit extra when required.

We were on the 11th or something and, blood vessels almost bursting, Greg ripped one down the fairway. I bent down to stick my tee in the ground and winked at John. I gave it extra and middled it perfectly. 'Christ! Off the heel again,' I said in a stage whisper as the ball flew 30 yards past Greg's. Another wink. You could hear the spectators murmuring: 'Look, Sam's hit it past Norman and it was off the heel!'

We used to have great times with Greg in his early days on the European Tour. Only his good friends like Queenie could get away with calling him 'Hollywood'. He brought glamour to the game as well as being a great player, as his Open Championship successes and long periods as World No. 1 confirmed.

It may also have been at Southport that I won so much money on horses – a few grand at any rate – that the local bookmaker could not settle. He told John and me to come back in three hours, by which time he would have raised the money. We went next door to a pub, had fish and chips and used the wrapping paper to carry home the cash.

That was the side of gambling which I found I had to control, i.e. stop, in the early years of my professional career. First, though, to meet Bunny halfway, I thought that I would just cut down, punt not so frequently and reduce my stakes. My favourite bet was a £2, sometimes £4, yankee on the horses – six doubles, four trebles and an accumulator; 11 bets totalling £22 or, in the case of the larger stake, £44. The first day that I tried out my new discipline – and I swear this is true – instead of my usual £2 yankee I did a 1p yankee. Total bet 11p. The punters who fill bookies throughout the land day in, day out would just laugh at anyone putting on such a ridiculous bet.

Sod's Law was bound to intervene, of course. All four selected horses won. Eleven winning doubles, four winning trebles and a winning four-timer. I collected £58 for my 11 pence stake. The day before I would have won either £11,600 or £23,200, depending on which of my usual outlays I had chosen. Did I say the amount does not matter? Never mind playing for pride not pounds, I had been playing with pence.

But Bunny was insistent. This hard but fair 65-year-old man had been through the mill in bookie terms with greyhounds when based in Glasgow. He gave up the big time and 'retired' to a small shop in Largs. As fascinated as I was at the gambling stories of this man whom I loved to death, I began to take heed of his dire warnings. It took ten years for me to get the message. I had become a prime candidate for Gamblers Anonymous. Although I was neither winning very much nor losing very much, I began to appreciate that it was taking over my life.

Gambling is just as much of an addiction as drinking or smoking. Whereas an alcoholic falls over, literally or metaphorically, a gambler stands up all the time. The key aspect about gambling is that no one need know. Only the gambler knows how much he is betting and on what; only the gambler knows how much he is losing. You can hide it far more easily from your wife and kids than you can a slurred word or a shaky step or smoke billowing through your nostrils.

I gave up betting for 12 years and I started again. I am probably as addicted to gambling now as I was then, except that with maturity has come self-control. I regard gambling as my hobby. Hobbies have to be paid for and, to that extent, I suppose I have lost money since I resumed. In fact, I've definitely lost. But not that much. My friends tell me I am a good gambler, brave enough and not too foolish. I think I am pretty good at it, though I realise it is always dangerous for the person himself to nurse that belief.

One thing about which I am under no delusion. You cannot win at gambling. You can win sometimes but not all the time and probably not even most of the time. It is just such enormous fun. I bet on football, occasionally on golf and on horse racing when I receive a tip from a friend. And since my appearance on *Poker Million*, a tournament televised by Sky Sports, which Jimmy White won, much to everyone's astonishment, I have dabbled in playing poker on the Internet. As I say, it's fun – the consistent and continuous credo of my life.

With gamblers you tend always to hear about wins rather than losses. I suppose I am no different. My biggest potential loss was in a pub in North Berwick, when I was playing pool with the proprietor. Half-pissed, I found myself in a double-or-quits game where, had I lost, it would have cost me £10,000. I won, and came out even.

The most I ever won was £11,500 on four European football matches. A yankee, needless to say, in which I took all four matches to be draws. The first three came up and for some reason there was a one-hour delay on the fourth, an Italian game. Roberto, from my favourite Italian restaurant in Virginia Water, and a few other friends were in my den at home playing a card game called kaluki. We sat there playing cards, having a drink, working out what I might win and staring at this Ceefax picture on my television screen. I don't think the screen changed for an hour. It was a 0–0 draw.

I am not sure that Seve Ballesteros would fancy watching an unchanging screen for 60 minutes but, former caddie that he once was, he used to love a wager. I remember being in a room with Seve at the French Open when he wanted to bet on his ability to throw a coin into a tiny square in a carpet, using backspin.

Seve was indirectly involved in my not winning a penny from my biggest successful bet. The explanation for this apparent riddle lay in Seve's insistence that Miguel Angel Martin be replaced in the European team prior to the 1997 Ryder Cup. Months earlier I bet £1,000 at even money – my largest ever bet at that time – on the Spaniard making the team. From that day on, partly to do with an injured wrist, he never won a euro yet still he made the team. But because he was forced to step down and did not hit a shot, the bookmakers refused to pay. I lost my money.

As it happened, I was something of a man in the middle of the whole affair. I must have received 50 faxes from Miguel asking me to help him sort everything out. He trusted me. I did my best for him, and not because of the money I had riding on his appearance. I don't think Ken Schofield had any alternative in the circumstances. Miguel was injured and the captain did not want an injured player on the team.

Funnily enough, back in 1993 I was involved in a related situation. A badly septic toe forced me to withdraw from the Sunday singles. Had I not played on Friday, all those who had backed me to play in the Ryder Cup that year would have lost their money. Of course, that was the furthest thing from my mind at the time. As a Ryder Cup trooper I was just desperate to do my bit for the cause.

7

Ryder Cup at last

My Ryder Cup career might have begun sooner but for Ken Schofield. At least that is what he insists every time we share a glass of wine and reminisce over the old days. I never say anything to disabuse him of that notion.

The year was 1977, the place was Wilmslow and the tournament was the Greater Manchester Open. Ken, in his comparatively new role as the young executive director, was driving around in his buggy during the final afternoon with the late Lord Derby, the PGA patron. He happened to be right on the spot when I needed a ruling.

'Tony Gray was the tournament director, and if there was one other official on site, then that was it,' Ken recalled.

'Nothing like the army of officials who emerge from behind bushes and trees these days. The Tour was still part of the PGA then and I was wearing the distinctive maroon jacket. Sam recognised the colour and the face and quite properly asked for a ruling. Basically, he wanted to know if he could have a drop from a path or some sort of artificial surface.

'That was where things began to go wrong. I tried to be helpful by assuming the role of referee with no competence to do so. I suggested that he play two balls, which he did. He scored a par 3 with one ball and 5 with other. I went on to tell Sam that I was pretty sure 3 was correct and he should score the hole thus.

'Tony Gray later corrected that ruling. It should have been a 5. I am not exactly sure if those two strokes actually cost Sam a place in the 1977 Great Britain and

Ireland team – the last before continental Europeans came on board – but that is how I have regarded the situation ever since. I got flustered. If it happened nowadays, I would have a manager suing me and the Tour.'

The story gets retold late at night after we have shared a few glasses of red wine. The time is long overdue for me to declare that it was not Ken's fault and I do not hold him responsible. The writ is in the post.

Ken has been a good friend over the years, someone in whom I can confide, someone who more often than not knows how to handle any situation.

Like the occasion at the very posh Club de Campo in 1982 when I won the Benson & Hedges Spanish Open, having lapped the field. I think I played all four days with the best of the Spaniards and won by eight strokes. Stevie Martin, a good friend of mine from Dundee, and one of the finest iron players I have ever seen, stayed behind after his round to share in my celebration. Stevie became pretty tired and emotional, so much so that he threw up on the lawn outside the clubhouse, pungently close to where the crested-blazered dignitaries were drinking aperitifs ahead of a grand dinner.

Ken spotted the problem and acted swiftly with the minimum of fuss. He put a chair over the offending mess and said: 'I think we'll call that GUR.' Ground under repair. Perfect.

I suppose I fell in love with the Ryder Cup about the same time everyone else of my generation did. There were the tears of Brian Huggett at Royal Birkdale in 1969 when he holed a 1-yard putt for a half against Billy Casper and thought, wrongly as it happened, that he had won the trophy for Great Britain and Ireland.

It beats me how anyone could get so emotional about golf!

But it was the supreme gesture of Jack Nicklaus, already my golfing hero, in the match behind which captured the imagination of a public beyond golf enthusiasts and epitomised so much of what is great about our sport. In giving Tony Jacklin a 2-ft putt on the final green for a halved tie and match, 16 points each, Nicklaus cemented his reputation for sportsmanship, laying down a marker for the spirit of the Ryder Cup. That legacy remains intact, even if the match has experienced a few shameful moments since.

I remember with fascination reading the reported conversations between Nicklaus and Jacklin while playing the final hole.

'How do you feel, Tony?' Nicklaus asked after calling on Jacklin to wait for him to catch up.

'Bloody awful,' Jacklin replied as the two men walked from the tee down the middle of the fairway.

'I thought you might,' Nicklaus said. 'But if it's any consolation, so do I. A bugger, isn't it?'

After holing a testing 4-footer for par, Nicklaus stooped forward to pick up his opponent's marker and, with a smile, offered his hand.

'I am sure you would have holed,' Nicklaus said, 'but I was not prepared to see you miss.'

From that moment on, the Ryder Cup held a certain appeal to romantics like me. An aura surrounded the match, despite the fact that only the introduction of Continental players in 1979 paved the way for making the contests truly competitive.

I desperately wanted to be a part of it. As I said, my desire was perhaps too strong. I yearned to make the team and, for long enough, I could not get in. As someone who enjoyed great camaraderie, I was always going to have an affinity for team golf. Gaining selection for the team confirmed your status in the game. You were one of the 12 best players in Europe, and not just at any given moment but over a two-year period of qualification.

So when I won the Irish Open in 1981, I was happier for the fact that it secured my place in the Ryder Cup team than for the victory itself.

It was my good fortune, or not, depending on your perspective, that I should make my debut at Walton Heath in September 1981, against what in later terminology would have been known as 'the dream team'. The American side that year was probably the finest ever to be assembled, over here or over there.

Together, they had already accumulated 36 major championship victories, with only three of the 12 still to win a major. Ben Crenshaw and Tom Kite proceeded to do so, leaving only Bruce Lietzke of their number without such a success at the end of his career. Most thought him well capable of completing the set had he opted to play more tournament golf.

In Tom Watson, Bill Rogers and Larry Nelson they boasted the winners of the US Masters, the Open Championship and the USPGA Championship that year. Their strength is best demonstrated merely by listing their names: the six aforementioned, plus, would you believe, Raymond Floyd, Johnny Miller, Jack Nicklaus, Jerry Pate, Hale Irwin and my buddy Lee Trevino. That calls for another 'Wow!' The late Dave Marr, one of golf's gentlemen, scarcely needed to be the intelligent and astute captain that he was.

John Jacobs, known as the 'father of European golf' because of his role as a trail-blazer in the 1960s and 1970s, was our captain. John remains a very quiet, lovely man, always with a kind and comforting word. Another true gentleman. His team was notable not so much for those present as those absent. There was no Seve Ballesteros, despite his 1979 victory in the Open and his US Masters triumph at Augusta the following year. A dispute over appearance money resulted in Seve playing only seven tournaments in Europe in 1981, mostly on the Continent. Although he won two of those – the Scandinavian Enterprises Open and the Spanish Open – it was decided that he should be denied one of the two wild cards.

People were already in awe of Seve. He was becoming a god on this side of the Atlantic, and the European Arnold Palmer, our king. We would have been nowhere in subsequent Ryder Cups without him. What he did for our Tour was immeasurable and unmatched. But in 1981 he sought the same kind of financial inducements being paid to American stars such as Johnny Miller, Lee Trevino and Tom Weiskopf. He wanted appearance money and the European Tour was not prepared to pay it.

In 1981, as with my captaincy two decades on, ten players were named straight from the money list. Whereas I enjoyed complete autonomy to make my two picks, John Jacobs had to abide by the decision of a selection committee of three: Neil Coles, the chairman, Bernhard Langer, the leader on the money list, and Jacobs himself.

While Jacobs was understandably keen to have Seve on the team, the committee opted for Peter Oosterhuis in his place, and Mark James, No. 11 in the rankings, instead of Tony Jacklin. It is fair to say that Tony was less than pleased.

In truth, Ballesteros and Jacklin would have made no difference to the outcome. Nor could Jacobs have done anything to alter the result. We were slaughtered. What is more, we knew we were going to be slaughtered. We were overpowered and overwhelmed. We were not good enough. Simple as that.

However, long before I lipped out from 12ft on the 18th for a birdie that would have given Howard Clark and me an afternoon fourball victory over Miller and Kite, I was hooked. The Ryder Cup was for me. I cried as the ball horseshoed the hole and stayed out. The bawling had started. It meant that much.

I have no idea to this day why Jacobs split Howard and me up for the morning fourballs on the second day. Howard was to become my favourite partner over the years, the best I ever had. He was rock solid, tough to beat and tough to please, as caddies discovered. You would never know, watching that mild-mannered, hugely informed and informative roving golf reporter on our screens these days, that as a prickly player he often wore his spikes on the inside of his golf shoes.

I was paired with Nick Faldo. First out and first finished by more than an hour as we were thrashed 7 and 5 by the lethal combination of Trevino and Pate. Trevino did all the thinking and Pate did most of the playing, as we discovered all too painfully the often sharp insight of a typical Super Mex quip.

'Jerry Pate is the best player in the world from the shoulders down,' Trevino said of his team-mate.

And, sure enough, Pate never hit a shot without Trevino telling him what to do. We would walk onto the tee at a par 3, for example, and Trevino would bark out his command. 'A 4-iron and hold it up,' came the order, only for the delivery to be swift and precise. Pate was the most magnificent shot-maker, with a swing to die for.

'A 5-iron and draw it,' might be the next instruction. And so it went on throughout the morning and during the course of the afternoon as the same American duo did for me and Oosterhuis, my third partner in three series. I was beginning to get a complex. We lost that foursomes 2 and 1.

To the singles and, as if I had not suffered enough from him, I drew Trevino in the top match. We bumped into each other on the putting green at Selsdon Park Hotel, where both teams were staying, on the Saturday night, an occasion for merry banter and mutual good-natured baiting.

'Sammy,' he said. He had called me Sammy, not Sam, since 1971 when Jimmy Letters, my first club sponsor, fixed me up with a practice match with him at a tournament in Dalmahoy, near Edinburgh.

'Sammy, I am going to beat the moustache off you.' The bushy black moustache had already become a caricaturist's dream, like the pencil behind the ear, the rolled cigarettes, the curly black hair and eventually the broomhandle putter. Each one to become my trademarks.

We were already five points in arrears prior to the singles. But I was more excited than I had ever been in my life when I woke up on the Sunday morning. I headed for the hotel car park, full of anticipation at the thought of playing in my first Ryder Cup singles. Head to head with Trevino, *mano a mano* as Mex would say, two practitioners of the money match playing for pride and honour.

Trevino was outside. 'Where you going, Sammy? he asked.

'I am going to the course,' I replied.

'Could you give me a lift?'

'Sure, jump in.'

So he got into the car and we went to the end of the drive, where you turn right for Walton Heath. I turned left.

'Hey, Sammy, where you going? Trevino enquired.

'Fuck you, Lee,' I said. 'I'm going home. I'm out of here. I'll settle for half a point.'

The ultimate practical joker and legendary

wisecracker nearly split his sides laughing. He took it in great part. Of course, there are some who wouldn't have, and there are many I would never have dared tease in that way. There are some, too, who might regard that as a sign of weakness on my part. I was just having fun.

I turned the car round, though I wish I had not. Trevino whipped me 5 and 3 in about two hours. If memory serves me correctly, we were back in the clubhouse having a beer before Nicklaus set out on match No. 12 against Eamonn Darcy.

That night I shaved off my moustache for the official dinner. It seemed like the right thing to do in the circumstances. It has been on and off since, mostly on. I feel naked without it.

As splendid an individual as John Jacobs was, and is, he was not in any way aggressive. The European team needed aggression if we were to mount a challenge to the Americans. The European team needed Tony Jacklin.

Becoming a Ryder Cup player makes a professional feel better about himself. He walks that bit taller and casts a slightly bigger shadow of intimidation. I certainly grew in stature after making my debut in 1981. Similar to my first tournament win in 1972, victory over Brian Barnes in 1975 and my success in the Australian PGA Championship in 1980, gaining selection to the Ryder Cup team gave a boost to my career.

The 1980s, in particular the first half of the decade, were to become a highly productive period of my professional life. From 1981 to 1985 inclusive I finished 6th, 3rd, 6th, 2nd and 5th in the Order of Merit. I won nine of my 21 European Tour victories in that five-year spell, seven in seasons '82, '83 and '84. Statistically at least, I played the best golf of my life in 1982, when I ended the year with a stroke average of 70.14.

However, I have always considered 1995 by far my

best year – the year I won three events, had 13 top ten finishes, and enjoyed my best Ryder Cup performance-wise. I might have won the Open Championship had I putted as well as I played tee to green, and I accumulated more than three quarters of a million pounds in prize money. A pretty good advert for the over-40s.

The year of my Ryder Cup debut also produced my highest finish in the Open, 5th at Royal St George's behind Bill Rogers, the best placing by a home-based Scot at that time since Eric Brown's 3rd way back in 1957. The highlight was undoubtedly my hole in one at the 16th on the final day. There are few greater thrills than achieving a hole in one in front of packed stands in your own Open. There was no way I was going to react with restraint.

When I saw the ball disappearing into the hole, I dropped my 7-iron and ran to grab playing partner Lee Trevino. I put my arms around him and lifted him into the air.

'Watch my back, Sammy,' he screamed. 'Watch my back.' This was at a time in Trevino's career when it was all he could do to get out of bed in the morning, never mind swing a club.

Rogers was playing a long way behind me and was several strokes in front. But I reckoned at that stage on two more birdies giving me a squeak at the title. It was not to be. What I thought was an exquisite floated approach to the 17th came up 20 yards short of the green and I had to settle for par. And I signed off with a costly double bogey 6, having caught the rough with my drive, found a bunker with my second and nearly hit my escape shot out of bounds.

The excellent annual handbook for the European Tour shows that the gap between Sandy Lyle and Sam Torrance for second position in the Order of Merit (behind winner Greg Norman) in 1982 was £1, £61,518 to £61,517 in favour of that lovely, easy-going lump of a lad who could hit the ball a country mile with a 1-iron.

Actually, the exact margin was £1.33p and that was determined only the following day on the exchange rate between the pound and the escudo. That was the difference between my being invited to what would have been my first Masters and not, since the letter everyone in golf coveted was sent only to the top two in our Order of Merit at that stage. Although I had won the weather-curtailed Portuguese Open by four strokes from Nick Faldo, I needed Lyle to finish one place lower than he did. Yet even that was not the full story. Sandy holed 10-ft putts on the last two greens to deny me.

And there was more. That same year – in an echo of my unacceptable behaviour in walking out of a tournament in India – I picked up my ball while leading during the second round of the Sanyo Open at Sant Cugat and went home. As it transpired, had I made the cut and pocketed even the smallest cheque, I would have finished ahead of Sandy in the Order of Merit at the end of the year.

I headed for John O'Leary's house in Richmond and from there I telephoned a journalist friend in Scotland before flying there the next day. I told him what I had done, confessed the error of my ways and asked him as a favour to go easy on me. I landed at Glasgow Airport to read a headline to the effect of: 'Torrance Slinks Back into Britain.'

I had the previous week secured just about the easiest victory of my career in the Spanish Open at Club de Campo. My front-running credentials were never better demonstrated, though the lack of leader boards or any other method of receiving information left me utterly oblivious to the fact. All I knew was that I held a single stroke advantage going into the final round and was three under par for 12 holes.

A mighty drive down the 13th fairway led me to a glimpse of the first leader board. I could see the name Torrance at the top but could not quite make out the margin. Suddenly, the figure came into focus. Blow me, I was 10 in front. I never hit a decent shot after that but I hung on to win by eight.

There were to be two more victories in 1983, a Ryder Cup year of course. My first victory in Scandinavia was achieved over an American and on pretty dreadful greens. I have won on a few occasions in my career on bad greens, primarily because I did not allow them to bother me. It was not uncommon then for a Yank to cross the Atlantic and win. But I managed to edge out Craig Stadler at Sven Tumba Golf and Country Club, a tough course built round a lake.

A successful defence of the Portuguese Open was notable for the winning score and a most curious meeting with American extrovert Danny Goodman. The most glorious summer's evening at the halfway point in the tournament saw Goodman sitting on the balcony with a face so miserable that you worried about leaving him alone with the belt on his trousers.

'Are you all right?' Mark James asked.

'Yeah,' he replied with a face like Victor Meldrew. 'I don't know what to do. I have just been left $20 million. All I have got to do is prove my sanity.' For once I was speechless. Mark, too.

If I tell you that my winning score that week was two under par 286 and that I was the only player in red figures, you will gain some understanding of the severity of a most peculiar course. Troia, in the Algarve, was really one large bunker. If you missed the fairway, you landed in deep sand, often in footprints. It would have taken 500 men and 500 rakes to have kept the sand smooth. Add to that the usual southern Portuguese wind and it made for a treacherous combination.

There was not the all-consuming interest in the Ryder Cup 20 years ago that there is now. For the profile to change the Americans needed to be beaten, and for the Americans to be beaten Europe needed the aggression and professionalism of Tony Jacklin. Having been omitted in 1981 under controversial circumstances, he needed to be persuaded to take charge.

Once on board, he blew stronger than an Algarve hurricane through the preparations for the match at PGA National in Florida. Everything became first class, from travel on Concorde to finest quality golf shirts, cashmere sweaters and smart suits. Our golf bags and hold-alls were made of the best leather. His attention to detail included the purchase of specially absorbent shirts to combat the humidity in daily temperatures well into the 90s. There were also extra pairs of golf shoes to cope with wet conditions underfoot. You were made to feel special, made to feel part of a great team. Most of all, you were made to feel you could win. We travelled to West Palm Beach with victory on our minds.

Another indication of a change in priorities, helped by a £300,000 sponsorship from Bell's Scotch Whisky, was that for the first time we were allowed to take our own caddies, all expenses paid.

It helped, too, that in Jacklin we had our own hero, a man who had been there, done it and worn the T-shirt with his victories in the Open Championship and the US Open. We looked up to him, respected him and wanted to play for him.

In the red corner, as it were, stood Jacklin's old adversary Jack Nicklaus, whose home was just 20 minutes away from West Palm Beach. It was somehow appropriate, given what had happened at Birkdale 14 years earlier, that both men should make their captaincy debuts in the same match.

Probably the most important contribution Tony made came before a ball was struck, before we crossed the Atlantic, before even the team was selected. He persuaded Seve to return to the fold. The Spaniard, who had won his second Green Jacket earlier in the year, was worth a whole lot more to the team than the bare, though impressive statistic, of four points out of five.

Seve hit what probably remains to this day the greatest shot in Ryder Cup history. He had hooked his tee shot at the 18th hole of his singles against Fuzzy Zoeller into deep rough and could only move the ball forward a few yards into a fairway bunker. He was still 240 yards away from the green and facing seemingly inevitable defeat. But he launched himself at his ball with a 3-wood and from the fringe left, pin high, chipped and putted to secure half a point. The distance, the lip of the bunker, the equipment and the situation made the shot one of sheer genius, executed by probably the only man capable of playing it. You have to realise that the club he used, an old wooden-faced Toney Penna No. 3, was so unforgiving it was hard enough to hit the ball properly from the fairway never mind from sand.

From day one, everything felt very different from how it had at Walton Heath. Tony instilled in us a belief that was translated into results. I paired up with José Maria Cañizares for a first day morning foursomes 4 and 3 defeat of Ray Floyd and Bob Gilder. The afternoon fourball saw me teamed up with my good friend and vice-captain to be Ian Woosnam.

Woosie was to become one of Europe's greatest players, a world No. 1, the Masters champion and one of the so-called 'famous five' who were born within 11

months of each other. It can only be coincidence that
between April 1957 and March 1958 countries as diverse
as Spain, England, Germany, Scotland and Wales produced, in order of seniority, Messrs Ballesteros, Faldo,
Langer, Lyle and Woosnam.

Woosie was making his Ryder Cup debut and,
having sat out the morning series, had become as fidgety
as an expectant father by the time we gathered on the
putting green prior to our match with Ben Crenshaw and
Calvin Peete. I could see that he was nervous and jumpy
and in need of some reassurance.

'Don't worry,' I said. 'I'll sort you out. It is not a
problem. We'll get on the first tee and I'll rip it down the
middle.'

That seemed to lift him a little. So I drove first and
proceeded to hit my ball straight right, out of bounds.
I glanced sheepishly at Woosie, who gave me a wry smile
and an unspoken message along the lines of, 'You prat.'
Whereupon, he fired a 1-iron down the middle of the
fairway, caressed a 9-iron with that effortless swing of
his to about a yard from the flag and holed the putt for
a birdie. That's the Ryder Cup for you. Out of the
shadows come heroes.

As it happened, I birdied about seven or eight of the
last ten or 11 holes in a terrific match that finished all
square. That was probably my best burst of golf in a
Ryder Cup.

Woosie had been my partner earlier on in the week,
not in crime but in an embarrassing misunderstanding.
The European team had been invited to dinner at the
yacht club a short drive from our hotel. I noticed Fuzzy
Zoeller giving directions to someone else and suggested
to Ian that we just follow his car. Nothing was said. We
jumped in the car and waited for him to leave.

We had been driving for more than quarter of an

hour – a little longer than expected – when we pulled up at this magnificent property. I remember Cal Peete getting out of one car, though we were first to get to the door. I rang the bell and the door was opened by none other than Jack Nicklaus, looking somewhat bemused, it has to be said.

'Is this the yacht club?' I asked rather pathetically.

'No, I live here,' the great man replied. 'But come in.'

He took us into his home, where the American team were gathering for a little soirée. Jack poured us a drink and pointed through his window to the yacht club on the other side of the lake.

A lot of guff has been said and written about the social demands of Ryder Cup week. Most of the complaining comes from the American players, who try to suggest that evening functions interrupt their preparations for the event. What rubbish! We are talking about a welcome dinner, a gala dinner and, perhaps, a get-together after the match is over. That's surely not too heavy a schedule to undertake. This is the Ryder Cup, for heaven's sake! Tell me what hardship there is in sitting down to dinner with your friends and team-mates. Most evenings it is just a question of a quiet dinner, a few jokes and laughs with your fellow team members and wives, and off to bed pretty early, sober and exhausted. You are far too tired for anything else.

As for the gala dinner, I have always felt enormous pride walking to the table as a member of the European team, hearing the roaring and cheering from people who have paid quite a lot of money to be present.

And yet the Americans moan and whine. What on earth is their problem? Do they think it is beneath them? It is not as if they have to sit with the general public.

These gripes have increased as money in golf has grown and the Ryder Cup itself has become an enormous international sporting occasion, probably third behind the Olympic Games and the football World Cup in its status. The events at PGA National that 1983 October weekend barely scratched the consciousness of the American public. Back in Europe, though, excitement was mounting. We led 4½–3½ after the first day. It was 6–6 at lunchtime on the second day and 8–8 going into the singles on Sunday.

I was drawn against Tom Kite, eighth match out. One down playing the 18th, I looked to be out when I hooked my second shot into thick rough about 90 yards from the hole. I was allowed relief from casual water but because I would have been required to drop the ball onto a down slope I decided to play it where it lay. I somehow contrived a wonderful pitch stone dead, maybe 18 inches from the hole, for a birdie and a halved match. I was ecstatic. Nicklaus was in despair. It was now 13–13 with two games remaining.

First Lanny Wadkins manufactured a breathtaking pitch over a bunker at the 18th, a 578-yard par 5 to secure a half point against Cañizares, prompting the most unusual sight of Nicklaus sinking to his knees and kissing the spot from where the shot was played.

Then Bernard Gallacher, who had been struggling to find his form all week, lost to Tom Watson on the 17th green. I still think Watson stretched the rules that day. Having missed the green on the right, he did not play his chip for ages, waiting to see what happened in the match ahead. It was a bit odd and a bit off, making Bernard wait. I always thought play was supposed to be continuous.

We had lost by a point, 14½ to 13½. We were heart-broken. We really felt we should have won. I am sure that we failed to close the deal because of inexperience and not having been in that position often enough. But we took great heart from the occasion and became stronger for the defeat. The Americans were always pretty aloof in those days and quite rightly so, given their generations of domination. That all changed in '83. They got the fright of their lives, believing for much of that final day that they were about to lose on home soil for the first time in history.

'The Ryder Cup will never again be a foregone conclusion,' a relieved Nicklaus commented. 'Gentlemen,' he told a group of British golf writers, 'what we now have is a real match again.'

Nicklaus, who had been instrumental in the introduction of European players to the event, never said truer words. We left Florida with our belief that we could beat these guys even stronger. My experience of the Ryder Cup is that when you are on a losing team you become even more determined to gain selection for the next team.

I was desperate to be at the Belfry in 1985, though, of course, I had no idea it would change my life.

8

The putt that changed my life

I might never have been in a position to hole the putt that changed my life. I might even have missed the 1985 Ryder Cup.

My love of fun and of having a good time has got me into a few scrapes over the years, but rarely had I come closer to real disaster than one autumn night in the Swiss Alps.

The Tour had rolled on and up to Crans sur Sierre, a popular Alpine ski resort a couple of hours' drive from Geneva and for years – before I think the course was ruined – home to one of the most enjoyable events on the calendar. The scenery is magnificent, the nightlife lively, and what golfer does not like to belt the ball 10 per cent further at an altitude of 4,000ft above sea level?

It was the Tuesday before Ryder Cup week, a time to unwind, a last chance, some of us decided, to let our hair down before the most important three days' golf in the year. The tournament started on Thursday, by which time all socialising would have ceased in light of our forthcoming trip to The Belfry.

But for the moment, a crowd of like-minded revellers had repaired to the George and Dragon, an English pub popular with the caddies, for a bit of rest and recreation. One drink led to another and before long I was on top of a table, stripped to the waist – a habit of mine, it seems – giving it plenty.

The pub resounded to the chorus of 'We're gonna beat the Yanks, we're gonna beat the Yanks, ee aye addio, we're gonna beat the Yanks.' Suddenly, in walked

Tom Kite, who took one look at the scene and, clearly struggling to believe his eyes and ears, turned round and left. That, of course, prompted another mighty roar from the assembled company, including quite a number of my Ryder Cup team-mates, whose anonymity remains preserved with me.

I viewed Kite's swift departure as one up to Europe. I punched the air and made contact with one of those whirligig fans. Losing its cool, it took a chunk out of my hand. There was blood everywhere. It could have been disastrous. It would not be too much of an exaggeration to envisage an injury that could have forced me to withdraw from the Ryder Cup. It would have been even conceivable to imagine a really disastrous, career-ending outcome.

Did I care? Not at that moment. I just wrapped it up with something and carried on drinking. There will be many who might regard our behaviour as loutish or at best inappropriate, given the importance of the following week. In fact it represented a release, an opportunity for the kind of bonding that would prove invaluable during the contest. Those of us present that night – and, frankly, those members of the team not there – knew we had a great chance of an historic victory. Little did I think that when the dream became reality I would be the man in the spotlight. That week and that putt were to change my life.

There was never any question that Jacklin would be reappointed as captain, but no shortage of debate about the system of selection. I can't remember a Ryder Cup when controversy has not raged concerning the method of picking 12 players, or should that be ten or what about 15?

My view has changed recently, not so much with my experience of captaincy as with a recognition of the significance of the world rankings and the fact that many of our leading players are competing in the USA. Originally, although it gave me a terrible dilemma over my selections, I was a defender of using the European Order of Merit to provide the bulk of the team as a way of protecting our tour. But it was frankly silly that I had to use a wild card on Sergio Garcia, at the time ranked No. 4 in the world.

I think they have got the balance about right now. Five spots for our tour, five straight from the world rankings and two picks to give the captain a measure of flexibility.

Jacklin had inherited his team in 1983, with all 12 players chosen straight from the money list. His preference would have been to select the whole team, something the Ryder Cup committee and players' representatives would never agree to. Not then, not now. The compromise in 1985 combined the top nine on the money list with three captain's picks. They were Nick Faldo, Ken Brown and, to the surprise of many, José Rivero. Remarkably, the Spaniard represented Europe's only player new to the Ryder Cup in a team that included nine of the dozen golfers narrowly beaten two years previously. That was to prove a crucial factor in our famous victory.

The automatic selections (in alphabetical order) were: Seve Ballesteros, José Maria Cañizares, Howard Clark, Bernhard Langer, Sandy Lyle, Manuel Pinero, Sam Torrance, Paul Way and Ian Woosnam.

The USA, captained by Lee Trevino, fielded four newcomers: Peter Jacobsen, Andy North, Mark O'Meara and Hal Sutton. Those with previous experience were: Ray Floyd, Hubert Green, Tom Kite, Calvin Peete, Craig Stadler, Curtis Strange, Lanny Wadkins and Fuzzy Zoeller.

Heightened expectation at the possibility of the Americans being beaten for the first time in 28 years generated large, excitable crowds, who eagerly applauded the home players onto tees and greens. If their enthusiasm occasionally strayed over the line of normal spectator etiquette, prompting the odd cheer at an American mistake or loss of hole, then it was understandable. Some of the US team complained, most volubly Peter Jacobsen, though I always thought it revealing that Trevino was to describe his players as 'a lot of cry-babies'. It made for an electric atmosphere that, except for a disappointing first day, nudged the needle on the amp gauge higher and higher as we edged towards victory.

We did not exactly enjoy a flier. Clark and I went down 3 and 2 to Stadler and Sutton as Europe lost the morning foursomes 1–3. Clark and I lost again in the fourballs, this time on the last green to Floyd and Wadkins, but by the end of the first day we had narrowed the deficit to 3½–4½.

The turning point came at lunchtime on the second day when, on the 18th green in that often lonely place between the lake, the giant scoreboard and the packed grandstand, Stadler missed the kind of short putt that would be a 'gimme' in most friendly club games. It was well inside the 'grip', the standard measure of concessions, perhaps less than 2ft.

'I was going to give him the putt,' Sandy Lyle told us at lunch. 'And then I thought, "Oh, I'll just let him tap it in."'

The Walrus became the Egg Man, to borrow from the lyrics of Lennon and McCartney, as he stubbed the ball left off the hole. He turned round, stuck his left hand down the back of his neck, and walked away in disbelief and despair.

Watching on a television in the clubhouse was Sir Henry Cotton, who turned to my manager Derek Pillage and said the prophetic words, 'That's going to cost America the Ryder Cup.'

In that instant, the momentum switched towards Europe. That unexpected half point for Langer and Lyle, who had holed a huge eagle putt at the 17th, brought the scores level. After three matches in a row, including a victory that morning with Howard over Kite and North, I was rested for the fourth series. By evening we led 9–7. We were in sight of an historic win and there was a tangible sense of destiny in the team room that evening.

But first Tony had to decide on his singles order. Among all the discussion there was a general agreement that Wadkins would be sent out first for the Americans, both as a quick player and just about the meanest gunfighter in their midst. Trevino would have been looking for him to do exactly the job *I* sought – and was given – from Colin Montgomerie all those years later.

'I want Wadkins,' a voice from the corner of the room said.

Manuel Pinero stood up, a bit like the wee slave soldier in *Spartacus*, and repeated a request that sounded more like a demand. 'I want Wadkins.'

Nobody in their right mind would want Wadkins. Wadkins was tough. Wadkins was someone you would not want in your worst nightmare. He had shown his calibre with the chilling pitch that effectively won the match in 1983. If you wanted someone, you would have picked, er, my eventual opponent, Andy North.

Sure enough, the draw came out and the little Spaniard's name was opposite that of Wadkins at the top of the order. Pinero not only got the opponent he wanted, he got the victory for which he, Jacklin and the team hardly dared hope. 10–7.

An out-of-sorts Woosie lost to Stadler, only for Way to beat Floyd. 11–8. Ballesteros halved with Kite in an amazing match before, in quick succession, Langer crushed Sutton and Lyle disposed of Jacobsen. 13½–8½. Europe needed just a single point to win the Ryder Cup for the first time since a Great Britain and Ireland team prevailed in 1957.

I was next.

Maybe because of what happened that Sunday or a Sunday 17 years later, I have always felt a great affinity for The Belfry, both the hotel and the golf course. Given the history, it was perhaps not suprising that when I signed a new sponsorship deal in 2003 it was with The De Vere Belfry.

Somehow, something always happened when the paths of The Belfry and Sam Torrance crossed, from my winning putt to my rugby tackle on a plant pot in 1993, from the septic toe that forced me to miss the singles that same year to my victorious team captaincy in 2002.

I had been going there since the mid-1970s when, to be honest, the course was neither good enough nor mature enough as a venue to stage the Hennessy Cognac team competition. But Dave Thomas has done wonders over the years and it is now a very fine test of golf.

'Look out for my young brother,' Manuel Ballesteros said to me, long before Seve came on Tour. 'He is going to be something special.' He certainly did not smell like anything special. My first ever encounter with the great man was at Dalmahoy, when he let rip with the most disgusting fart. 'That's diabolical,' I said, pretending to be offended. 'I eat food, not flowers,' he replied.

Seve had already demonstrated his brilliance by the time we met in the Hennessy at The Belfry in 1978. Within a year he would be Open Champion. There was an incident that day. There had to be. This was Torrance at The Belfry.

I was one down playing the 17th. He was on the

front edge of the green in two and I was to the right of the green. I completely fluffed my chip a matter of a few feet, though enough to move my ball nearer to the hole than his. He rolled his long putt stone dead, to be conceded a birdie 4. Lo and behold, I chipped in for a half to take the match down the 18th.

I was off, like a horse bolting through the tape. I reached the teeing area, placed my ball on a tee and was about to hit when I realised there was no one around. I spotted a puzzled-looking Seve and a knot of spectators about 80 yards away. In my eagerness and excitement, I had gone to the 9th tee. Anyway, he three-putted the last and we halved our match.

I managed to go to the right tee on Sunday, 15 September 1985. Just getting to the 1st tee had been a glorious struggle, fighting my way through the avenue of cheering spectators who had come in their thousands in anticipation of the greatest Ryder Cup day in Britain for a generation. You could sense there was something in the air.

There must have been something in my cereal that morning. I played awful. I was three down after ten holes to North, who had scarcely hit a shot. I remember urging myself to keep concentrating, keep trying and hopefully my luck would change. It did. A par was good enough to win the 11th, and at the 15th North missed a short putt for a half. I was now one down playing the 17th.

I knew exactly the position. I knew we needed one more point. Tony was there, walking with my match as if to indicate its importance. I hit a good drive up the par 5 17th, while North fired his ball through the fairway into the thick rough. He managed to move his ball only 40 yards or so with his second shot. I had only to knock my second shot into the gap and I would be left with a wedge to the green. He was still well over 200 yards away. The advantage was mine. Christ, did I not hook my second shot into the long stuff.

'What have I done?' I thought.

From nowhere, it seemed to me, considering his unimpressive ball-striking all day, North flushed this long iron, which flew arrow-like towards the pin. His ball bounced short of the green, rolled past the flag and stopped just off the putting surface, though only 15ft from the flag. Now I was in trouble.

I found my ball in rough that was long and wispy rather than deep and thick. In my favour I was only 100 yards from the hole. A difficult shot, but playable. I was thinking about what was at stake and of all the people I wanted to win for and I hit an unbelievable shot to just 8ft away from the stick.

North hit the hole with his putt but the ball stayed out. I had my putt to go all square, head to the last hole, and have the opportunity of securing the point we required to win the Ryder Cup. No pressure then. My hands were shaking, my club was shaking, everything was shaking. It felt like the hardest putt of my career. But I knocked it straight in and made for the 18th tee. Not the 9th, as I had done against Seve years earlier.

I remember taking out my driver and passing it to Tony Jacklin with the words, 'You hit it'.

'Don't be daft, laddie,' he replied. 'You have got it in you.'

I hit the drive of my life.

In those days, before club and ball technology changed the character of holes, the 18th represented a greater challenge than now. It was not uncommon to be hitting a 4- or 5-iron, even a wooden club, for your approach over the lake to the green. I cut the corner so much with my drive, hitting it so far down the fairway, that I needed just a 9-iron for my second.

North, meanwhile, skied his drive into the water. The best he could do was a bogey. I knew then we had won the Ryder Cup. I was not going to screw this up. All I needed was a par from the centre of the fairway.

I walked from the tee and crossed over the first part of the burn with tears streaming down my face. I looked to the right and saw all the American wives in a stony-faced row. I did not want to let them see me crying, so I managed to hold it together for just a few more moments.

My second shot was straightforward, were it not for the circumstances. All I was thinking was 'Don't duff it'. I could thin it and it would get up there somewhere. Don't hit it fat, don't put it in the water. Keep your head still, the same basic that boys and girls are taught when they first pick up a golf club. The same basic that I must have heard a thousand times from my gravel-voiced father growing up in Largs.

I made a lovely connection and knew immediately that I had nailed it. The ball flew over the water and onto the green, about 6 yards from the hole. I remember managing a sigh of relief and raising my arms in the classic gesture of triumph before being grabbed by Woosie. I clattered his head accidentally with my 9-iron but I bet he did not feel a thing.

North was further away in four and was conceded a short putt for a double bogey 6. I had three putts to win, three putts for the Ryder Cup. What luxury!

Unbeknown to me, back at a 17th green almost forgotten about in comparison to events unfolding in the natural amphitheatre of the 18th, Howard Clark, my partner of so many foursomes and fourballs, was lining up a 4-ft putt that would have clinched the match. To him would have gone the glory. But he missed.

A BBC television executive later told me that they recorded his putt to show after mine, regardless of whether he was successful or not. Although you cannot stage-manage live sport with any precision, the scene around the 18th was exactly how a film director would have choreographed the climax. The huge leader board, the lake, the grandstands, the crowds, the captains, opposing team-mates – they were all gathered together in that spot at that moment.

And in the middle was a hairy Scot with a red sweater at least two sizes too small.

Three putts for the Ryder Cup. But I did not even want to two-putt. If the 17th had been the hardest putt of my life, this was the easiest. I rolled it towards the hole, watched it start to take the gentle right to left break and raised my arms again, putter erect in my left hand, as it fell into the cup. It was by some margin the best moment of my career. And it remained that until 17 years later at the same green on the same course.

'This was the day European golf came of age,' Jacklin said. 'The team was my inspiration and it shows the world how good we really are. We have so much talent, more than even we realise.'

A night of all nights followed. The celebration of all celebrations. It seemed that everyone ended up in the swimming pool, though one of the journalists playing snooker in the hotel late that evening resisted my attempts to throw him into the water. To this day I tease Bill Elliott about how he did a runner in order to avoid getting his nice suit wet.

The party continued until five or six in the morning. A few hours' sleep and it was off to a champagne brunch with John O'Leary. Monday afternoon saw us drive back to London and another all-night session with my great friend Mike Kemble at his house in Woburn. Dennis Taylor celebrated his famous final-frame defeat of Steve Davis in the World Snooker Championship in the same house.

Somehow, I boarded a flight from Heathrow to Spain the following day for what turned out to be a third celebration in a row as some of the Ryder Cup team hooked up for the first time with their friends and fellow professionals who shared in the triumph. This was a reflection of the growth and increasing strength in depth of the European Tour, and everyone basked in the after-glow of victory over the Americans.

The Wednesday pro-am proved little more than an excuse for a fourth night of revelry, which for me ended at about 3am. I simply could not drink another drop. I could not get any more in. I stopped drinking for a month after that to recover from the biggest hangover of my life.

Yet I never felt a thing. I was carried along in a state of euphoria that mirrored exactly how European golf felt in the heady aftermath of our success. It totally transformed my life. Not so much financially – for five years after that I did not have a club contract – but certainly in terms of public profile. I could not go any-where without being recognised and congratulated. My popularity soared, both in my native Scotland and beyond. That was not a problem for me. As a pretty outgoing sort, I welcomed the attention and enjoyed interacting with the golf fans. It was certainly not going to change me.

I may never make the return journey from Sunningdale to Largs, but then I don't need to. I am still there. I am still the guy who likes nothing more than a social drink and maybe a game of darts with my mates in the nearest local.

Life has a strange way of tripping you up just when you are running your fastest. Less than a month after holing a winning putt at the Ryder Cup I was failing to hole a crucial putt in the Dunhill Cup. It remains the biggest disappointment of my career.

The stage was set for another Torrance triumph, one where, as a proud Scot, I could, metaphorically at least, wrap the St Andrew's cross round my shoulders. The inaugural Dunhill Cup at St Andrews in October 1985 was the perfect time, place and event for the golf-mad Scottish public to acclaim the Ryder Cup heroes, and maybe one hero in particular.

Sandy Lyle led the three-man Scottish team, which also included Gordon Brand Jnr; England fielded three of the victorious Ryder Cup team in Nick Faldo, Howard Clark and Paul Way; Spain could also claim three, namely Seve Ballesteros, Manuel Pinero and José Maria Cañizares; and, of course, Ian Woosnam represented the heart and soul and spine of the Welsh team. Only three of the team from The Belfry were missing: Bernhärd Langer, José Rivero and Ken Brown.

Scotland had beaten Brazil, though only narrowly, and Japan, a much more comfortable 3–0, on the way to a semi-final match against an all-Ryder Cup USA team of Mark O'Meara, Raymond Floyd and Curtis Strange. There was a high level of anticipation and excitement at the possibility of Scotland winning this new team competition on home soil.

Sandy had lost to O'Meara, and Gordon looked to have the measure of Floyd. It fell to me to see off Strange, who, of course, would cross my path in rather more dramatic circumstances a generation later. We already knew and liked each other. I have always had an admiration for tough cookies.

This will sound like terrible arrogance but I was playing great at the time. I mean I was king. He could not beat me. That is honestly how I felt. We were tied going up the last, the widest and most celebrated fairway in golf. Over the Swilcan Bridge I walked, heading towards my ball and a win that Scotland expected. I certainly did.

He handed the advantage to me by leaving his approach in the Valley of Sin. It is a difficult two putt from there, though Costantino Rocca in the 1995 Open and Paul Lawrie in the 2001 Dunhill Links Championship were to prove it was possible to single putt.

I was even more in the driving seat when I knocked my second shot about 10ft below the hole, leaving a straight uphill putt. Perfect. He left his first putt 4ft short and finished out for par. All I had to do was hole an easy putt for a winning birdie. A golfer needs confidence, not over-confidence. Not only did I miss that one, knocking it clumsily past the hole, but I missed the downhill return too.

I could have died. I just wanted the hallowed turf to open up and swallow me. From having experienced the highest point of my life I now had to endure the lowest. I was inconsolable.

The following year was not a good one. Domestic problems, combined with what was to become regarded as the customary Torrance non-Ryder Cup year slump, saw me fail to win any tournament for the first time since 1977. For the next decade, with the exception of 1990, I was to finish higher in the Order of Merit on the odd years than on the even ones, it probably being no coincidence that in each case Ryder Cup selection was at stake.

If 1985 had not ensured my enthusiasm for the event for all time, then the experience of 1987 at Muirfield Village provided further cementing. To this day, I regard our victory there, an historic first in the United States, as Europe's greatest.

Most people who were there talk about the European celebrations as much as anything. In a huge storage room for buggies in the bowels of the magnificent complex was situated the so-called International Tent, in effect the meeting place for thirsty European supporters. That was to prove the gathering point for the most extraordinary scenes ever witnessed at a golf tournament, certainly in America. Hundreds of fans, carrying flags, wearing caps and scarves – for all the world like a good-natured football crowd – swayed together in repeated choruses of 'Eee aye addio, we've won the cup'. Some were standing on tables, others were on chairs. I could not help thinking back to that night in an English pub halfway up a Swiss mountain when we sang 'Eee aye addio' about what we were going to do to the Americans.

Our supporters appreciated it when into their midst, led by the likes of Woosie, Jesse and me, came the players. Shirts were tossed into the air – mine of course – and champagne was sprayed everywhere. I would have removed every stitch of clothing if I could have got away with it. Golf had never seen such patriotic fervour. For about half an hour, until we were dragged away to the victory dinner, we had a ball.

The enormity of the achievement should not be underestimated. This was Muirfield Village, the course Nicklaus designed and built, a regular stopping place on their Tour, a venue chosen for revenge. Nicklaus had resumed the captaincy with that in mind.

But our team was very strong: Seve was still in his pomp; Nick Faldo had just won his first Open at Muirfield; Bernhard Langer would finish the year ranked third in the world, one place ahead of Sandy Lyle, who within six months would win the Masters at Augusta; Woosie was the World No. 6 while a 21-year old José Maria Olazábal was emerging as a real talent. Competition to get into the starting line-up was intense.

Tony Jacklin, captain for a third time, took me aside on the eve of battle and, in his most sombre voice, declared, 'I'm resting you for the first day – you're playing.' His timing was perfect in that the second half of his message came just as he saw my jaw drop and deflation spread across my face. His tease reflected all the nudge, nudge, wink, wink team-room talk about how Suzanne and I could not keep our hands off each other, having recently started a passionate love affair. We had just become famously engaged on Concorde on the official flight across the Atlantic and, frankly, were in a constant state of physical excitement.

As it transpired, I played only on the Friday morning prior to the Sunday singles. Everybody was playing great. I was bursting to play but others were ahead of me. That is the way it goes. I realised long before I became Mark James's vice-captain or I myself assumed the captaincy the importance of those sitting out a series maintaining the group ethic and remaining supportive members of the team – not always easy in such an individualistic sport as golf.

The golf that week was just the best Europe had ever played. A 4–0 whitewash of the Friday afternoon fourballs gave us what proved to be a decisive 6–2 advantage. But it was the Saturday afternoon series of fourballs that produced some sensational low scoring and caused Jacklin to comment, 'I never thought I would live to see the day when I would see golf played like this.'

Woosie and Faldo were out in a better ball 29 and eventually 10 under par for the 14 holes required to dispose of Tom Kite and Curtis Strange; Andy Bean and Payne Stewart also reached the turn in 29, the foundation to a 3 and 2 victory over Eamonn Darcy and Gordon Brand Jnr. But it was Langer's 8-iron approach to the last hole in the setting sun and fading light that lived longest in the memory. Wadkins, who surprisingly did not win a point until the 12th of the singles, hit his close enough to guarantee a birdie. Langer's ball finished inside that of Wadkins, just a couple of inches from the hole.

Europe led 10½–5½, needing just four points from the 12 singles. It was to prove quite a struggle, with Darcy becoming a less unexpected hero in hindsight when you consider the subsequent exploits of fellow Irishmen Christy O'Connor Jnr, Philip Walton and Paul McGinley.

It is said that Darcy's whole body was shaking – and only his putter remained steady – when he sank the most slippery of 6-ft putts on the final green for a crucial, if not precisely Ryder Cup-winning, point against Ben Crenshaw. I had seen Olazábal with that putt the previous day and knew that if he had missed, the ball would have rolled 15ft down the slope. An ashen-faced Darcy was still gripping the putter tight in his hand at the back of the green amid all the mayhem.

'Geez, that thing,' I said to him, grabbing his putter. 'What was the problem?' I asked as I put a ball down on the same spot and stroked it into the hole with one hand. It seemed funny at the time. I did not mean to make light of what I knew to be a horrendously difficult putt. All the more so since an hour earlier I had experienced my first wriggling snake – not Feherty's adder but the involuntary twitch of the putter that had sent Mr Lu's ball scurrying across the green at Muirfield in 1972.

I had been one down with one to play against Larry Mize. He hooked his drive into a hazard and, after much toing and froing and dropping and redropping, he holed a 50-footer, no less, for a bogey 5. I hit my tee shot down the middle and fired a glorious 5-iron just 12ft below the hole. I had two putts for a half point we looked like needing, according to the scoreboard.

My hands were shaking, and they kept shaking as I struck the putt. I had no idea when I hit the ball whether it would go 20ft past or move just a foot. It rolled stone dead. It had looked to an observer the perfect putt. I knew that it had been anything but. I knew how it felt and, what is more, I remembered how it felt in the weeks and months to come. I identify that moment as the start of my serious putting problems.

Darcy was never the same player after that. He, too, was to find life difficult on the greens.

It had been one of the greatest weeks of my life, a privilege to be a member of a great side. The crowds at Heathrow greeting our triumphant return were unbelievable. It was one of the happiest periods of my life. I may have acquired the beginnings of the yips but I was in love.

9

Suzanne

The first time I set eyes on Suzanne was at a party at the London home of Robert Windsor and Grace Kennedy. Robert was a great friend of snooker star John Spencer, Grace a good-looking, talented singer.

In walks this gorgeous woman wearing a long skirt with a slit up the side, which revealed the suggestion of a magnificent pair of legs. Dancer's legs which, of course, they were, prior to Suzanne working on television and in films.

'Wow! Who the hell is that?' I asked John O'Leary.

Pretty soon I was flicking at her skirt with my snooker cue in a flirtatious and mischievous manner. We hit it off immediately and spent the night together on the couch, top to tail. Definitely no hanky panky.

Suzanne was in the process of breaking up with the actor Patrick Mower. By the time we met again my first marriage was ending very publicly in a ghastly tabloid tangle that I do not intend to discuss for the sake of Suzanne and my three gorgeous children, Daniel, Phoebe and Anouska. Together, they have given me a happiness that I could scarcely believe possible.

But when I caught up with Suzanne again in 1987 I was in a bit of a mess. An emotional wreck at the best of times, I was drinking too much and my golf was suffering. Suzanne was introduced to golf in an indirect way by Eric Morecambe, having done three Eric and Ernie shows after they had switched from BBC to ITV. She had just done *Carry On Emmanuelle* and, thinking she was French, they cast her in one of the plays 'wot Ernie wrote'. In fact, she had pretended to be French in order to get the film role. A skimpy dress, a bit of an accent and suddenly Suzanne Morris, the daughter of Mary Bonner, from Airdrie, and Henry Morris, a north London billiard hall owner, was a Parisienne actress.

As a result of her association with Britain's greatest ever double act, she was made a Lady Taverner; the fourth, if memory serves me correctly, after Lady Thatcher, Rachel Heyhoe-Flint and Joan Morecambe. She used to do a lot of charity work for them.

The Taverners were involved in a golf short being filmed at Turnberry. When John Cleese dropped out someone thought about Suzanne as a replacement. She says she was obviously there for decoration and concentrated on just looking good. Nice clothes and a decent swing. But she did take a couple of lessons.

So there she was on the Ailsa Championship course at Turnberry, playing the first round of golf in her life and, bizarrely, achieving a hole in one at the 4th, a par 3. Some very good golfers play from schoolboy to OAP and never manage a hole in one. Unfortunately, they were not filming at the time but there were plenty of witnesses. She was so naive that when she got to the bar later in the day she remarked to the people she was with that she thought someone would buy her a drink in the circumstances – she didn't know that she was supposed to buy all the drinks. But she got the golf bug for a while and received loads of invitations to take part in pro-ams.

I would see Suzanne from time to time at those pro-ams, always in company. She was this really bubbly person, fun to be with, part of the crew. There was nothing more than that. Then she disappeared for a couple of years. I found out later she had moved to California to study acting.

The first I knew of her return was while in

contention during the closing holes of the final round of the 1987 London Standard Four Stars event at Moor Park. I heard a voice shout, 'Hi, Sam,' and saw this woman running from behind the ropes onto the fairway. I ushered her back to the gallery, promising to see her later. There was definitely a spark there. It was impossible to look at Suzanne and not feel a stirring of desire. But I had a tournament to win first.

As it happened, I lost in a play-off to Mark McNulty. And that night I lost my heart.

We met in the celebrity tent where the pros and celebrity amateurs mingled. Although it must have been obvious to everyone how well we were getting on, we tried to achieve a measure of discretion as we arranged to meet outside. I went out one exit and Suzanne disappeared through the kitchens. We were kissing under a tree in the pitch black as a van slowed down some 50 yards away.

'Night, Sam,' a voice shouted through the driver's window.

The van moved down the road a bit before stopping again.

'Night, Suzanne,' the same voice called.

We were rumbled. We went our separate ways that night but the spark had now ignited. And we still hadn't been on a date. We put that right within a few weeks.

We might well have got together even earlier. Suzanne told me how she saw me playing golf on television one day and decided to pay me a visit. It was a matchplay event at St Pierre. I was three up on Jeff Hawkes with five holes to play, looking good to face Seve the next day. She telephoned a friend at the BBC and made all the arrangements for the following day, not expecting me to lose on the final green. It was not exactly in my plans either. I went home and she stayed where she was.

In those days, when playing at Moor Park or at other tournaments in the London area, I would stay with my dear friend Chris Rudge at a magnificent pub called the Rose and Crown. Chris – or Grandad, as I call him – drives for me nowadays, to functions or speaking engagements when some socialising is required.

I was at the Rose and Crown the evening I was due round for dinner at Suzanne's house in West Hampstead, a beautiful five-bedroom flat she bought from Sheena Easton, the Scottish singer who moved to the States and bizarrely hitched up with Prince.

To this day, Suzanne thinks I took fright. I remember having a few too many, maybe because I was a little apprehensive. She was waiting in her flat, all dolled up, and I rang to say I couldn't make it.

'Sorry?' she replied, a bit puzzled at my reticence.

'I can't come.'

'Why?'

'I haven't got a car.'

'I'll come and pick you up.'

'No, it's all right, I'm on my way.' That was all the encouragement I needed. I knew she meant business.

At which point I jumped in a taxi with a pint in one hand and a bottle of champagne in the other. Stopping only to buy a box of after-dinner mints – the great Scottish romantic that I am – I was soon at her place. She was standing on the balcony looking like a million dollars.

That was us off and running. We were both outgoing, chatty people who liked to party, stay out late and live life to the full. Within weeks she was off and running, after an example of my natural exuberance and sense of fun threatened our relationship. I was playing at Royal Birkdale and Suzanne was still coming to terms with such expressions as the two-tee start. When I putted out at the 18th, she headed straight for the bar and became puzzled when I did not appear.

'Is there another bar?' she asked of O'Leary.

'No, this is it,' he replied.

'Are you sure Sam will come in here?'

'Yeah, when he's finished. He's got nine more to play.'

Which was why I saw her running down the side of the second fairway trying to catch me up. It was my birthday that week, usually the prompt for some of my old mates from Largs to appear for a surprise celebration. Sure enough, half a dozen of the lads arrived for a party, which included the almost compulsory kissogram. Apparently, I returned the kiss rather too enthusiastically and started chasing the woman around the room. Suzanne was not impressed.

I discovered just how unimpressed the next morning when I awoke to find her gone. She had been due to leave that day to rejoin the cast of *Stepping Out* on tour in Scotland. She was on stage that evening at the Adam Smith Centre in Kirkcaldy. But it was my birthday and I had not expected her to leave without waking me.

I was lying in bed feeling sorry for myself when these things started arriving at regular intervals. Balloons, champagne, presents, even chocolate buttons, which I just love. She had obviously arranged everything in advance and not been able to cancel. My self-pity soon turned to guilt and, pausing only to sample the champagne, I persuaded my friends from Largs to drive me from Southport to Kirkcaldy.

We got there after curtain-up. I went straight to the stage door and persuaded the man to show me to Suzanne's dressing room, where I hid in the wardrobe. Suzanne always teases me about that. 'It's Scotland,' she says. 'Of course Sam Torrance could get into the star's dressing room and into her wardrobe. Anything you like, Sam. Do you want us to stop the show, Sam?'

I waited until the interval when she returned to her room for a change of clothes. As she opened the wardrobe to fetch a gown, I jumped out in front of her. I think she was wearing nothing but a face of terror.

'Don't ever leave me again,' I said. And she hasn't.

That week she stepped out of *Stepping Out*, to the horror of one angry producer. Bill Kenwright, London's most celebrated impresario, has apparently forgiven her desertion, though in acting terms it is considered even more taboo than a golfer walking out of a tournament.

Unbeknown to me, she flew from Glasgow to London, London to Geneva and then travelled by train and coach to surprise me at the European Masters at Crans Sur Sierre. Imagine my astonishment and delight when, sitting in a coffee shop on the main street of this little ski village, I looked through the window and saw Suzanne and O'Leary walking up the hill. I let them walk past before startling them from behind with the old Scottish greeting 'Oi'. Within weeks, Suzanne and I were sitting on Concorde on our way to the Ryder Cup.

'What would you say if I asked you to marry me?' I asked in one of my moments of spontaneity, as Concorde soared across the Atlantic. I had planned nothing.

'I don't know,' she replied. 'Yes, I suppose.'

'Okay, will you marry me?' I asked.

'Yes,' came the answer.

I needed a ring. I had not brought one with me. So I removed the little rubber band from the wee rose that British Airways give you with your meal and placed it on the appropriate finger. Suzanne still has the now well-worn, rubber band.

It was more than seven years before we were to marry but we are as much in love today as we were when we became engaged at 50,000ft and at mach two.

Apparently, Suzanne had been subconsciously rehearsing for the day in the early throes of our relationship. There was one section in *Stepping Out* where her character would be scribbling down on paper notes of a dance routine. She came off the stage every night with pages of 'Mrs Torrance' and 'Suzanne Torrance' and 'Mrs Sam Torrance', the doodling of someone falling in love.

Tony Jacklin seemed happy for us, though I worried that our high profile and high altitude union might in some way deflect from the task ahead. A cartoon in one of the newspapers that week showed Suzanne draped round me in seductive pose while I addressed a putt. 'Not now, Suzanne,' the bubble says, 'I am putting at the Ryder Cup.'

It worked out terrifically well. We won and Suzanne won the friendship of players and partners whom she had not known prior to the trip. It must have been difficult for her, stepping into such a close-knit group of people obsessed by golf and, at that moment, with the job of beating the USA for the first time on their own territory.

We were all over each other. I could not keep my hands off her and I had to endure a lot of stick from my team-mates when I arrived for our meetings and meals with a fairly dishevelled appearance. The opening ceremony proved a special moment for us. We walked, hand in hand, round the back of the 18th green in front of the big clubhouse and up to the stage. The reception from the spectators was fantastic.

We looked at each other with the same thought in mind and said 'yes' before spontaneously running back round the clubhouse to the beginning and starting the walk all over again.

We were young lovers who had both been round the block. We had both lived more than a little and were ready to settle down, albeit not to a life of pipes, slippers and aprons. Not the least attractive aspect of Suzanne is her ability to be one of the gang, to party with the best. She can be 'one of the boys' as well as the most gorgeous, sexy woman. We used to leave little love messages to each other, on eggs, behind doors, beside toilets, anywhere really.

Our first place together was her Hampstead flat but that did not really work for me. Parking was impossible. I would come home from a tournament on Sunday night and have to park what seemed miles away. My little Porsche was always getting broken into. It was a bit of a nightmare.

I wanted us to live in Largs where I was born and brought up and where for 20 years on Tour I returned with never less than enthusiasm. I loved my enormous white house on the hill, opposite Kelburne Golf Club on the other side of the tracks from where I grew up. Even though I would spend a lot of time away playing golf and in a London flat during the height of the British season, I never thought about moving. Largs was home. I wanted it to be our home. And I wanted my child to be born in Scotland. So a pregnant Suzanne came to live in Largs. And Daniel came sooner than anyone expected.

When Suzanne went into labour five weeks prematurely, her first thought was for me. 'Tell him not to panic, everything will be all right,' was how she insisted I be told of the news. She knew I would panic.

'Don't panic,' the man in charge of the courtesy cars at Fulford said as I arrived at the Benson & Hedges tournament on the morning of 4 August 1988. 'You are about to become a father.' I had sensed there was something wrong that morning. Curiously, I had told the driver on the way to the course that I had felt strange and uneasy.

I panicked, of course. 'How do I get there?' Planes and trains were discounted. It became quickly apparent that I would have to go by road. The sponsors gave me a car and a driver and we set off for the maternity hospital at Paisley, halfway between Largs and Glasgow. With the mobile phone not then the everyday gadget it is now, there were frequent stops and telephone calls to check on progress. I arrived just in time – or 20 minutes late – depending on your point of view.

'Childbirth is not a spectator sport,' said a great hero of mine, Billy Connolly. Actually, I was to discover it is as I was present when Phoebe came along in 1992 and Anouska three years later. Daniel was washed and cleaned and ready to pose with the proud father when I swept into the hospital. 'Give me that baby,' I said, and the resulting photograph of him in my arms sits in its frame in the Tartan Room of our home in Virginia Water.

Wetting the baby's head is a tradition pursued perhaps more vigorously in the west of Scotland than anywhere else in the world. There was no way that Sam Torrance, the traditionalist, was not going to toast the arrival of his son and heir. This was in the period before all-day opening and it took some cajoling on the part of Suzanne's brother Stuart, Danny, a cousin, and me to persuade the owner of a large discotheque nearby to provide us with drinks throughout the afternoon.

After an early evening visit to the hospital to check that Suzanne was fine – and she seemed to understand – it was back to the club for more celebrations. Next thing I knew it was morning and I was lying stark naked in Suzanne's bed at the hospital. Suzanne was nowhere to be seen, and Daniel, being premature, was in an incubator in

Above: Me and my cousin Barclay Duff (right) at two years old on the Largs seafront. I thought I'd try zebras before horses.
Left: With another cousin, Sandy McLennan, and my mother at Rossendale when I was about seven.

Above: From left to right, Dai Rees, Bernard Gallagher, me and Mike Travers at Teignmouth Golf Club 1975.

Right: My first professional win (thanks to Davy McCleland, runner-up) – the Under-25 Matchplay Championship at Birkdale in 1972. Lord Derby makes the official presentation.

Opposite: Willie Aitcheson and me in 1972.

Opposite: Father follows in son's footsteps!
Above: My father trying to stop me tilting. This picture looks pretty tame, normally he would hold my hair and it was agony!

Above: Top of the swing in 1976 – the Benson & Hedges at Fulford.

Left: With Jimmy Letters, brother of John Letters, the famous club manufacturer who got me my first job at Sunningdale.
Below: Posing with Angus McKenzie (centre), the man who started me on tour, and Manuel Ballesteros, Seve's big brother.

Above: With my great mate John O'Leary and my dad.

the special baby unit. I couldn't find my car keys and one of my shoes was missing.

Suzanne claims I came back at about 2am, professed my undying love for her and basically pushed her out of her bed. Maternity beds do not tend to be made for two. She decided it would be more comfortable if she found another place to sleep. She wandered down the corridor and lay down on another bed. The nurses discovered her in the morning only after a little searching.

They found me naked, hairy of course, and barely covered by a sheet. The nurses loved it. Suzanne got her camera out and took pictures of all of them gathered around me in her bed.

My keys eventually materialised – in the ignition of my car parked in front of the hospital in a space reserved for a doctor. The sun-roof was open, the seat reclined and on the floor was the missing shoe. I must have tried to sleep and reckoned a bed a better bet.

I was just the happiest man alive. Friends bought me a T-shirt with the words 'I am a dad' on it. I wore it with pride. Together, Suzanne and Daniel changed my life totally. I realised at that moment that I did not need anything else in my life. I had my golf and I had my family and I had new responsibilities. The visits to the pub at teatime and the marathon snooker sessions would have to stop.

We are blessed to be the parents of three lovely children. Amongst the happiness and great joy, however, has been some sadness. Suzanne has suffered five miscarriages since Daniel was born, and on two occasions was perilously close to death.

I was playing at Valderrama in southern Spain when I received word that Suzanne had had a miscarriage and lost pints of blood. My mother had been told to tell me that Suzanne was unlikely to survive the night. But Mum could not bear to give me such bleak news over the phone, reasoning rightly that I would not be able to make it back to Scotland any more quickly.

I was at home – though I'm not sure I was any help – on another occasion when Suzanne gave birth to a still-born child. Years later I now wonder if I ought to have found the strength to look at the baby when a doctor gave me the opportunity. I could not at the time.

Suzanne had another miscarriage in Cannes, an episode that turned into something of a French farce without the humour. They wanted payment on the spot but not by credit card. They insisted on cash. So I nipped out to a bank after asking a nurse to look after Daniel. I was coming in the front door of the hospital and I could hear this baby crying. I knew it was mine, I could just sense it. I took the lift to the fifth floor but I couldn't get out because the door was jammed. Something was blocking it. I pushed and pushed and it opened enough for me to see a trolley bed blocking the door. It turned out to be Suzanne, flaked out, with Daniel going bananas.

Suzanne has always said that I was born to be a dad. I don't know if Suzanne was born to be pregnant but she spent the best part of ten years in that condition!

As much as I loved living in Largs, I wanted to spend more time with Suzanne and Daniel. Moving south became the only answer as it gave me as much as a day and a half extra at home in between tournaments.

Suzanne changed me and she probably saved me. She gave me a new outlook on life and a stable environment. I had been Jack the lad and I would always be someone up for a laugh and a joke and some fun. But she gave me what had been missing from my life – happiness. If you are happy and contented, you are bound to work better. I have no doubt that the main reason for the resurgence of my career in the 1990s and for the fact that I played the best golf of my life into my 40s was down to my relationship with Suzanne.

She taught me about worrying. She said worrying was 'the interest you pay on the inevitable'. Having been a star in her own right, someone used to working in front of the public, she could share what I was going through. Not that I was going through anything other than life. She reassured me of my ability and never nagged when I came home drunk after a session with the boys.

We continued to have fun together and as a family. And it was together that we tackled the job of the Ryder Cup captaincy. I said publicly right from the outset that Suzanne and I were in it together, a statement that raised a few eyebrows from those who would have wives and partners nowhere near the Ryder Cup.

But the wives play a very important part in the week in terms of helping to set the right tone, establish the right atmosphere in the team room and, frankly, keep the players contented. I believe Europe has, over the years, made the women feel an integral part of the match and not just decorative appendages.

Suzanne and I discussed every aspect of the 2002 match. We used to sit in my dressing room at home for hours in peace and quiet when the kids were at school and nursery, discussing everything from outfits to my two picks. She may not have appreciated the golfing nuances in the choice of two from Jesper Parnevik, Sergio Garcia and José Maria Olazábal, but she always had something to say that was beneficial to my thinking.

My moment of glory in victory was also very much Suzanne's. I could not have done it without her.

10

The broomhandle

If the pencil behind the ear, roll-up cigarettes and moustache are my trademarks, the broomhandle putter has become my crutch.

To Arnold Palmer it should be tried 'only in the privacy of the bathroom'. Tom Watson, another traditionalist, said he would rather be seen retired than use it, and left-hander Bob Charles, one of the greatest ever putters, campaigned to 'ban the broom'. The R&A always seems to be reconsidering its legality and desirability.

Even my mate Monty, in an example of cutting off his belly-putter to spite his golf, has called for the governing bodies to pass legislation against the extended clubs.

But to me the long putter was a career-saver, a tool to preserve my ability and one that, despite sniggers and scoffs from some quarters, I used without ever the slightest tinge of embarrassment.

'Are you not embarrassed?' people used to ask me, the way you might question a strapping teenager pulling one of those airline bags on wheels.

'Don't worry about me,' I always replied. 'I was much more embarrassed by the twitch.'

The twitch, or the yips, is not a pretty sight and an even more grotesque feeling. I averted my gaze, as one might react to any horror, at Mr Lu's wriggling snake in 1972; and I experienced a sense of nausea 15 years later when thinking about my putt against Larry Mize at the Ryder Cup.

My father remembers I was still shaking ten minutes after holing the putt. Eamonn Darcy, faced with an even more bottom-clenching putt on the final green at Muirfield Village, was much later still gripping tightly onto his putter handle as if stuck on a never-ending white-knuckle ride. Which, in a way, is what the yips can be.

In between my first sighting of the serpent and my first actual confrontation, I had frequently been reminded of its existence. I remember the teenage Bernhard Langer suffering in a Great Britain v Europe Hennessy Cognac match at Lille in 1976. The poor German kid was in tears.

Six years later I was playing with Langer in a PGA Championship at Hillside when he struck a 15-ft putt on a flat green straight off the putting surface. If you are capable of doing that, how on earth can you control yourself to win a tournament? Yet Langer has won more than 60 tournaments around the world, including two Masters titles, curing himself of putting troubles with astonishing regularity. There can be no greater testament to his mental strength and fortitude.

Maybe Bernhard subscribes to a recently published view of the Mayo Clinic that the yips is a form of repetitive strain injury caused by constant gripping and regripping of the club; in essence, a physiological rather than a mental problem. I doubt it. I have always thought the twitch a product of the mind, a nervous reaction to your situation.

For most people, it is caused by years and years of pressure, holing 3-footers to save anything from par to your career. In the case of Langer, I think it was the result of a young German suddenly transported from a country virtually without golf onto the professional tour. The move was so big, so early. That he became one of the greatest ever European players again testifies to his resilience.

I was never a great putter, even when at my peak. I was good when on song and pretty ordinary when not. My lack of consistency on the greens made it one of the weaker areas of my golf. Ranking my own game from best to worst, I would start with driving, then, in order, bunker play, short irons, putting and finally long irons. I hit my 2- and 3- irons so low that sometimes I needed a wall behind the green in order to stop the ball. As low burners from the tee, however, they could be most effective.

Dad's assessment of my slow, languid stroke sounded a familiar theme. He said I had a young man's putting stroke. I stood far away from the ball and did not look down the line.

Although the Mize putt in 1987 left a mental scar, I had already taken a few blows over the years. I was well on the road to disaster by then. As early as the 1982 Open Championship at Troon I was putting badly enough to ruin any chances of achieving my ultimate dream. Jim McAllister, one of my oldest friends, a great fan and for years the professional at Haggs Castle in Glasgow, having watched every hole I played that year, declared to my father, 'Your boy played well enough to win the Open, but he putted terrible.'

My unrefined golf course management might also have contributed to a 12th place finish. Dad still bemoans a second shot of mine he witnessed at the par 5 along the railway line which, with my length, I could reach with a 5-iron but which was causing problems for most of the field. Standing behind the ropes as the most passionate of spectators, he lost the flight of the ball and had to ask a policeman where it landed.

'It's on the railway line,' the constable replied.

'Why the hell did you put the ball on the railway line?' Dad later asked me, as if I had intended to.

'I was trying to fade it into the flag, Dad, but just faded it too much,' I answered.

'Why did you no just hit the ball in the middle of the

green and birdie it with two putts? Everyone else was taking 6s, 7s, 8s and even bloody 10s.' We had lots of conversations like that over the years.

I had worried that my father, the traditionalist that he is, might have disapproved of the long putter. I expected the sarcastic question, 'What are you going to do with that? Catch some fish?'

But he was fine. As a new father at the time, I was beginning to understand why. The long putter helped me, so he was happy. He had been watching his son go through hell on the greens and he had been going through more hell than me. He was delighted with any cure.

Although the theft of my favourite Arnold Palmer putter from the pro shop at Walton Heath in 1988 did not help, it was not the cause of my problems. Matters finally came to a head at a tournament in France in March 1999. I finished fifth in the AGF Open at La Grande Motte, Montpellier, despite playing well enough tee to green to have won by about ten strokes. I still had a 10-footer on the 72nd green for second position. But I missed that and the one back. That was it as far as I was concerned.

I had tried the long putter during two weeks of winter practice with my father in Florida, having previously read about Orville Moody's use of the broomhandle on the US Seniors Tour. I saw one in the professional's shop and gave it a go. No great shakes, I thought.

Desperate situations require desperate measures, so back at home in Largs I remembered the long putter... and climbed on to the snooker table – as you do.

Nowadays, I have a high-quality synthetic putting green in my back garden, which simulates the speed of greens as fast as those at Augusta. The truest and fastest surface I could practise putting on in Largs at that time was my snooker table. Happily, the ceiling was high enough for me to stand up to my full 5ft 11 inches. I needed a new weapon, and not the kind you bought over the counter. In the week following the tournament in France, instead of heading for Sardinia, I took an old Ping putter, stuck it in my vice and lengthened the shaft by 2ft. I stood on the blue spot and hit golf balls as hard as I could into the corner pockets. There was no scream of 'Eureka' from the room but I never missed. Trial and error determined that I was more comfortable with the handle held right up to my chin.

I was using a pendulum motion and a pendulum swings more naturally from that position, provided you let the club find its own plumb line. The idea is to let the club dangle behind the ball, then place your feet accordingly. I have stuck with that method ever since, and for all those who have switched to the long putter, very few have chosen to copy me.

Putting is two hands trying to work as one. The twitch is when one hand takes over from the other and the circuitry from brain to hands blows. My method is essentially one-handed putting. Other variations, like the belly putter, have the weakness of requiring both hands.

The time to test it in public under competitive conditions drew nigh. At the beginning of April I took the broom to Jersey, where I have many good friends and where the competition was not, perhaps, the hottest. I remember missing the green at the first hole, chipping to 4ft – the horror distance for anyone at the start of a round – and knocking it straight into the middle of the cup. I ended up birdieing the last four holes of the tournament and finishing fifth, just two strokes behind the winner, Christy O'Connor Jnr. I putted beautifully and never looked back.

By which I mean I achieved a level of competence that allowed me to sustain my career into my 40s and earn more than £3 million in the process. I have never been as good a putter as I was on my good days with the short stick, but I'll never be a bad putter again. I am a solid putter now who could probably hit as good a putt to win the Open as in the first round of an ordinary tournament.

Only once did I revert to the short putter in a European Tour event. Mucking around, not much more than that, I won a bit of money on the practice putting green ahead of the Lancôme Trophy with the short putter, holing putts from all over the place. That persuaded me, stupidly as it transpired, to try it in the tournament itself. I even made a few birdie putts. My first twitchy three-putt, however, reminded me of why I had changed. That was the long and short of it.

I was tempted on another occasion in the French Open at Le Golf National in 1998. I had scored 63 using a short putter in a pro-am at Sunningdale the previous week, despite four-putting the 2nd green. I took the short putter out again a few days later and carded a 65 off the championship tees at Wentworth. But the short putter only lasted eight holes, and by the time I reached Paris my opening 64 of what was to become my last European Tour victory was achieved with the trusty broomhandle.

As I told reporters at the time: 'I gave the short putter up as a bad job because I could not bear to be waiting for the twitch to return. So out the little one had to go.'

As far as I was concerned, there was never a question of tradition being flouted. I was happy with the fact that I could compete again in the game I loved. I am sure I would have eventually found a way out of my troubles but I doubt if I would have won again. As it was, by 1988 I was pretty much dead in the water, talking about packing in tournament golf but deep down never really contemplating it.

I am sure it was a question of pride with many people. Tom Watson would have won four more majors in my opinion if he had gone to the broomhandle when he developed the yips. I tried to persuade Langer for years that it was for him. It took a long time before I won him over. Woosie is back and forward between the long and the short, never fully committed to the switch. I keep telling him how brilliant he is with it.

My great friend David Feherty eventually ended his resistance in 1996. When I presented him with one of my old broomhandles at the Scottish Open at Carnoustie he reacted as only he could. 'I hope it doesn't realise it is me who is using it now,' he said. 'I may have to grow a moustache and put on a bit of weight so that it keeps on behaving.'

Others, like Peter Senior, who also tucks it under his chin, were quicker to follow my example. Professionals always show an interest in anything new. As soon as I made an appearance with the broomhandle, they began sniffing around, circling like an animal looking to mate, having a shiftie, then perhaps having a go. Initial reticence soon disappeared when they saw the improvement in my putting statistics. My attitude was that I would give anyone a lesson anytime. If you wanted to putt with the broomhandle, you came to Sam. No professional would wish the yips on another because once you succumb, it takes over your golfing life and ultimately your life as a whole. Every time you play you are dreading getting to the end of the fairway. I had got to the stage where I hated the prospect of going out to play. Although I never thought I was not strong enough to get over it, I did despair.

Apart from Orville Moody and a few other senior golfers in the USA, there was no one else using the broomhandle when I began. There were no coaching manuals and, indeed, no coaches teaching the method. There was not even a recognised method. No one was making or selling the club. I was really the first to take it round the world, and certainly the first to play with it in the Ryder Cup. I won tournaments with it.

But I was not the first. Peter Senior of Australia won the 1990 European Open at, of all places, Sunningdale, using the same club with which I started. I could not resist claiming a share of the credit and pointing out the irony to the assembled media. 'I gave my old putter to Peter when my new custom-built one was ready and it won before I did,' I said.

My time would come. But I had already secured my fifth consecutive automatic selection to the Ryder Cup team, something I could not have achieved without the product of hours of experimentation at the vice and on the snooker table. My Ryder Cup journey would have ended had the long putter not entered my life.

It is no exaggeration to say that the introduction of the Continental players in 1979 and then our victories in 1985 and 1987 had transformed the Ryder Cup from a match between cousins – in which only one cousin seemed too interested – into a contest that fascinated the whole global family of golf. Even those not qualified to play, such as Ernie Els and Nick Price, would make sure they were near a television set for the biennial clash of tours and, to some extent, cultures.

The contest at The Belfry in '89 was billed as the Match of the Century, an illustration not only of the hype now being generated but also of the genuine scale of the event. My research into the Ryder Cup as captain drew me to contemporary reports of just how massive it had become.

When the tented village was erected that year – 226 structures covering 350,000 square feet – it became the biggest ever at a sporting event in Britain. The total of working personnel, including everyone from caterers to tournament staff, nudged up to the 5,000 mark. There were 380 writers, including the unprecedented figure of more than 50 from the USA. Just six years earlier you would have had to look pretty closely in any of the American newspapers for a Ryder Cup report. It commanded the same column inches as the British Dominoes Championship might receive in one of our tabloids.

In the end, Europe retained the trophy after a nail-biting 14–14 draw. The cliché was trotted out by US captain Raymond Floyd: 'The one winner was the game of golf.' Everyone could pat each other on the back and congratulate themselves on a wonderful tussle.

Yes…and no. Never mind the heroics of '85 and '87, this was the '89 European team, a new team, a different team, another team, one that was devastated at not winning. Retaining the Ryder Cup seemed pretty scant consolation at the time for a side that lost the last four singles, three of them on the 18th green. I was one of the quartet, though in going down 3 and 1 to Tom Watson, I never reached my Holy Grail of 1985. We let the Americans off the hook. We were overtaken by complacency at the end, a disappointing way for the most successful term of captaincy in the history of the event to end. Tony Jacklin called it a day after a narrow defeat at PGA National, victories at The Belfry and Muirfield Village and a draw back at The Belfry. As the ultimate professional, there was probably no one more upset not to secure another win than Jacklin.

Our motivation had been sharpened when Floyd introduced his players at the gala ball in the Metropole Hotel outside Birmingham as 'the 12 greatest players in the world'. You can imagine how that rankled with our players, not least Nick Faldo, who had won the first of successive Green Jackets at the Masters earlier that year. In Faldo, José Maria Olazábal, Ian Woosnam and Seve Ballesteros, we could boast four of the top ten ranked players. Even Sandy Lyle was the world No 11 at the time and, sadly, his form had dipped so much that he informed Jacklin he did not want to be considered for selection.

I was one point out of two coming into the singles, after partnering Gordon Brand Jnr to victory in a Friday afternoon fourball over Curtis Strange and Paul Azinger and a Saturday morning foursomes defeat by Azinger and Chip Beck. All eyes had been on my broomhandle putter that week and I was not best pleased to three-putt the 18th on Friday from one of the lower tiers. I have always found the broomhandle least effective when the hole is on a different level from the ball. But Gordon played a wonderful winning bunker shot.

Watson and I clashed – and I use the word advisedly – twice in Ryder Cup matches, once on the course and once off. His refusal of my request for autographs of his team at the gala dinner came four years later. In 1989, he upset me during our singles match.

Although he had begun to suffer his own putting problems, Watson putted brilliantly against me, holing everything, often from much further away than me. I had one of those days when my best putts seemed to shave the hole or lip out and I was three down at the 11th. When I came out of a bunker at the 12th to about 2ft, I expected the putt to be conceded. I would not have minded being forced to hole out if the request had not been accompanied by the unnecessary comment: 'I should probably give you that but I think I will test you.' As it happened, Watson sank another 10-footer to win the hole.

Anyone standing on the 13th tee that day might have seen smoke coming out of my ears and not put it down to where I kept my half-puffed roll-ups. I nearly drove the green and chipped to 3ft for a win. I birdied the next to win that as well. But I just could not buy another putt and eventually lost on the 17th green.

By then, with the trophy retained, Europe led 14–10, needing just another half point for victory. The BBC's excellent Steve Rider made one of the few gaffes of his career when interviewing Tom Kite behind the 18th green and talking about a European victory. 'Not yet,' came the terse reply from Kite. 'Let's get that straight.' And he was to be proved correct as Brand Jnr, Faldo and Woosie all lost in front of the clubhouse.

Woosie was to reveal that he had been offered a halved match by Strange on the 15th, something that was not in any case allowed by the rules. Strange, one down at the time, proceeded to birdie the last four holes. The champagne tasted a little flatter that evening – though not by the end of the night.

Thanks to the long putter, my official earnings now rose from £42,252 in 1988 to £170,650 in 1989. But still a victory would not come. I was definitely getting closer, never more so than at The Belfry, the scene of so many of my triumphs – and quite a few of my disappointments.

A nocturnal encounter with a flower-stand was still three years away when I stood on the 10th tee during the third round of the English Open. I drove over the water and onto the green at the famous par 4, before rolling a 20-ft eagle putt right to the edge of the cup. It stopped agonisingly short, close enough to give me the impression that it might fall in at any second. It did, but several seconds too late, as it transpired, and not, according to the saying, a second too soon.

I had waited too long, more than the maximum permitted ten seconds. Not that I knew the rule. Referee John Paramor informed me of my error a few holes later and I was penalised a stroke. Fair enough, I thought. I was just delighted not to be disqualified. But that stroke was to cost me the tournament.

The final day was one of those joyous occasions that you can relish even when victory proves elusive. I was playing in the last threesome with my great friend Mark James and Seve Ballesteros, a legend with whom I had spent many a late night in deep discussion. Up ahead, and making a charge, was David Feherty, who had become my Tour travelling companion and greatest mate.

By the 12th, Mark's shoulders were slumped and his head was threatening to take its leave. 'What's the matter with you?' I asked. The words and the tone could only have been used by friend to friend. 'One more birdie and you're lying second.'

Feherty held the clubhouse lead by the time we reached the 18th. He was level with me and Mark, now not second but in a tie for the lead. We needed par 4s to force a play-off with Feherty, who was standing behind the green knowing that bogeys were distinctly possible on such a dangerous hole. We both hit good drives into the fairway. Mark struck a fine second shot to about 30ft from the stick; I hit a lovely, high, floaty 4-iron – not my shape of shot at all – right over the pin to perhaps 15ft. He holed for birdie, I holed for birdie and Feherty, denied even a play-off, cursed for Ulster.

The play-off lasted one hole, though the resulting friendly banter has continued to this day. I maintain that Mark's putt would have rolled off the 10th green into the water – okay, gone 10ft past – had it not hit the centre of the cup and dropped for a winning birdie. I was getting close.

I had not won a tournament of any description for more than three years when I took the Mercedes German Masters title at Stuttgart in October 1990. The first prize of £75,000 was the biggest cheque of my career at that stage. But I was much more concerned about adding to my list of victories and proving that with the help of the long putter I could overcome the yips. A course record-equalling 65 in the second round put me into contention. The £2,000 rolling prize for course records had risen to £14,000. 'Don't worry, lads, I'll break the record tomorrow,' I told the press in buoyant mood.

True to my word, I carded a 64 in the third round, which would have secured a nice bonus had Woosie not entered the fray. Ian Woosnam produced a final round 62 which won for him the kitty and heaped a great deal of pressure on his friend with the extended putter and stretched nerves. I hung on, but only just.

The last piece was in place as regards my switch to the long putter. I had needed a total of only 50 putts during my second and third rounds in Germany, probably the lowest consecutive putting stats in my career. There was no going back now. I was to receive some money from a club manufacturer for endorsing the broomhandle but all attempts at merchandising seemed to fail. The average handicap golfer has never bought it in any numbers. I gave my name to the Sam Torrance putter but I have never received a penny by way of commission. Frankly, that was of little concern. The fact that my competitiveness was extended well into my 40s was enough for me.

There was, however, no shortage of 'Sam Torrance putters' on the market at one time, nearly all frightful-looking monstrosities and nothing to do with me. There were golf shops all over Scotland selling long putters under the name 'Sam Torrance' that I had never seen, let alone endorsed.

Every Christmas, John Wilkie, Peter Hart and myself would head for Glasgow on the pretext of doing some festive shopping. Of course, it was just an excuse for a bevvy. I persuaded the boys to go into a well-known sports shop and ask for a Sam Torrance putter.

'Yes, we sell those, very popular,' the shop assistant said.

'Are you sure?' the boys asked.

'Yes, I'll just go round the back and get one.'

I was standing at the desk when he returned with some ugly-looking thing that had nothing to do with me. You should have seen the lad's face when he spotted the moustache and the grin.

I have tried many versions over the years, the key element is to find the right weight balance. Otherwise, it is all just a case of the next gimmick. The two-ball has become very popular in the last year or so. I have never really had a sentimental favourite. I don't think of golf clubs that way. It is true to say that, like the snooker player with his cue, a professional hates to lose his putter. But that also applies equally to driver and sand wedge. If a pro loses or has stolen any of those three, he is in trouble. Or he thinks he is in trouble, and that can be just as bad.

I was coming up for my 20th year on the European Tour, my 21st as a professional. And in two decades I had played in just one major championship – the 1985 Masters – other than my continuous run of Opens. I had not competed in a single US Open or in even one USPGA Championship. That is how it used to be. An increase in invitations to Ryder Cup players in recent years and the growing importance of world rankings in determining the entry list for all four majors have changed that. But it is worth remembering that an American player of the same stature as me, playing in the same era, would have participated in three times the number of major championships.

So, while others were at Augusta in the spring of 1991, I was taking part in the Jersey European Airways Open over the humps, bumps, runs and hollows of the delightful La Moye Golf Club. I held off Mark Davis by one stroke for my 14th victory in Europe. That was to be my only win of the year but I managed enough high finishes, including second place in both the British Masters and the French Open, to make it comfortably into the European team for my sixth Ryder Cup in a row.

Kiawah Island, 1991, 'The War on the Shore', as it was dubbed by a media combining the conflict in the Gulf with a few heated arguments on the course, a rowdy crowd and Corey Pavin's bizarre taste in camouflage caps. I know things went on in a fairly hostile atmosphere, but I do take the rather unfashionable view that there was nothing too untoward. I never witnessed anything remotely as bad as what was to occur at Brookline eight years later.

With David Feherty gaining one of the automatic selections, I now had my absolute dearest friend in the world on the team. Of course, he was anxious to know what it's like.

'It is like having a kid,' I told him.

You cannot explain to someone who does not have a child what it is like having a child. You cannot explain that love, that feeling. It is exactly the same with the Ryder Cup. He was very expectant, no pun intended, because of that and I think he understood what I meant afterwards.

We were pretty inseparable in those days, an obvious combination for Bernard Gallacher captaining the side for the first time. We practised together and were cocky enough to challenge Seve and Ollie to a money game. Big mistake. We lost a few hundred quid that day.

Our first outing was in the afternoon fourballs against Lanny Wadkins and Mark O'Meara.

Feherty was ghostly white. He says it was easily the most terrifying moment of his career. I tried to offer him encouragement and little pieces of advice. I told him to make sure he arrived on the tee last in order to make the applause for us the last thing they heard before hitting. His first Ryder Cup putt was a cracker, a 15-footer that finished 3ft short and 4ft wide of the hole. He almost missed the ball, hitting the ground in front with his putter head.

I put my arm round him and squeezed. He looked a strange shade of green. I began to roll a cigarette as we walked to the second tee.

'Just think,' I said to him. 'You're on the same team as Seve, Faldo, Langer, Olazabal, Woosie, Monty and, most impressive of all, me!'

'Aye, I suppose I am,' he replied, trying to smile.

'This only happens tae a few people, so you'd better be up tae enjoyin' it.' Feherty swears that I paused for effect, flicked open my old brass Zippo, dragged deeply on the Old Holborn, and blew smoke in his face before adding, 'So dinnae be a prick or ah'll join Wadkins an' O'Meara, an' you can play the three of us.'

My God, Feherty was nervous. But he played fantastically well, especially on the inward half, as we recovered from three down to take the match to the 18th. David was faced with a 10-ft birdie putt for half a point. For the first time in the entire day he asked me to read the line.

'Left edge,' I said. I was very positive. 'Just knock it in.' And he did. We played once more together in the second morning's foursomes. But we did not gel, as sometimes happens in that most difficult of disciplines, and we went down 4 and 2 to Wadkins and Hale Irwin.

Gelling is not what you would call an exact science. It is when you hit a bad shot and your partner hits a good chip or vice versa; or when he hits it 8ft past and you hole it. You can't always predict who will gel. Who would have predicted Lee Westwood and Sergio Garcia becoming such a strong combination in 2002? Not the captain, for a start.

I don't think it is necessary to be friends or have similar personalities. Not liking the guy might even help. He hits a good drive; I'll hit a better second. That sort of mentality.

Of course, the contest had well and truly kicked off on the first foursomes of the first morning when Seve and Ollie locked horns with Paul Azinger and Chip Beck over a ball-changing row.

'San, San, big problem,' Seve said, continuing his lifetime habit of getting my name wrong. 'San, get Bernard now. Big problem.' I had been walking with this match and was on hand as message boy. Bernard, however, could not be contacted on the radio. It transpired that his radio had been switched off amid concern that David Stockton, his opposite number, was able to tune into our frequency and listen to our every ploy. I left the match and ran to find Bernard behind the 9th green.

It took 20 minutes of fierce argument on the 10th tee to sort everything out. The Americans had been switching balls but nothing could be done about it. Europe was three down and Seve was fuming. There used to be no more formidable combination in golf. Suffice to say, Europe turned the match around with some of the best golf ever played in a Ryder Cup.

I lost my singles to a revitalised Freddie Couples on another dramatic Ryder Cup final day, with the result not determined until the final putt on the final green of the final singles. Poor Bernhard Langer, now no longer the innocent German kid, was crying again. I know of no other golfer who could have suffered the disappointment of missing the putt to lose the Ryder Cup and go on to win a tournament just seven days later. Then again, no one other than Langer has suffered so many bouts of the yips and recovered each time. His association with the broomhandle lay ahead.

I have been using the club since my teenage son Daniel began walking. And like any son wanting to copy his dad, he was using the broomhandle almost before he had tried the conventional putter. He wanted to use it because I used it. But I do not think it is a good idea to go straight to the long putter. Putting the normal way teaches you so much about chipping and playing little shots from the side of the green. I think it can detract from young people's short games if they go directly to the extended putter.

Daniel is, in any case, a beautiful putter.

An unexpected bonus at the end of 1991 offered me a first opportunity to captain a team. I was asked to take charge of a six-man European Tour side for the Asahi Glass Four Tours World Championship at Royal Adelaide. My reaction was something along the lines of: 'What, me? Are you sure? Does a captain not have to be responsible?'

We were essentially six mates on a golfing holiday, having a bloody good time on and off the course – Paul Broadhurst, David Feherty, Colin Montgomerie, Ronan Rafferty, Steve Richardson and yours truly as player, captain and social secretary. The Aussie media gave us frightful stick for having sent a weak side, with Broadhurst clashing verbally with a TV crew as we arrived at the airport. We ended up beating the best in the world, or at least the best that the organisers could muster on the other side of the world in November.

My tactics were simple: 'Right, the round's finished, let's have a beer. Relax, boys, we can do this. Take it easy, have another drink, we'll beat them no bother.' I remember Broadhurst coming from three strokes behind with three holes to play to beat Jim Gallagher Jnr of the USPGA Tour and clinch our place in the final against the Australia/New Zealand Tour. Broadhurst, now coached by my father, incidentally, scored better than anyone during the week.

Jamie Spence, who was playing in a tournament the following day, came to watch and ended up in a karaoke bar singing 'Campbeltown Loch, I wish you were whisky' with me.

And no, for once I managed to get through a week without being found walking naked along a hotel corridor...

11

Flying rugby tackle

Did I tell you about my sleepwalking?

I had become so adept with the broomhandle that I could use it in my sleep. What I had always found a lot harder was staying in bed in my sleep. Walking was a different matter. My sleepwalking became a subject of national concern – at least to those interested in golf – when barely a month prior to the 1993 Ryder Cup I walked into a giant plant pot in the middle of my room at The Belfry hotel.

When I say walked, I mean ran. When I say bumped, I mean collided. And when I say asleep, I may well have been awake. The fact is that I mistook a 4-ft-high plant pot standing in the middle of my bedroom for a masked intruder and I launched myself at it with the best flying rugby tackle of my life. Actually, the only flying rugby tackle of my life. Suddenly, I was fully conscious, lying in agony on the floor surrounded by hundreds of pieces of broken pot and shredded shrubbery. For months afterwards, every time I hit a ball into the trees, a playing partner would come out with something like, 'Careful, Sam, it's a jungle out there.'

There will be many of you out there, like most of my friends, who will immediately conclude that I was drunk. I was, in fact, as sober as a judge (a metaphor that has always puzzled me, given my encounters with members of the legal profession). The diagnosis was a fractured sternum, not an injury you would recommend to anyone just a few weeks away from a Ryder Cup match.

This was merely the latest in a number of nocturnal

accidents that the media branded as my sleepwalking exploits. I was happy to use the expression myself. On reflection, I am not sure it was anything more complicated than a very sleepy person getting up for a pee, sometimes drunk, sometimes not.

The mishaps and illnesses seem to have increased as the years rolled by. My mother does not recall a particularly accident-prone child, always skinning his hands and knees, though there was the occasion when a beer lorry rolled down the steep hill at Routenburn Golf Club and smashed into my bedroom with me in it. I escaped with a fright and a case of Pale Ale. No, I'm just joking about the beer.

My sound fitness and good health, not to mention stamina, was proved by the fact that I missed only two events in my first ten years on the European Tour. That was the result of my first 'sleepwalking' incident in the early 1970s. I tripped over my packed suitcases on the way to the toilet in the middle of the night, kicked the wall and ended up breaking my toe.

There was the previously mentioned 'pissing in the pot' incident at Disneyland, a nocturnal meander in all but time. It may have been the afternoon and broad daylight, but I was asleep and sozzled.

That was followed by another instance in Dublin when I was locked out of my room wearing nothing but a bushy moustache. Again, that was a case of my needing the toilet and taking the wrong turning. I resisted the temptation to join the booming disco downstairs, choosing instead to knock on Ian Woosnam's door. He took me in and telephoned down to reception for a spare key. There were other examples, like the time in the south of France when I found myself naked on the balcony and locked out of my third-floor room in the middle of the night. I had gone out for a fag on a warm evening. An hour and a half later I was shaking with cold as none of my shouting and screaming had succeeded in attracting help. Just when I was on the point of smashing the glass door with the chair, I saw what turned out to be golf photographer Steve Munday walking up the road. He alerted management to my plight.

My broken sternum had mended by the time Tom Watson's team arrived at The Belfry in September 1993. Although I had not played competitively for a month, I practised well and felt ready to make a valuable contribution to the team. As it was, I managed only one foursomes match and had to withdraw from the singles through injury – a different injury.

My weekend of despair lay ahead. I was in jovial mood at the gala dinner, the £150 per head bun fight for sponsors and patrons of the Tour, attended by the two teams. As I said earlier, I have always considered the whines about these sorts of occasions – primarily from the Americans – ludicrous.

My humour changed later that evening after suffering the embarrassment of asking Tom Watson for an autograph and being refused. I had walked from my seat to his to make the request and did not enjoy walking back empty-handed. Watson had not wanted his players 'bothered' by signature-seekers and told me that making an exception for me would open the floodgates. He was perfectly polite and, I thought, completely wrong.

This is the same man who, when making his debut in 1977, said, 'They always have a menu with the names of the players on it; we send them round the tables and they are all autographed. That's a nice thing to have and save from the Ryder Cup.'

I was fuming and enough people became aware of the situation for the media to generate a full-blown diplomatic storm the following day. I went to the press centre the next day to play down the incident for the sake of the team and the event. Bernard Gallacher, also trying to defuse the situation, later added, 'If that's going to be the only major incident of the week, that'll be fine.'

But he knew my feelings. 'I have never seen Sam more angry or embarrassed,' he said later. 'He went across the room to the American table in a spirit of friendship to ask Watson to autograph his menu and Watson refused.'

My attention was soon diverted from intended or imagined slights to a sore toe, which was beginning to cause some discomfort. I had suffered from an ingrown toenail previously and I knew the feeling. I took my shoe and sock off to discover a tiny blister right on the tip of the nail. There was practically nothing to see, so I thought nothing of it. You do not tend to feel physical pain during Ryder Cup week, only mental anguish. Adrenalin kills all aches.

By the eve of the contest, however, it had become a bit worse. I had not told anyone at that point, thinking the problem not serious. I then informed Bernard, declaring I would be fine for the morning foursomes. 'Jesse' James and myself were drawn against Lanny Wadkins and Corey Pavin in the opening tie of the match. Come the morning, the toe was really sore. I probably should not have played.

It was a difficult call to make when the Ryder Cup had become such an important part of my life. I would have walked over burning coals for the cause – and it felt as if I was. The moment everything fell apart came at the 8th. I will remember it to my dying day. Jesse had hit a great drive down the middle of the fairway. I was left with a 5-iron to the green. When I transferred all my weight to the left side of my left foot on the downswing, I felt a sharp pain, causing me to block the shot and send the ball flying 30 yards right of the green. A horrific shot like that was simply not in my repertoire.

I never hit a decent shot for the rest of the round. I was hopeless, absolutely hopeless, an impossible situation in foursomes. After losing the next five holes, four of them to pars, we eventually went down by the margin of 4 and 3. I felt so sorry for Jesse and so disappointed that I had let down Europe and my great friend Bernard Gallacher.

When I took off my shoe, there was gunge and stuff caked to my sock and pus oozing out of my toe. 'Pus in boots,' Feherty called it, the master of black humour.

The decision was taken to have the nail removed under local anaesthetic at Birmingham Hospital that evening. A painful little operation, I can tell you. The hope was that I might recover sufficiently to play in the singles on the Sunday. There was no chance of taking part on Saturday and, to be honest, little expectation of my being fit for the final day. I thought I was finished for the week.

Watson was called into a room on Saturday night and warned that the 'sealed envelope' rule would probably have to be invoked. For authentication purposes, I removed my shoe to reveal a bandage soaked in funny-coloured pus.

'All right, all right, you don't need to show me any more,' Watson said.

Two years earlier, Steve Pate, who had been involved in a car accident on the way back from the team dinner, pulled out of the singles suffering from bruised ribs and an injured hip. Pate had actually played in the Saturday afternoon fourballs, surprising all the Europeans by being one of the few to reach one of the longest par 5s – with a drive and a 5-iron! Poor David Gilford was the unfortunate guy to be named in the European envelope. He was allocated a half point against Pate and not allowed to strike a ball.

Sunday morning dawned with no great change in my condition. Although I struggled to put on my golf shoe, I still hoped to get to that first tee, perhaps by using painkillers. I was desperate to play. I would have taken pills, had injections, anything. But, rightly, Bernard was not keen to take a chance on how the painkillers might affect me. I hit a few balls on the range but knew my fate when I struggled to walk back to the team room.

My faithful caddie Malcolm Mason, optimistic when leaving me on Saturday evening, had discovered that I was withdrawing as he made his way to the team room. 'Sorry, Malcolm, I can't play,' I said when we met. The highs have more than outweighed the lows in my career but this was one of the lowest points. Lanny Wadkins, one of Watson's picks, had volunteered to have his name placed in the American envelope and we were awarded a half point each.

It proved the worst possible start to a less than perfect day as we lost 13–15 with no fewer than eight of the 11 singles being decided on the last green. I was desperate for Bernard to have a third chance at being a victorious captain and just as desperate that my contribution would be considerable. Happily, it all came together two years later in what was to be my last Ryder Cup as a player.

The Ryder Cup was bound for Valderrama in southern Spain in 1997, so when I limped out of The Belfry in September 1993, I had no idea that I would ever be returning on Ryder Cup duty. I could not at that time have imagined coming back as captain, let alone as a victorious one.

There were bound to be tournaments there and, knowing me, a few scrapes and bumps to come. Little did

I know that subsequent visits to The Belfry would see me play a character in a Stephen King horror film one year and be forced to withdraw when in contention 12 months later.

Nothing to do with sleepwalking and struggling to locate the nearest toilet on these occasions. I was unloading some luggage from the back seat of my car at the start of the 2000 Benson & Hedges International week when I cracked my head on the edge of the door. There was blood everywhere. Instead of practising, I spent the day being stitched up by a doctor and resting.

A year later I pulled out at the halfway stage of the same tournament suffering from a rib muscle injury, despite holding a share of third place. I was falling apart. Every year there seemed to be something. A springing rib and damaged vertebrae sidelined me for five weeks at the start of 1999, preventing me from defending my French Open title; I lost even longer in 1994 due to a skin problem and an operation to remove five cysts from an eye; I pulled a muscle picking up my daughter one year and, having flown all the way to Dubai, turned right round to fly home again having damaged my back pushing a luggage trolley.

And still my mum insisted I had never been accident-prone.

By the early to mid-1990s I had begun to accept the widespread view that, subconsciously or not, I seemed to reserve my best form for the periods of Ryder Cup qualification, generally the odd-numbered years. From 1987 to 1995, with the exception of 1990, my odd years proved considerably more productive than the even ones.

For example, 1992 was a disaster. My final placing of 62nd in the Order of Merit was at that stage my worst in 20 years on the European Tour, and there was to be nothing so bad until 1999. At the time I put it down to a combination of factors: despite stroking the ball well I was having no luck on the greens; I became a daddy for the second time when Phoebe was born; I moved house from Largs to Virginia Water, a wrench for someone as fiercely Scottish as me; and, of course, there was the almost compulsory injury, this time a broken rib incurred while slipping on the stairs. All of that resulted in official earnings of little more than £80,000, just three top ten finishes in my usual full programme of 27 events.

There was one highlight, in July 1992, that went almost unreported outside my native Scotland. Sixty still represents a magical, almost mythical, barrier for the professional golfer to break. It remains enough of a rarity for television commentators and producers to become very agitated when anyone gets within touching distance. Rarer than both the 147 maximum in snooker and the nine-dart finish in darts.

I managed a 58. Moreover, I did it after two swift pints of Guinness and without a single practice shot. I always thought that the greatest advert for the dark stuff.

The occasion was the centenary pro-am of Bathgate Golf Club, a club between Edinburgh and Glasgow justifiably proud for having produced two Ryder Cup captains, Eric Brown and Bernard Gallacher.

I flew north on the Monday of the Scottish Open at Gleneagles in the company of Bernard, Ronnie Corbett and Bruce Forsyth. We were running late, arriving just half an hour before our tee-off time. No time to hit a ball and no time to have a practice putt. No time for lunch. Time, however, to down two pints.

The elixir obviously took a while to kick in since I missed a 10-ft eagle putt at the 1st and a 3-ft putt for birdie at the 2nd. After that, I went bananas, playing the next seven holes in 7 under par to be out in 28. The inward half was almost stately by comparison, with birdies coming at the 10th, 12th, 15th and 16th. That left me needing just a par 4 at the last to break 60.

My drive at the 18th was perfect, straight down the middle, leaving just an easy 90-yard sand wedge to the pin. There was a bunker to the right and one to the left. Nothing could be more straightforward. But I was nervous. Boy, was I nervous. The thought of a 59 suddenly got to me. I pushed my shot 10 yards right of where I intended and close enough to the bunker for concern. But the ball bounced on the top of the bunker, kicked left and rolled right up to the flag. I was left with a tap-in for a birdie 3 and a 58.

Little Ronnie could hardly contain himself with excitement. I also played with Jim Gallacher, Bernard's older brother and the club captain that year. Both he and Ronnie signed the card that hangs on the wall in the clubhouse.

For the record, my 13 under par score read 4, 4, 3, 2, 3, 3, 3, 3, 3, -28; 3, 3, 4, 3, 4, 4, 3, 3, 3, -30.

Yet 1993, with the Ryder Cup clock ticking, produced three victories, including what I like to refer to as my 'alcohol double', in Italy, Spain and Germany. There were April wins in the Kronenbourg Open and the Heineken Open Catalonia, and a June success in the Honda Open. Three titles in the space of 11 weeks took me to the top of the Order of Merit and virtually guaranteed a seventh Ryder Cup appearance in a row.

The Gardagolf Golf Club at the Italian resort of Salo, high in the hills above Lake Garda, is a place of stunning beauty, not that professional golfers are renowned for looking beyond their yardage charts and the out-of-bounds posts. If a lake is not a water hazard, they are not interested. Scenery is for holidaymakers. It may have affected my focus occasionally but I always liked to look around and get around.

If the slick greens were not exactly to my taste, the strong winds of the weekend delighted me and, as it happened, fellow Scotsman Mike Miller, who finished runner-up, one stroke behind. Costantino Rocca had drawn level at the start of the final round but he drove out of bounds at both the 4th and 5th to fall out of immediate contention.

It was my 16th victory on the European Tour, my third in Italy if you include the unofficial Radici Open, and my first since Jersey two years earlier. It moved me from 31st to 21st in the cup rankings, at a time when I had some catching up to do. I had failed to accumulate many points when counting began towards the end of 1992. Again, I won my weight in a sponsor's brew, this time champagne. Again, Malcolm and I were encouraged to load the golf bag with bricks.

Later that month, in a Barcelona still jumping in the aftermath of the Olympic Games, I won again. The great Catalonian city had hosted the Summer Olympics, though it looked a candidate for the Winter Olympics during a final day abandoned due to vile weather. The sloping fairways looked like ski runs as hail, rain and lightning reduced the occasion to a 54-hole event.

I did not much care if the shipbuilders Noah & Son had been required as I sat in the clubhouse playing cribbage, waiting for officialdom to declare me the winner. My second-round course record of 63 at Ocona Montanya, home for the equestrian events in the Olympics, began with seven 3s in a row, better even than when I scored 58 at Bathgate! Another story.

I duly collected the £50,000 and points with a one-stroke victory over American Jay Townsend, the man from Jupiter. Jupiter, Florida, that is. Billy Foster, one of the great caddies, with experience of seven Ryder Cups, carrying for Gordon Brand Jnr, Seve Ballesteros and

Top: Winning the Irish Open at Portmarnock in 1981. I may use this pose again…

Opposite: Grumpy old men – with Malcolm Mason my longest-serving caddie.
Right: Winning the Jersey Open in 1991. Suzanne gives me a hug wearing the latest in headgear!
Below: My winning captaincy, the 1995 Dunhill Cup with Monty (right) and 'Hot Pie', aka Andrew Coltart.

Opposite: My mum, dad and their dog, Major.
Above: The in-laws – Suzanne's mum and dad, Mary and Henry.
Below: Our wedding party gathered at Skibo Castle in 1995. The ceremony was planned as a surprise for Suzanne.

Above: Suzanne changed my life, so did the other two subjects in this picture – my son Daniel and the broomhandle putter!
Opposite: With Daniel and my daughters Phoebe and Anouska at the Skills Challenge at Wentworth.

Above left: Cutting the cake at our wedding at Skibo Castle.

Above right: Arriving for the 1989 Ryder Cup at the Belfry with one-year-old son, Daniel. Who would have thought that these two would become captain and lady captain?

Right: Alone at last – me, the wife and the cup.

Darren Clarke, worked for me that week while Malcolm went on honeymoon. The agreement was that Billy and Malcolm received 5 per cent each of prize money. Victory came despite suffering a displaced rib lifting luggage the previous week. But manipulation by a physiotherapist at Sunningdale did the trick.

I had a sore wrist, heavy cold and streaming hay fever when winning again in June at Hamburg's Gut Kaden course. The German galleries had come out in their thousands to welcome home Bernhard Langer after his victory in the Masters at Augusta. But he just missed out on joining a four-man play-off involving Ian Woosnam, Paul Broadhurst and Sweden's Johan Rystrom. A 35-ft birdie putt at the first extra hole, the 18th, secured a cheque for £83,000 and top place in the Volvo Order of Merit.

I told reporters, 'It just did not happen last year [1992]. But here I got the right putt in at the right time and I know that Ryder Cup place is mine.'

12

The wedding

What on earth was all the fuss about Madonna's wedding in Skibo Castle? Been there, done that, worn the morning suit.

If she had got in touch, I could have told her not to worry. Suzanne and I were married at Skibo, one of Scotland's largest, most impressive baronial houses, on 14 January 1995, six years before the Ritchies-to-be and a global media circus descended on Dornoch on the Firth.

The plan had been to lure Suzanne to Scotland for a surprise 40th birthday party, only to compound the deception by making the occasion a surprise wedding. Excitement was mounting among the few in the know when I received a telephone call in December from the owner, Peter de Savary.

'I'm sorry, old boy,' he said, 'but Skibo has burned to the ground.'

I am exaggerating in the telling, of course, though with Peter around there is usually no need to. Only someone with his sense of mischief would choose to open his Carnegie Club at Skibo on April Fool's Day in 1995. However, on this occasion he was not fooling. A fire had broken out in the kitchens during renovations, causing what turned out to be £750,000 worth of damage.

'Don't worry, your wedding will take place as scheduled,' he assured me.

Peter was incredible. He made it appear as if his sole aim in life was to have Skibo Castle looking its most magnificent for the marriage of Suzanne Danielle (née Morris), dancer, actress and mother, to Samuel Robert

Torrance (nae problem). He was true to his word.

There was a moment, though, when I wondered if I should not have pursued a less ambitious method of making a gold ring out of the rubber band I gave Suzanne on Concorde more than seven years earlier.

I had previously visited a clergyman in a church near my home in Virginia Water to discuss the situation. He said he could not conduct the ceremony because I had previously been married. Unless...

'Unless you wish to make a donation to the church every month. Then I will marry you,' he said.

That was Christian of him, I thought. So I turned my attention to Scotland and the place that philanthropist Andrew Carnegie described as 'heaven on earth'. Peter de Savary, who bought the 7,000-acre estate in 1990, was thrilled by the idea and could not have been more helpful.

I told Suzanne only that we were doing something special for her birthday, something that required a new dress. We went shopping to Browns in London's South Molton Street, one of her favourites, where I enlisted the help of the staff. While Suzanne was changing in a cubicle, I let them in on the secret. She ended up buying a wedding dress not knowing she was buying a wedding dress. Later that week, Lesley Gallacher, Bernard's wife, took her shopping for accessories and persuaded her to buy shoes that she described as being a bit 'weddingy'. Lesley was in on the secret, of course.

We headed for Heathrow on the Friday, leaving the kids with friends also in the know. The children were to follow the next morning. I arranged the check-in so that when we boarded the plane she still didn't know where we were going. She guessed somewhere in Scotland but the flight was longer than to Edinburgh or Glasgow. Eventually, we landed at Inverness, to be met by a Rolls-Royce. It was late in the evening by the time we arrived at Skibo.

Now I had a problem. I had to go to the registry office in Dornoch to sign something that allowed us to be married the next day. She was none too amused when I told her that I was going out. Even less so when I returned several hours later. Well, the office stayed open late and the staff were so kind and I felt it was only right to take them and the driver from the hotel for a drink and, you know, we met a few ghillies and one thing led to another...

Suzanne and I were on speaking terms again by next morning. Now I had to keep her in the room as everything was made ready downstairs and the 50 or so guests started arriving. Breakfast in bed, of course, followed by a hairdo and a massage.

'I have arranged for them to come to the room,' I told her. 'No need for you to go anywhere.' By this time she was very suspicious. Bizarrely, she was telephoning Lesley Gallacher, telling her about the wonderful location and the splendour of the castle, at the very moment the Gallachers were coming up the drive.

Eventually, I allowed her out. She walked down the staircase to the hall to be greeted by our friends and children, Daniel and Phoebe. Anouska, our youngest daughter, was on the way, if you know what I mean.

I handed her a flat box, the sort that might contain a necklace. There was a note inside, saying: 'Will you marry me now?'

She said, 'Yes, of course,' but even looking around at all our friends and family, the penny did not drop. She thought I was asking whether she would agree to marry me after all our years together and after all I had done for her birthday. She did not know I meant 'now' as in now, this very minute.

Everyone was standing in the hall at the bottom of these huge stairs, cheering and clapping. It was a wonderful moment. Well, of course, given my limitless capacity to cry on almost any occasion, I was a complete wreck throughout the ceremony and even the next morning.

The minister was doing his thing about the 'death do us part' and all the phrases you have to repeat. And, of course, I couldn't get a word out because I was crying. And my mother was wailing away too. The bride is the one supposed to cry but someone had to keep control.

The next morning I had to stand up at the brunch and give a speech. It was a case of 'I love you' and I was off again, tears streaming down my face. Very sweet, but I was not going to get away with that with so many mates there. So they all threw their napkins at me. I was covered in gleaming white napkins.

It was great, like one of those old weekend house parties. But it had to end, as the marriage nearly did on the way home. Suzanne experienced air rage before anyone invented the phrase as her husband became a bit too merry on the way back to London. I would like to thank British Airways for allowing one very ecstatic, very drunk, newly married Scotsman on board when, according to witnesses, they might justifiably have refused. Like all our arguments, however, the row was intense, brief and quickly forgotten. And before you start feeling too sorry for Suzanne, just remember she is more than capable of giving as good as she gets.

There was the occasion at a Ryder Cup in America when she insisted on getting out of the car in the middle of nowhere. She had celebrated a little too enthusiastically and was feeling sick. There she lay at the side of the road in the desert and there she wanted to remain. It took the best efforts of Laurence Levy, a very dear, now departed, photographer friend of mine, and me to carry her back into the vehicle.

Our first anniversary back at Skibo, staying in the same room and with some of our closest friends as our guests, was not without incident. I made one of my more dramatic entrances when I walked into the bar that evening with a chunk of flesh hanging off my forehead. I had walked into a bedroom wall. There was blood everywhere. My excuse was that I was chasing a ghost in the old haunted house.

It was Lesley Gallacher who tore a strip off me, ripping away the hanging flesh from my head. The bandage was suitably impressive, like something an Indian spinner might wear. As it happens, I was in Brunei the following week, where the combination of heat, humidity and air-conditioning accelerated the healing process dramatically.

That was January 1996. Nothing bad happened in 1995, with the possible exception of a few three-putts in the final round at St Andrews, which ruined my best opportunity of winning the Open Championship. Otherwise, it was the most fantastic year of my career, a year launched by my marriage to Suzanne and illuminated by the birth of my third child, Anouska. This was no coincidence. I was happier than at any time in a very happy life. I always feel that you play your best golf when most contented. Family life did not make me soft; it inspired me.

By the end of the year I would win three tournaments on the European Tour, mount my strongest challenge in the Open, run Monty to the last hole of the last round of the last tournament in the Order of Merit race, lead Scotland to victory in the Dunhill Cup, produce my best playing performance in the Ryder Cup and, oh yes, win more than £1 million in prize money.

It began in the first week in May at the Conte de Florence Italian Open at Le Rovedine on the outskirts of

Milan. Ironically, I was within half an hour of withdrawing due to a problem with my upper thigh tendon. I decided to play on, though not before cancelling a £100 bet on myself at 16 to 1. But a third-round 63 contributed greatly to a two-stroke victory over José Rivero, the man I had beaten in a play-off for my first Italian Open title in 1987. A first prize of £61,000 boosted my Ryder Cup points, while the gift of my weight in wine did the same to my cellar.

The organisers were great. They weighed not only a substantial Scotsman but a golf bag packed to bursting point with shoes and balls, etc. and his even bulkier caddie, Malcolm Mason. Nor was the weight of the bottles counted in the equation. I am partial to a beaker of the warm south, next to Guinness my favourite drink. Just keep me away from whisky – it does not agree with me!

The Murphy's Irish Open at Mount Juliet was a much bigger affair, with a £100,000 first prize and the imported presence of Greg Norman, then the World No. 1, and Craig Stadler. In the end it was three European Tour regulars who fought out a three-man play-off: Howard Clark, Stuart Cage and yours truly. Stuart found the water at the first extra hole, the 18th, leaving the Ryder Cup partners of many a fourball and foursome to battle it out for the title.

'As good a shot as I have ever played,' was how I described at the time my high, floating, 240-yard, 3-wood approach to the second play-off hole, the 17th. It has scarcely diminished with time and a fading memory. Howard holed a 20-ft putt for a birdie 4. But I found the centre of the cup with a 9-footer for a winning eagle.

That win, my second of the season and almost on a par with the Australian PGA success in 1980, an earlier 5th place in the Deutsche Bank Open and 11th in the Scottish Open at Carnoustie, put me in a great frame of mind for the Open Championship at the Old Course, my favourite of all British links courses. Rounds of 71 and 70 in difficult weather conditions established my best-ever position at the halfway stage of an Open. A third-round 71 kept me in contention, despite being five strokes behind Michael Campbell, following his extraordinary 65. While Michael faded right from the start of the final round, a birdie at the 3rd moved me closer to the lead. I had another great birdie chance at the 5th but the wind was blowing and my broomhandle putter was beginning to move round and about rather than to and fro. The pendulum action is difficult to maintain in strong winds.

I three-putted the 8th, 9th and 13th and hit a wayward drive into an unplayable lie at the 12th. My challenge was over, as John Daly went on to beat Costantino Rocca in a play-off. A birdie at the final hole proved no consolation.

There was still an Order of Merit to be won and the challenge of a fellow countryman to repel. But Monty's reaction to missing the halfway cut at St Andrews was both predictable and sensational. His next six tournaments were to yield two victories, the German Open and the Lancôme Trophy, two second places, in the Scandinavian Masters and the USPGA Championship, and prize money of £450,000. He broke 70 18 times in 24 rounds of golf.

All summer it seemed as if it was me and Monty battling it out at the top of the leader board. I managed four second places, a third and five other top tens, as for about the first time in my career I maintained my form throughout a whole campaign. A third victory came the week before the Ryder Cup in the British Masters at Collingtree, perhaps the most obvious example of my ability to putt on poor greens.

The Masters had been a special event for me over

the 15-year period it had been held at Woburn. I stayed every year with a dear friend, Mike Kemble, and, although I had never managed a win, I was hardly ever out of the top ten. I loved it at Mike's so much that I telephoned him to voice my regret.

'It's not going to be such a great week,' I told Mike.

'Don't be so daft,' he replied, 'Collingtree is nearer my house than Woburn.'

To celebrate I picked up the £108,000 first prize with rounds of 67, 66, 68 and 69, one ahead of Michael Campbell. That put me in front of Monty again and on that numbered cloud, judging by the joyous tone of my press conference.

'I haven't been so happy since my children were born,' I said. 'My dad always told me I'd play my best golf in my 40s and he was right. This win is more special than anything else in this wonderful season.' Little did I know there were further wonders to come.

Maybe Dad thought I wouldn't mature properly until my 40s. Forty- and 50-year-old golfers are certainly healthier, fitter and more aware of dietary matters than they used to be. But at the other end of the scale youngsters are coming through so quickly and so strongly, seemingly neither impressed nor intimidated by their elders. I reckon that your peak as a golfer might range from 28 to 34. I had some great moments at that age but also some bad stuff that perhaps prevented me playing my best. I had no regrets. In the words of the American T-shirt, shit happens.

Europe had won the Ryder Cup and Scotland the Dunhill Cup by the time Monty and I got together for our golfing equivalent of High Noon at Valderrama, a perfect venue to sort out 'The Man' from the men. My advantage over Colin was £4,000 going into the Volvo Masters, with Bernhard Langer, £60,000 adrift, a third possible Order of Merit winner, given the size of the first prize.

A third-round 74 severely damaged my chances. But a final-round 68 – the lowest of the day – in very difficult conditions, exerted the most intense pressure on Monty. He needed to play the inward half under par on a day of high scoring. He holed a 15-ft second putt for par at the 10th and made a birdie at the long par 3 12th with the pin in its most difficult front/left position. I thought he would do it and I was proved right, but not before a few dramas.

Having finished more than an hour ahead of him, I sat holding hands with Suzanne in the press tent, drinking coffee and smoking my roll-ups, looking as optimistic as I could in the circumstances. The first of two key moments arrived at the 17th, the hole that Seve redesigned/destroyed depending on your viewpoint. There had been ten 7s, three 8s and one 9 there, as player after player ended up in the water guarding the front of the green. A par 5 would keep Colin on course.

But his ball lay 2ft above his stance, in a fluffy bit of rough, sitting down, 82 yards from the front of the green. He had no margin for error. It was definitely make or break time. Suddenly, the television screen showed a ball in the air. It was lit like one of those scenes from a baseball match – would the ball go fair or foul? Would it land on the green and stay there or spin back into the water? And whose ball was it anyway? We had not seen who had hit the shot. Dramatically, it bounced just on the putting surface and somehow stayed there, almost defying the slope.

'Please don't be Monty's ball,' I found myself thinking.

The camera panned back to show Monty looking mightily relieved. He thought he had gripped down the shaft and hit it perfectly. I thought he was a bit fortunate. That's golf. His par was secured.

He needed to par the last for a third Order of Merit success in a row, a sequence previously achieved by Peter Oosterhuis and Seve Ballesteros in the 1970s. A 3-ft putt would have tested many, but not Monty.

'C'est la vie,' was my rather weak immediate reaction to the journalists who surrounded my table. I could not tell them how I really felt. I was totally and utterly gutted, as disappointed as at any time in my career. I had been trying for 25 years to win the Order of Merit and I knew that another opportunity would not present itself. I was 42 years old. Tiger Woods was 19 and about to turn professional. Golf was about to become a 'cool' sport; youngsters would flood into the game.

Monty knew the score. 'I feel for Sam,' he said. 'He's played so well, so bravely all year. This is going to be hard for him to take. He's had the best season he has ever had, he led us to the Dunhill Cup and he had a great Ryder Cup. To shoot the best score of the last day, to finish third and still not win the Order of Merit has got to be hard for him.'

There was, however, much to be proud of, much to look back on, not least a Ryder Cup that, thankfully, erased the memory of my personal nightmare at The Belfry two years previously. Although I did not know at the time that it would be my last Ryder Cup as a player, I realised the opportunities to make up for '93 would be few. My determination to perform to the best of my ability at Oak Hill Country Club had everything to do with what had happened last time. I wanted to redeem myself.

If 1993 was my worst Ryder Cup, a complete horror story, 1995 was to prove my best.

Oak Hill, Rochester, where Curtis Strange won the 1989 US Open, is in New York State, almost 400 miles from New York City, not too far from the Canadian border. José Maria Olazábal had been one of Bernard Gallacher's picks but a foot injury forced his withdrawal. He was replaced by Ian Woosnam.

Despite the fact that I had been a more successful fourball player than foursomes player over the years, perversely I was to win my two foursomes matches and lose the fourballs, one with Rocca and the other with Monty. Tino and I beat Jay Haas and Freddie Couples on the first morning and enjoyed a 6 and 5 thrashing of Davis Love and Jeff Maggert on the second morning. I was happy for Tino, who undeservedly had copped all the flack for our defeat in 1993. He took it really badly, retreating further into a shell almost forced on him by his lack of English.

Rocca is a bit of a loner who likes to eat on his own. There is so much between us since '95, however, that we never meet without giving each other a cuddle. The Ryder Cup forges life-long relationships.

One cuddle nearly broke one of my ribs. It was more of a bear hug, but you make allowances when someone holes in one during the Ryder Cup. It must have been even more satisfying for him coming against Love, the player he lost to in the singles in 1993. I had quite a job calming him down. It was early in the round and we had a three-hole advantage to protect.

Monty and I had been nipping Bernard's head to play us together in the fourballs. We were both playing fantastic golf that year, and particularly at that stage in the season. We'd been at the top of the Order of Merit and the top of leaderboards every week for virtually the whole of 1995. We thought no one could beat us. Brad Faxon and Freddie Couples did on the second afternoon, by 4 and 2. The irony was that Monty and I both broke par and individually both scored lower than our opponents. They just dovetailed perfectly, ham and egging it as they say in the USA. It was unbelievable. When Faxon was in the trees, Freddie would birdie; and when Freddie had the ball in his pocket, Faxon would birdie.

There was a good example of what went on at the par 5 13th. Faxon was out of the hole and Freddie was in thick rough at the side of the green. Monty had hit his approach to about 4ft from the flag. I lipped out but was stone dead for a birdie 4. Couples chipped in for the half. The crowd went nuts, with Faxon and Couples high-fiving all over the place.

I walked onto the next tee and went straight up to Couples and whispered in his ear, 'Fuck you.' It is the kind of thing you can say even in the Ryder Cup cauldron if you are me and talking to a great mate. You have to pick your moment and your victim. I wouldn't say it to Scott Hoch, for example. But Freddie took it very well. He told me later that he had told this to some of his team-mates, who had taken it seriously and poured scorn on my behaviour. Freddie put them right.

Anyway, Freddie knew I had something on him, something that would probably have offended the more sensitive members of his team. I just thought the whole incident a hoot.

Picture the scene. The eve of the match; the players have gone to bed early, excited and nervous about the day ahead. We have left the team room to the wives and girlfriends, who are enjoying a bit of a session. It is a tough week for them as well, and they need to wind down on occasions. The usual culprits are leading the festivities: Lesley Gallacher, Jane James and, of course, Suzanne, who is a girl after my own heart.

The girls are a bit hyper and the team room is close enough to our bedrooms for there to be a few telephone calls asking them to tone the noise down. Per-Ulrik Johansson's room is the nearest, and his need for them to be a bit more quiet is understandably the greatest.

I have already told them to calm down. I am lying in bed now, a bit uptight about the impending contest. It does not matter how many Ryder Cups you play, the hours before the start produce a powerful cocktail of fear and excitement. I am lying in bed and I can hear them carrying on.

'Wooah!' A roar spreads through the bedroom complex like fire sweeping down a corridor. I'm thinking, 'Why can't these women keep quiet?'

'Woooaah!' Another roar, only louder. I am now thinking I have to have a word. But I can't be bothered.

'Wooooooaaaah!' This one is like a bomb going off and I'm up. Shorts on, T-shirt on and I am down the corridor to the team room. The door is locked. It is never locked. I hammer on the door.

The door opens and Jane James is standing right in front of me. Suzanne is at her side.

'What the bloody hell is going on?' I ask. 'Do you women not realise it is the first bloody round of the bloody Ryder Cup tomorrow. What's going on?' I may have been a bit stronger than that.

Jane and Suzanne are nervously glancing to their left as if someone is hiding behind the door. I look behind the door. Someone *is* hiding behind the door.

'Sammy, Sammy,' a familiar Californian drawl pleads.

'It's okay, Freddie, no problem.' I love Freddie Couples. There are few finer men in golf.

The following morning I walk onto the range, where some of the American and European players have already started practising. I stroll casually past the American area when Freddie Couples, my foursomes opponent in about an hour, runs towards me.

'Sammy, Sammy, I am so sorry about last night,' the wee darling says.

'Freddie, please. Relax, it is not a problem, not a problem.' I milk the situation for all it is worth. There are a few puzzled American faces.

As it turns out, Freddie being Freddie, unable to sleep, decided he wanted some pictures signed. So, Freddie being Freddie, he thought 10.30pm was not too late and he headed for our team room. Only, Freddie being Freddie, he went down on his hands and knees, crawled into the room and, still unnoticed, jumped up in front of the women with a deathly scream. The roar I heard was the women's reaction.

The story indicates the great and genuine spirit between the two sides that has existed in all the matches in which I have been involved. It is not all 'War on the Shore' and 'Battle of Brookline'. These are exceptions to the norm. A terrific camaraderie has always existed and long may it continue to do so.

But I still wanted to whip Loren Roberts in the singles. We were 7–9 down going into the last day, needing 7½ from the 12 singles to regain the Ryder Cup. When Seve, cutting a swathe through the undergrowth, lost the top match to Tom Lehman, we were confronted by that proverbial mountain. But, as one American scribe wrote, 'Oak Hill, turned Soak Hill in the rain, became Choke Hill.' That's how they saw it. We thought we played pretty well.

The thing about Loren Roberts at that time of his career was that he didn't miss fairways and he didn't miss greens and he putted like God. A tough combination. Not for nothing was he known as the 'Boss of the Moss'. But I was in control the whole way, playing solidly and well if not sensationally. By the time I reached the 16th I was 1 up, comfortable with my game and comfortable with my emotions. I hit a perfect tee shot, leaving an 8-iron to the green. As Roberts prepared to strike his second, I walked forward about 25 to 30 yards and across the rough to the ropes, where Suzanne was watching.

'Watch this,' I said to Suzanne.

I just felt as if I were in the zone. If you have never been in the zone on a golf course, you will not have a clue what people mean by that expression. If you have been in the zone, you will know precisely the feeling. It is a question of being ready to hit exactly the shot required and knowing that you will execute it to the inch. You are so pumped up that nothing can get in your way. I guess Tiger feels like that most days.

I have felt that way maybe three times: against Doug McLelland at that matchplay final at the start of my career; against Antonio Garrido at Gleneagles in a Double Diamond event; and against Roberts that day.

I was so ready.

My 8-iron never left the flag. It carried the thick collar of rough, hopped up to the pin and checked a few feet from the hole. I sank the putt for a winning birdie. A 3-wood to the top of the hill, a gorgeous 5-iron onto the green, two putts and my 2 and 1 victory was sealed.

When Philip Walton holed the putt that won the Ryder Cup he became the first man in history to do so with a broomhandle putter, and in the process completed a singles sweep for the men with the long sticks. Mark James defeated Jeff Maggert 3 and 1, I did my bit and the Irishman edged out Jay Haas on the final green. Philip might have been using a curling broom for all he knew. He seemed almost unaware of the situation, though that was probably just his little boy lost look.

'I've got two putts for it,' he told his caddie, Bryan McLauchlan. 'I think I'll take them.' It seemed an eminently sensible approach when faced with a 12-ft

Above: Remember this?

Opposite: Waving the Scottish flag as I've always done at
Muirfield Village during the 1987 Ryder Cup.
Above top: The 2002 European Ryder Cup Team. The faces say it
all – we are going to win.
Below: The opening ceremony of the 1995 Ryder Cup at Oakhill.

Above: Team joy. Philip Walton sinks the winning putt at the 1995 Ryder Cup. *Right:* Who'll get to *keep* their hands on it? US captain Curtis Strange and me holding the Ryder Cup.

Left: Suzanne leads out the ladies for the opening ceremony of the Ryder Cup 2002 at the De Vere Belfry. *Below:* Daniel and me relaxing after the opening ceremony.

Above: The heat of the battle. A study in concentration – with Paul McGinley (behind), Jesper Parnevik and Suzanne.
Opposite: I love this green!

Above: Winning the Ryder Cup in 2002, and *(below)* winning the Dunhill Links in 2003. Dreams do come true.

uphill, slightly left to right putt. Before you could say third-time-lucky-and-I'm-not-being-captain-again, Bernard Gallacher was lifting Walton rather clumsily into the air and shouting in his ear, 'You've just won the Ryder Cup.' Philip, ever one for the puzzled expression, looked surprised.

A month later, seven of the triumphant European team were at St Andrews for the Dunhill Cup. Walton lost on the final green to Andrew Coltart as Scotland beat Ireland in the semi-final to reach a third final in 11 attempts. How the Scottish golfing fans longed for a victory at the home of golf. We had lost on both occasions to England – in 1987 and 1992 – the latter a match I missed.

Surely we could not lose in 1995, the year Torrance and Montgomerie were carrying all before them. As it happened, all three of us finished with four wins out of five, with Andy seeing off everyone except the mighty Ernie Els.

It fell to me to clinch the win and lift the trophy as captain after a 68–70 defeat of Mark McNulty. He was a class player, someone against whom I could not afford anything but my best. Happily, I felt inspired, not least by the reception I received from fans all the way round. The walk up the widest and most celebrated fairway in golf was incredible, just a taste of what it might be like to win an Open Championship in Scotland in front of 'my ain folk'. The experience was unbelievable. I may even have shed a tear or two.

13

'Guid drink'

In Scotland, 'He likes a guid drink,' is a common enough description of a person. Although it is not exactly a compliment, there is nothing really derogatory in the words. It tells of someone who drinks steadily and occasionally too heavily, someone who gets drunk rather than being a drunk.

I think it is fair to say that I like a 'guid drink'. I always have, though always for reasons of conviviality rather than out of habit. Those who know me best will say that alcohol is as much a part of me as my curly black hair, moustache, raised eyebrows, pencil behind the ear, roll-up cigarettes and broomhandle putter. As David Feherty put it, 'The pint and the punt are essential parts of Sam.' I never disagree with Feherty.

My grandfather liked a 'guid drink'. My father used to like a 'guid drink'. They both grew up in the same west of Scotland working-class culture of heavy binge drinking, which began on pay day and ended when the money was spent, often that same night. The pubs closed at 9pm in those days, preceded by a last-20-minute rush in which pint-laden tables would fill up with small glasses of whisky.

My father, who has always considered the businessman drinking daily more dependent on alcohol than the working man and his binges, has stopped drinking more often and for longer periods than me. His longest dry period was between 1976 and 1990. He has not touched the stuff for the last six years. I am very proud of how he has put his problems behind him and established a reputation as a golf coach recognised by everyone from the aspiring young Scottish amateurs he teaches to Tiger Woods himself.

'Tiger, I have never seen a great golfer improve as much as you have,' he told the World No. 1 on the practice range one day.

'Coming from you, Bob, that means a lot,' the perfect gentleman replied.

As ever, he was trying to make a point. 'Tiger, as great as he is, knows his faults and he is working on them, one by one, I think he can become nearly unbeatable. Mind you, no one will ever beat Ben Hogan in my eye.'

My father has been obsessed by Hogan for 50 years. He has had Sean Connery staying in his house, but nothing has come close to impressing him as much as the time he met Hogan and shook his hand. He collects anything to do with Hogan.

I stopped drinking once, for 22 months. When I say I stopped drinking, I mean I stopped drinking completely and without the slightest lapse. Not a drop of alcohol passed my lips for almost two years, as I demonstrated again the strong will and determination that serve as a counterbalance to the weaker elements of my character. If I set my mind to do something, I will do it.

I decided to go on the wagon after failing to make the Ryder Cup team in 1997. Although I had been feeling bad about myself for some time, having put on weight and gone to seed a little, the decision was entirely down to failing to gain selection for the match at Valderrama.

That hurt. It hurt despite the fact that I never really got close, either for automatic selection or for one of the wild cards chosen by Seve Ballesteros. It hurt, too, that after seven Ryder Cups in a row, I did not merit a private word or a telephone call from Seve informing me of the situation. I think it is important to take time to offer some words of consolation to people when they experience disappointment. I am not trying to make myself out as some kind of saint, but I must have contacted eight players to tell them they had been considered, and excluded, prior to announcing my team.

Seve would have been totally wrapped up in his team and how to beat the Americans, and rightly so. But he might have managed a minute or two for those not in his team, especially those with something of a history in the event. A call from the great man himself would have been nice. Just to acknowledge that I had tried my bollocks off and hadn't made it. Thanks for the effort but no thanks. No more was needed.

As it happened, I had been drawn to play with Seve for the first two rounds of the last counting event, the BMW International Open in Munich. I think I was probably still within mathematical reach of the team and, I would like to think, on the list for a possible wild card. My cause was scarcely helped at the 11th hole (my second) in the first round. I pushed my tee shot at the par 5 a bit right into the trees and hacked my ball back onto the fairway. When I went to prepare for my third shot, I realised I had played the wrong ball. That cost me an 8 on the way to a really disappointing 75. Seve never said a word. At that stage, there was nothing for him to say. I was totally dejected.

But I decided to go for it in the second round, if only to demonstrate to the Ryder Cup captain that I could still play. I scored 66, though it was not good enough to survive the halfway cut. I thought there might still be a glimmer of hope. But it was not to be.

I thought then that Seve might have invited me to come along and help in some capacity. I knew he would want his own fellow countrymen in Spain, but I thought we were close enough for me to be asked to provide some assistance. But it was not to be.

Instead, I received an offer from the PGA to be their guest, staying with officials in a hotel about three quarters of an hour from the course. That was not for me.

For the first time in my life I watched the Ryder Cup on television from the sofa in my den at home. Every single minute of it, from the first ball struck to the last putt holed. I became a golf fan for three days, complete with a steady flow of drinks and snacks and an open line to my bookie. I didn't move from the Friday morning until the Sunday night except to go to bed, take a couple of showers and change tracksuits. I found it fascinating to watch. At the same time I was disappointed and a little upset. There was a huge part of me wanting to be there.

And I decided there and then that even though I would be 46 years old by the next Ryder Cup, I wanted to win back my place in the team. To that end, I stopped drinking. It was entirely my decision, unusually something I did not discuss with Suzanne.

It took Suzanne a week to suss that something was up. 'What are you doing, darling?' she asked me one day.

'Oh, I want to make the Ryder Cup team, so I'm not going to have another drink,' I replied in a manner that belied the momentous nature of my decision. There had not been too many days in my life when I did not have at least one drink.

I started going to the gym. Four times a week I went to my gym and Queenie went to his, and we would meet at Sunningdale afterwards for breakfast. He used to tease me that I was starting to wear black to make me look even more sleek and fit. I never did weights. That was too much like hard work. I ran on the treadmill, for up to an hour at a time, and I went on the rowing machine for 15-minute sessions.

I got very fit and became very happy. I lost two stone. I went to the gym four times a week in an effort to regain my place in the Ryder Cup team and I failed miserably. I went to the gym four times a week and I did not even come close.

I did, however, manage a tournament victory, ending a 33-month barren period similar to the one I suffered in the late 1980s. Except I was now a 44-year-old accident-prone hypochondriac with a bad back, dodgy knees, a long putter and a bad memory. But I had not forgotten how to win.

With the decision to stop drinking came the realisation that I had become a little complacent, a little too sure of myself. During the winter after missing out on the Ryder Cup, I underwent surgery to remove bone growths from both feet and did not hit a ball for three months. That was the lowest point. I could not walk and I could not play the game I loved. I lost three months and two stone but found the determination to work on my golf, particularly on my chipping – an area I had neglected.

I had been around long enough to know that a win can happen at any time when you are least expecting it. When I started 'ripping it', as they say, at a pro-am at Sunningdale and later that week at Wentworth – I scored 63 and 65 respectively – I arranged for a sponsor's invitation to play in the French Open at Le Golf National on the outskirts of Paris. I had not even entered.

France was a thrilling and vibrant place to be that summer. The World Cup had captured the imagination of the country. Parisians still crowded into their pavement cafés but the national sport of people-watching was forsaken in favour of watching football. The smallest bars installed the largest television sets. Monty had given me a lift over from Farnborough in a private jet that probably would have done Andrew Coltart, Adam Hunter and Dean Robertson very nicely indeed on their travels.

My three misguided fellow countrymen set off on a 350-mile round trip by car to Saint-Etienne to see Scotland lose a Group A decider to Morocco. *Sacré bleu!* By the time they returned, after driving through the night, they discovered that part of the clubhouse had been allocated to the South Korean football team. The *Coupe du Monde* was everywhere.

An opening 64 validated the decision to add the event to my schedule. The most spectacular moment of the round came on the 18th when my second shot rolled onto a narrow wooden bridge and came to rest in a half inch gap between planks. The ball could have gone anywhere. In fact, I nearly holed it and rolled in an 8-footer for a closing birdie. But my shot of the week came later.

It had been my lowest competitive round since a 63 in Switzerland in 1995, as it happened the week preceding my last European win. When I reached the 17th on Sunday afternoon, I knew that one more birdie would clinch victory. It came there and then thanks to a 7-wood approach that flew 207 yards into the wind to finish just 18 inches from the flag. That was the best I had played under pressure for years and years.

I flew home, opened a bottle of champagne for Suzanne and some friends and poured myself a cup of tea.

Boring. That's what my friends said of me throughout that period, without ever putting undue pressure on me to revert to my old ways. I was feeling great. I had regained my appetite. I did not miss a thing. I still went out and still had fun. But I was not as much fun, or so my mates would tell me. In fact, everyone said I had become a boring old fart. Feherty was merciless, insisting that people were inclined to fall on their swords in my company.

But I could still find a few *bon mots* for my friends in the media. I went to Dublin the following week in buoyant mood.

'I've never won two weeks running,' I told a press conference. 'Mind you, I've never been sober two weeks running either. This time I've brought my best game to Ireland. Normally, I just take a hangover to Ireland and bring back a bigger one.

'At the age of 44, I realise that golf and drink don't mix. At 24, you can get away with it. When you are younger you can have the odd beer – even get drunk now and again – without serious effects. But at 40 your body does not always recover like it used to. And I suddenly realised I did not have much time left. I am now fitter and positively bouncing round the course. The other good thing about winning the French Open is that it gives me another three years before people start reminding me how long it has been since I last won.'

Now that I have turned 50, they have stopped bringing up the subject. That was to prove my last European Tour win and it came in a non-Ryder Cup year and before the start of the counting events.

My victory in the French Open was enough to tip the balance in favour of Mark James for the captaincy. Ryder Cup officials had suggested that the position go to who-ever was less likely to make the team. Victory in France made me the likelier candidate, so on 24 August, my 45th birthday, I withdrew from the running and offered Mark my full backing. Although nothing was written down, it was accepted that I would be captain in 2001.

It is not that I played badly in late '98 and throughout the first half of '99, I just never managed to convert good positions into the victories or the high finishes required to establish a position inside the top ten of the Ryder Cup points table.

There was also another injury – my back this time – that prevented me from even defending my title in France. For the sake of the sponsors, I flew out for the tournament, only to fly straight back again after a couple of interviews and appearances.

My bid to regain my Ryder Cup place effectively ended when I was forced to pull out of the Open Championship at Carnoustie in July 1999 through injury. It brought to a shuddering and emotional end a run of 27 consecutive appearances in the greatest championship in the world. Each time I was not exempt, I managed to qualify, something of an achievement in itself considering how many pursue so few places.

My experiences at the Open ranged from being in contention in 1995 to being disqualified in 1978 in the most bizarre circumstances. It came to light after the championship that I had played a ball from over the Swilcan Burn at the first hole of the second round without realising that I was out of bounds. Two weeks later, while at the German Open, I received a very polite letter from Keith MacKenzie, the then secretary of the Royal & Ancient, informing me that I had been disqualified and that they wanted their money back. I had to return a cheque for £50.

As it happened, if I had been disqualified there and then, the halfway cut would have been one stroke higher and people such as Tony Jacklin, Ben Crenshaw and Lanny Wadkins would have survived and, who knows, one of them might have gone on to win the Open.

I was exempt in '99, but injured. I telephoned Suzanne with the bad news.

'I can't play, darling,' I said. 'I'm not going to be in the Ryder Cup now. I know it. I won't be in the Open next year. Everything's gone. My career is over.'

She listened to the words of a very distressed golfer,

46 in a month, not wanting to face up to the fact that I would never play in another Ryder Cup.

'I think you should have a drink,' Suzanne replied, taking instant stock of the situation.

'I think you are right,' I said.

I knew it was the right thing for me at that time. I was, frankly, desperate for a drink. But Daniel was with me. So instead we bought some fish and chips and sat on the rocks at the beach eating our 'carry oot'. It can mean food or drink in Scotland. I have to remember to ask for a takeaway in England.

We flew home the next day. That night Suzanne and I shared a bottle and a half of wine. I also had a can of beer. I was completely and utterly sozzled, as you can imagine. I had not touched alcohol for almost two years. It felt like a release, a huge release. I knew I was not going to make the 1999 team and I knew I would never make another team.

We had a great night and several great nights for several weeks. The word got around that I was off the wagon and all of my friends wanted to have a night out with me. I could not go anywhere for ages without people pouring drink down my throat. As soon as I walked into a bar or a clubhouse or a friend's home it would be 'Have a drink, Sam.'

I was legless for weeks, just on the number of drinks people wanted to buy me.

14

Man of God

The telephone rang late one October afternoon in the snooker room at the far end of my house. Much of my life is in there: the full-sized pool table, the bar in the corner, photographs of my career and my family, either mounted on the wood-panelled walls or filling box after box.

There are enough trophies to stock a silversmith's, enough videos to do justice to your neighbourhood Blockbuster shop. The Ryder Cup is everywhere in this sanctuary. You can almost smell the freshly mown grass and hear the roar of the crowd.

'Oh, hello Tom,' I said, recognising the American voice. 'I'll take the call upstairs, if you don't mind.'

What I had to say to Tom Lehman could wait another 30 seconds. But I did not want the possibility of the children or anyone else interrupting. So I headed upstairs to the master bedroom, motioning Suzanne to join me to provide moral support.

Tom Lehman and I had been trying to speak to each other for days, ever since I received a long, rambling letter from the American Ryder Cup player about the controversial 1999 match at Brookline and its aftermath. His letter, sent from his home at Scottsdale, Arizona, was dated Monday 27 September, just 24 hours after the most disgraceful and disgusting day in the history of professional golf. The spectators behaved like animals and some of the American players, most notably Lehman, acted like madmen.

Lehman was not alone in cavorting all over the 17th green after Justin Leonard holed what turned out to be the cup-winning putt. But it was the sight of him in full cry that prompted me to blurt out to the then Sky Sports presenter Andrew Castle the words that were to appear prominently in the next day's newspapers, at least on one side of the Atlantic.

'The US should be ashamed,' I said to Andrew Castle. 'It's about the most disgusting thing I've seen, and this is not sour grapes. The way they ran across the green was disgraceful. Tom Lehman calls himself a man of God but his behaviour today has been disgusting.'

Lehman's response to my 'man of God' quotation was to put pen to paper. Bizarrely, he misunderstood my remarks. He seemed to think that I was implying that to be a Christian was to be a 'wimp or a weenie'. His words, not mine.

We had left messages on each other's answering machines before we eventually spoke. I didn't wait for him to say his piece because to my mind he didn't have a piece to say.

'Tom,' I said. 'I've obviously upset you judging by your comments in the letter. I wasn't doubting your Christianity. I saw you run 50 yards from the 17th green, back down the fairway and stand in front of the crowd, fist pumping at them as if in a frenzy. I watched you, I saw you. And what I said was that your behaviour was not the behaviour of a man of God.'

There was dead silence for maybe ten seconds before he replied. I remember his exact words. 'Sam, you make a good point,' Lehman said. 'And I apologise from the bottom of my heart.'

His apology – readily accepted, I must stress – was coupled with an admission in the letter that contradicted the insistence of captain Ben Crenshaw that there was never any intention on the part of any of the American players to incite the galleries.

Lehman wrote tellingly: 'Our team needed some emotion, and I decided to help them get it. I played the crowd for all it was worth. I fist-pumped, I blew kisses, I waved. I played some great golf too.'

Lehman did play great golf that Sunday. So did most of his team-mates. But the comeback and their eventual victory will always be overshadowed in my mind by their loutish behaviour and the vicious personal abuse that by no means only Colin Montgomerie of our team had to endure from spectators. That was evil.

We have enjoyed an incident-free, unblemished Ryder Cup since then, as I knew we would, given the nature of British golf fans and the character of Curtis Strange. I am, therefore, reluctant to draw attention to a scar faded by time and, more significantly, the recent memory of a true sporting contest.

But it is worth revisiting Brookline's 17th green to remind us of what can happen when guards are dropped and to provide the perspective for remarks for which I have subsequently been criticised.

It became obvious early on that things were going on that were just not right. When Lehman walked onto the first tee and sang their national anthem, our eyebrows were raised. By the time David Duval was inciting the crowds with a bout of incongruous fist-pumping, things had become very smelly indeed. David Duval, for heaven's sake, a great man, whom I like immensely; yet, here he was, running along the length of the gallery, high-fiving with spectators and cocking a hand around his ear as if to exhort the crowd to more intensified hysteria.

Who's to say I would not have been doing the same thing in the circumstances? I am a devious bugger, after all. But it was just not right, not right on the day, not right any day. I would like to think I would never go that far.

Emotions had definitely overtaken the American players. They were hyper while we were docile. Maybe we should have stood up to it a bit more and given some back.

I was crouched at the side of the 17th green, with Suzanne at my side, when Justin Leonard holed that 45-ft putt and the American players and wives went crazy. They were acting as if they had won the Ryder Cup. Had that been the case at that moment, their actions would have been fine. Had the final whistle gone, they could have invaded the pitch with impunity. They could have danced on the green as well as the grave of European hopes.

But they had not won the Ryder Cup. José Maria Olazábal still had a putt to halve the hole and at that stage perhaps even clinch victory for Europe. The fact that he had been required to move his marker demonstrated that he was on the same line to Leonard, only nearer. An American cameraman taking pictures of the premature celebrations was to trample on that line.

With each second and minute that went by, Olazábal remembered less and less of what he had learned 'going to school' on Leonard's putt. All he could think about was the crap that was going on. Still, they continued celebrating. I actually had to pull Suzanne back, such was her fury.

What they did there was totally wrong. It was exuberant, it was emotional and it was in the heat of the moment. But it was disrespectful, even if no disrespect had been intended. Maybe they did think they had won. That would be giving them credit where no credit was due. But they hadn't won.

No criticism intended to my great friend Mark James but I sometimes wonder what would have happened if Seve Ballesteros had been captain. This was Olazábal, Seve's favoured son, the golfer he nurtured and brought into the Ryder Cup, teaching him all he knew about the event. This was happening to his man. Seve might not have let anyone leave that green until justice had been done.

Dare one say Brookline needed a Jack Nicklaus to allow the true spirit of the Ryder Cup to emerge from the mire? I think there was a case for Ben Crenshaw stepping in and giving Olazábal his putt. He was probably too preoccupied kissing the ground. Mark O'Meara had done something similar to Padraig Harrington with a tricky 3-footer after two pairs of feet belonging to American wives ran between the Irishman and his ball. The video shows clearly that O'Meara conceded the putt and apologised after seeing the women run in front of Padraig. That was the true spirit of the Ryder Cup.

It was not up to Justin Leonard to give Olazabal his putt. I think the situation had gone beyond that. Leonard was in no way to blame. He got carried away, but understandably and only for a minute.

'Let's get off this green – everybody back,' he was shouting, initially to no avail.

Now, it was my turn to shout. Which is not my style. Although I have been involved in a few controversies in my time, I neither like them nor court them. If I can avoid a fight, I will. But if one is inevitable, I will not be posted missing.

So it was not exactly me when I launched into a tirade against the American team. Lehman claimed in his letter that he guessed I would have been the source of the 'man of God' comment. Spouting my mouth off in front of millions, knowing that millions more would soon be made aware of my words, was not me either.

I was back in our team room, the converted professional shop, when Mitchell Platts, the European Tour's director of communications, came up to me.

'Am I in trouble?' I asked him.

'Not with me you're not,' Mitch replied.

That was good enough for me. As a former Fleet Street man and one of the shrewdest officials around, he knew the game. I realised I'd said something, but I felt it had to be said. I think from the feedback I later received, everyone back in Britain and on the Continent was thinking the same. Deep down I knew I was right and not out of order. But I remained apprehensive that evening and into the next morning. I was worried that I had blotted my copybook, anxious about having possibly abused my exalted position of vice-captain.

Then I heard that Tony Blair was backing me. 'Mr Blair caught it on the news and could not believe that all those golfers could run on to the green,' a spokesman for Mr Blair said. 'He did agree with Sam Torrance.'

That meant a lot to me. I had got the man who was running the country on my side. That was almost as good as having the backing of the guy running the European Tour. Ken Schofield was also most supportive.

'If anyone had taken a different view from Sam's, they would have been out of context,' Schofield said later. 'The emotions were such that, short of someone taking a gun, I think anything said was going to be acceptable. If anything was going to be said by anyone in the heat of the moment – and not just by Sam – it was then. Typical of Sam that he should feel bad and anxious. We told him not only did he say the right thing but he was the right man to do so.'

It had been a lively and disappointing end to what had been a terrific new experience for me. For the first time since 1981 I had been at a Ryder Cup not as a player. There is nothing better than being a player but being a vice-captain was pretty good.

One change revealed itself to me somewhat unexpectedly. When, on occasion, rested for a morning

or afternoon series, I would willingly lend moral support
to my team-mates as a spectator. But there is nothing
worse than going out and watching. You want it to be
you. You feel it should be you out there.

'Christ's sake! I can't believe the captain played him
rather than me,' would be the natural thought. 'It should
be me out there.'

The result is a negative feeling that you try to hide.
'Oh no, he's going to miss this,' was how I viewed almost
every putt.

When I became vice-captain, I could not believe the
difference. I was genuinely positive about every shot and
every putt. It proved a real insight into how I would feel as
captain. I never thought we would lose in Brookline and I
never thought for an instant we would lose at The Belfry.

The vice-captains' job – Ken Brown and I were
called assistants, to be precise – is to be the eyes and ears
of the captain. We did the same job for Mark as Woosie,
Joakim Haeggmann and Mark did for me at The De Vere
Belfry. The captain decides who you watch in practice
and you report back in sometimes blunt terms. As a
trustee and a friend you are expected to be utterly
honest, even brutally so.

'So and so played shite today, he's really struggling,'
could well be the verdict. You were no help to your captain
if you did not tell it exactly as it was, often in graphic
terms.

The rest of the time was spent interacting with the
players in whatever way was required. You might have to
mollycoddle someone and give him a big hug; you might
need to cheer up or calm down players according to
circumstance, give them a boost or slap them down. You
would do whatever was required for the good of the team.

There was one occasion with Jean Van de Velde
when, with hindsight, I might have done more. I think on

reflection I did not recognise the signs. It was the Saturday afternoon after play had started. I found Jean sitting alone in a cordoned-off area between our team room and the locker room.

'What's up? I asked.

'Nothing,' he replied.

'You sure? Everything okay?'

'Yeah, yeah,' he insisted.

At the time, I thought it was nothing more than a player needing a bit of time to himself. But looking back, I should have seen the guy was struggling because he hadn't been asked to play in the first two days. I should have taken him for a walk somewhere and explained to him how good he was, how he had done brilliantly to make the team, why he was not playing and how vital he would be to the cause in the Sunday singles. But I did not see it at the time.

Of the three players who did not play until the Sunday, Van de Velde had the most difficulty coming to terms with the situation. The Frenchman remained quiet, aloof, not really part of the team. Andrew Coltart was, by contrast, magnificent, a captain's pick who did not get picked until the last series. He seemed genuinely proud to be a Ryder Cup player and did all that was asked and expected of him throughout the week.

Jarmo Sandelin was a legend, one of the greatest team players I have ever seen. How he maintained his enthusiasm and good humour while sitting out the action I will never know. His party piece, if you like, would be to burst into the team room with the words: 'I love you here, I love you there, I love you every fucking where.' It just lifted the whole team.

Jarmo is as nice as they come, not deserving of the stick he received for a complete misunderstanding in his match against Phil Mickelson. Jarmo had hit the ball very close at the 2nd, probably no more than 2ft from the flag. He walked onto the green, reached into his pocket for a marker and discovered only a hole. Everything had gone, tees, markers, money, the lot. He looked in his golf bag and found only tees. Neither he nor his caddie had a marker or a coin between them. But the crowd began to boo him, thinking he was waiting for the putt to be conceded. Eventually, he had to borrow a coin from someone in the gallery. After marking the ball, he missed the tiddler, of course.

The incident involving Andrew Coltart was much more sinister. Andy played beautifully against the mighty Tiger Woods, only to find himself shattered by events at the 9th. Tiger had just chipped in to win a hole he looked like losing. Instead of being all square, my fellow countryman was two down. Then Andy hooked his tee shot marginally left at the par 5. I could see from the tee that there were problems in finding the ball. I drove ahead in my buggy to help in the search. Without success. Eventually, I had to drive him back to the tee to hit another ball. Only after he did so, and another ball was put into play, did we receive a signal that his first shot had been found – about 50 yards from where we had been directed by marshals to look. It was just off the fairway and plugged. The marshals had insisted that the ball had struck a tree. Balls that hit trees do not plug. They land more gently than those that fly straight from tee into the ground. I never saw the marshals high-fiving their delight at the outcome but, as they say, I know people who did.

Van de Velde was a bit negative, a bit down in the dumps about not playing prior to Sunday. As a result, he didn't give us the performance of which he was more than capable.

There was much debate about whether Jesse should

have blooded the three rookies, Coltart, Sandelin and Van de Velde, prior to the Sunday singles. As it happened, I played all my four newcomers at some point during the Friday and Saturday – Paul McGinley, Pierre Fulke, Phillip Price and Niclas Fasth – and none of them lost on the final day. That had been my intention. But it was in no way based on a feeling that Jesse had made a mistake in his battle plan at Brookline. I am not convinced either way.

What deserves to be stressed is that no Great Britain or European captain had ever established a 4-point lead against the Americans after two days. The job of the captain was to squeeze as many points as possible out of each series. The fact that we were 4 points clear going into the final day suggests Jesse could not have done a better job. If he had played Coltart, Sandelin and Van de Velde in the first two days – and, remember, he was juggling with seven debutants – we might not have established such an advantage. It remains a debatable point in which both sides of the argument have a sustainable position.

Come Sunday, everything went pear-shaped. The American team was transformed, as was the crowd, from enthusiastic golf spectators into a bunch of animals. We walked that morning 'into the bear pit', the phrase coined by former R&A Secretary Sir Michael Bonallack and adopted by Mark as the title of a book that was to give me many sleepless nights in the first months of my captaincy.

I would not go as far as to say the hostile atmosphere was deliberately engineered. But it was encouraged in various ways, from the distribution of American flags to the aggressive fist-pumping. Suddenly, a wonderful environment for playing golf had been turned into a very hostile environment, not in any way conducive to golf.

There is never any place on a golf course for the kind of shouting and booing and screaming and roaring that went on that day.

Monty, of course, suffered the worst, as he had done on numerous occasions in the USA. Never previously, though, had he experienced a level of abuse that forced his disgusted father to flee to the clubhouse. His wife, Eimear, demonstrated the self-control and patience of a saint in putting up with what she heard as she walked inside the ropes that day.

Monty was left alone in the middle of the 17th fairway when the mayhem at the green was cleared and Europe were beaten. But he still had a point to earn and a point to prove.

I ran after Monty as he walked from the green to the 18th tee. 'Come on,' I said, putting my arm round him. 'This is your record, your singles record. You get up there and win this.'

The Ryder Cup was lost but I wanted him not only to maintain his fantastic singles record but to make a statement to all the morons who had ever barracked him, on that day or any other day. A proud man, who had been denied his singles point by captain Seve Ballesteros at Valderrama, he needed little encouragement. Of course, the records state that he went on to beat Payne Stewart, who within weeks was tragically killed in a plane crash.

As soon as one Ryder Cup ends, speculation begins about the identity of the next captain. Although nothing had even been written down in black and white or stated officially, it had been intimated to me that I would be offered the captaincy for The De Vere Belfry in 2001. This was the second half of the double ticket, if you like, that had identified Mark and me as candidates for the position in 1999. First up, if you recall, would be whoever was the more unlikely to make the team as a player.

Once the committee had met to determine that I would be the next captain, I pressed for an announcement. I wanted an end to all the questions and speculation. I was very, very proud to be asked to be captain and I wanted the world to know, the sooner the better. So on 1 December, just ten weeks after defeat in Brookline, and at my suggestion, my appointment was announced.

'My two picks will be Lennox Lewis and Prince Naseem,' I quipped at the press conference, referring to the events still so painfully etched in our minds.

But it was very much just a joke. I knew that there would be no repeat of the disgraceful scenes when the match returned to England in 2001. I knew in Curtis Strange that the United States had chosen a captain who would uphold the traditions of the game with dignity and style. I knew that together, as friends and old rivals, we would get the Ryder Cup back on track. No one could have watched the events at Brookline and thought it did not need to be sorted.

It took what I have referred to as a 'three-second call' to Curtis to confirm what I already knew. We spoke for a few seconds longer than that, but not much.

'This thing has to get back on the rails,' I said.

'Absolutely,' he replied. 'No problem. We'll not be doing that again.'

And, apart from a few pleasantries, that was the sum total of our discussion on the subject at that time. We spoke on a few occasions subsequently but there was really no need. We had swept everything from the desk in that briefest of conversations. I had a job to do, he had a job to do; we would do a job together and it would be great.

'Auld yin,' I called him because of his grey hair, though, in fact he is 17 months my junior. Our professional careers had followed a similar span, crossing only occasionally at team events, such as the Ryder Cup and Dunhill Cup, and at Open Championships. We knew and liked each other. Our relationship was not such that we would meet for dinner and get drunk together, but we would never walk past each other. We'd always have a laugh or a joke or have something to say to each other. There was a definite friendship there. He was always going to be an easy man to work with. A great man to work with, as it turned out.

We faced each other a few times on the playing field, as it were. My defeat by him in the 1985 Dunhill Cup remains a painful disappointment in no way compensated for by my victory in the Asahi Glass team event in Australia. Later that week I enjoyed a final green success over Greg Norman, which knocked out the host nation and ensured a Europe v America final, which they won.

I considered Curtis a nice guy and a great player. I always admire great players. I did not mind his reputation for being a tough cookie one bit.

The Ryder Cup had become such a huge part of my life that I would be lying if I said that I had not entertained dreams of one day captaining the side. For a long time they were no more than dreams. When Ken Schofield and I enjoyed a late-night glass of red wine, I would ask him if he thought I might ever be captain.

'Yes, Sam,' he would say. 'I think you could be one day.' I always thought he was just humouring me to shut me up.

After the telephone call to Curtis, there was no need to consider drafting in Lennox Lewis and Prince Naseem in any capacity. But I would shortly have to nominate my vice-captains, or assistants, or whatever the current vogue title. There was never any doubt in my mind that I would ask Jesse to do for me what I hope I had done for him.

That desolate Sunday night at Brookline, when the contest was over and the aftermath preliminaries had been completed, we met in locker rooms that had already been stripped by thieves.

My captaincy, though successful, gave me an idea of what Jesse must have been feeling that evening. He looked as if he had been through hell, which in a sense he had. It broke my heart – and it must have broken his – that his term of office was ending without a victory.

'Sam,' he said, 'if you want some help the next time, I'm your man.'

He was my man, all right. If I was going to be captain, I wanted him beside me. I have always admired Jesse, more than virtually anyone on the tour. He has a great head. If you want to know what's right and what's wrong, ask Mark. That was the way I looked at it.

Jesse and Woosie were going to be my men. Ian Woosnam had been the best player in the world and, as his mates will testify, was always the best friend in the world. The twin imperatives for any captain nominating a vice-captain is to choose someone with Ryder Cup experience and someone you can trust completely.

Jesse and Woosie: what a team! We had been a team for years. We had played together and socialised together, spending many a late night in the company of our wives. We were very close – close to each other and close to the players who would be carrying the European flag into action.

Yet I was criticised for my choice.

Political correctness had infected the Tour to such an extent that some called for me to have a Continental player as a vice-captain. I was seething. I needed people I knew well and could rely on for the sake of the team, not some sort of token Continental to demonstrate that we liked Europe. As someone who joined the Tour at the beginning and travelled all over Europe for 30 years, making friends with countless players on the Continent, no one could doubt my European credentials.

As it happened, long after the initial criticism, Joakim Haeggman became one of my vice-captains and did a fantastic job.

Storm clouds were gathering. Little did I know then that much of my first year as captain was to be spent trying to dampen the embers of a fire that would not go out and, indeed, regularly burst into flames throughout the hot summer of 2000. And I don't mean the weather.

It was not so much a question of 'into the bear pit' but into the bin. Nothing more than a flippant remark concerning a light-hearted moment in the team room at Brookline was to threaten my captaincy.

The good luck message from Nick Faldo that ended up among the litter did not stay there. It was not until 1 August the following year that it finally disappeared, and only after I had asked one of my best friends to resign as vice-captain.

15

Jesse resigns

Nick Faldo is the best golfer there has ever been in this country. The best Europe has produced, better than Seve, better than anyone.

My admiration for him as a player could not be higher. I remember him hitting a shot 25 years ago that I knew I could never hit, one that put him in a different league from me and the rest of our peers. It was at the Greater Manchester Open at Wilmslow, the same venue and tournament where Ken Schofield gave me 'the wrong ruling'.

Faldo was faced with 200 yards to a pin placed on the middle-left of the green, guarded by a bunker. I saw the shot as a hard 4-iron drawing in from the right round the bunker. He played a 2-iron like a sand wedge. The ball soared high into the air and landed ever so softly, like an old dog slumping down in front of the fire, or perhaps, as we golfers say, like a butterfly with sore feet. It took my breath away.

Later, he was to take a good swing and turn it into a better swing so that a very good player could become a great one. There is a world of difference from what he did to the numerous examples of players with flawed techniques that work for them changing swings and struggling. I often think they should leave well alone. Not everyone has the drive, dedication and determination of a Nick Faldo.

There was no one stronger coming down the stretch than Faldo. We saw it in 1995 when he basically won the Ryder Cup for Europe.

But Faldo was to make my first summer as captain a misery as the controversy arising from Mark James's book *Into the Bear Pit* grew and grew.

Even during the match at The De Vere Belfry three years on, by which time the row had long been resolved and forgotten about, Faldo raised the subject. He told Sky Sports viewers that he would be visiting the European team room personally because he did not want to risk sending a message. The story was repeated prominently in several newspapers the following day. That was probably one of his 'funny' jokes. I must say I thought it rather bizarre, however, when one of his representatives, not him personally, telephoned the team room to ask if it was all right for Nick to pop in. How could it be otherwise for a stalwart of so many Ryder Cup matches, for Europe's record points scorer, for the winner of three Opens and three Masters? Of course he would be welcome. After all that, I thought it odd that I never saw him in the room. Nor did I speak to anyone who saw him. Not before the match, not while the match was going on and not during the celebrations.

At Brookline in 1999 he had sent a good luck message that was held up for the assembled company to see.

'What should we do with it?' a voice asked.

'Bin it,' someone replied in jest.

It was a joke, nothing more or less than a joke that might have been played on anyone. Yet that flippant remark, and its subsequent retelling in Mark's book, was to cause a diplomatic storm, the likes of which European golf had rarely witnessed. It broke out during the Volvo PGA Championship in May and it rumbled on and on and on for two months – it seemed much longer at the time – until 1 August, when Mark resigned.

Unlike many who were passing judgement on the

affair, I read the so-called damaging section of Mark's book. I found it more humorous than insulting, though, of course, it was clear that there was no love lost between the pair. The serialisation in the *Daily Mail* was the problem. When taken out of context under a sensational headline, the passage looked horrific.

'I binned Faldo's good luck letter,' the headline screamed, as everyone started to arrive at Wentworth for the flagship event of our Tour. Naturally, I was asked for my opinion. It was an occasion for a straight bat, a 'no comment' until the book had been read. I did look at the offending paragraphs. They amounted to nothing. Faldo obviously took a different view. He summoned his troops and just laid into Jesse. And he kept on and on and on until it became too big. I had no idea at the time that it would assume the proportions it did. I don't think Jesse did either. I know my old friend as well as anyone. If he had imagined the extra arms and legs which that 'bear' would acquire, I think he would have omitted the whole episode from the book.

But he genuinely did not believe he did anything wrong. And what is more, I still don't think he did anything wrong. I must make that crystal clear. I never for a second thought that Mark had crossed any line in his conduct. Yet I was forced to seek his resignation. Things became so smelly that I had to ask one of my best friends to step down. That was one of the hardest things I have ever had to do. Imagine having to go on live television and tell the world that I had asked my vice-captain – and, more importantly, my friend – to resign. What kind of start to my captaincy was that? But the controversy had to stop.

The Ryder Cup had suffered enough from the row over Brookline. The European Tour was receiving some bad publicity. Week in, week out, we were playing tournaments and reading newspaper reports not about who was leading, not about great golf, but about the latest development in the continuing saga. Golf, probably the least tarnished sport in the world, was being blackened almost on a daily basis. Officials were getting jumpy, sponsors were becoming angry.

A feud was encroaching on my captaincy. And it had to stop. I never fell out with anyone during the whole affair. But I agonised about what to do or what not to do just about every minute of every day. I seemed to be thinking about it every waking moment. I was confused, but never demoralised.

Naively perhaps, I thought the meeting at Loch Lomond in July would put an end to the whole thing. The tournament committee, chaired by Mark himself, met in a tent beside the loch with photographers trying to poke their cameras through the door. The vote was ten to nil in Mark's favour, a clear reflection of the comparative popularity of the two protagonists among fellow players.

Nick Faldo, as I have indicated, is a magnificent golfer, someone whom I have admired as a player for quarter of a century. I would never criticise him for his ability and achievements. However, he has managed to compile an impressive Ryder Cup record despite never gelling with his fellow teammates. The players know the truth of it and, like elephants, they never forget.

'It's over,' I declared after the meeting, as much in hope as in expectation. Still it did not end. I thought that the Open Championship would make it go away. Unbelievably, it still simmered throughout the week. If the Open was not big enough to end this nonsense, then action had to be taken

'Get him out,' my dad would say every day, either by telephone or in person. Not out of malice or dislike for Mark but simply as a loving father who wanted the best for his son. My friends took the same view.

'You have to dump Mark,' they would say. 'It is the only way.'

I was not yet ready to agree. I think at any stage during the process that Jesse would have stood down if I had asked him directly to do so. But I continued to pray that it would blow over. Remember, there was no way I could act dispassionately. This was personal. Jesse was one of my dearest friends. He still is, thank God. I would have hated it if I had lost my friendship with him over this.

It could have happened. I contemplated lots of options: I thought of letting the whole controversy run its course; I thought of saying to the Ryder Cup committee that if they wanted to sack him, they should sack him; I thought of sticking to my guns and insisting that he must remain my vice-captain; I even thought of issuing an ultimatum that if Mark was made to resign, I too would resign. I never did make that threat. And the meeting with the Ryder Cup committee did not reach the stage where my captaincy was on the line.

Frankly, I desperately wanted to be captain. I had dreamed of the job for years. I wanted it badly and I wanted to do the best job I possibly could. I was not strong enough to play any games of brinkmanship. So, hearing how strongly the Ryder Cup committee felt on the matter, I agreed that I would ask Jesse to resign. I telephoned him on his mobile. He was in Spain on holiday. To be honest, I cannot remember exactly what was said. It was all a bit of a blur, as emotional events can be. This was the last thing I ever wanted to do.

'Jesse,' I said, deciding my customary greeting of 'Jessica' was inappropriate to the occasion, 'this has got to stop. I'm sorry, you are going to have to resign.' Words to that effect. He agreed. There was not much more to say. I put down the telephone and readied myself for a live television interview.

The European Tour offered to put someone else up in front of the cameras. But I insisted. It was my call, my responsibility and my captaincy. It was time for me to take control. I could see then that for the good of the Ryder Cup the controversy had to end. Except that it didn't stop. Not entirely. For a while Faldo persisted in trying to have his pound of flesh from James with talk of breach of conduct, etc.

Although I asked Jesse to step down, there was never a second when I considered that this man would not be by my side at the Ryder Cup, helping to plot victory. This was politics, I could not say anything to him at the time. I could not say that I was asking him to step down but that actually I still wanted him to come; but that was very much in my mind. And, of course, he was at The De Vere Belfry in 2002, dressed in all the official gear, not as a vice-captain in name but as much an integral part of my back-room team as Ian Woosnam and Joakim Haeggman.

It was very big of Mark James to step down and be there for me at the match. I hope he knows how much it meant to me that he could share the victory he was denied in dreadful circumstances at Brookline. Even at the moment of triumph, I thought of him and that awful couple of months in the summer of 2000.

By the following summer, ever the diplomat, I was making encouraging noises about Faldo regaining his place in the European team. I had a good idea even at that stage who my picks were going to be, but I saw no reason to discourage Faldo from trying to gain selection. Faldo 2001 was nowhere near the force of Faldo 1995, but a Faldo on form would strengthen any team. I took the view that speculation never did any harm. Moreover, if a man makes my team, he has my highest regard. I don't care who he is and what differences we might have had in the past.

Right from the start of the counting process I had it in my mind that the two wild cards would probably be Jesper Parnevik and Sergio Garcia, a successful pairing at Brookline and two US Tour regulars who, if a major championship did not come their way, might not earn enough points for automatic selection. In fact, I told Garcia early in 2001 that he would be a definite captain's pick should the occasion arise. Although I never requested that he try to gain one of the ten places by coming over for the last counting event, the BMW International Open, he made the gesture.

I had always been a supporter of rewarding players loyal to the European Tour by selecting the vast majority of the team from the Ryder Cup points table, essentially the Order of Merit. Now that I was the captain and confronting the prospect of being without one of our world-class players, I began to change my mind.

It became pretty clear throughout the summer that I would be faced with picking two from three and having to line up without one of the threesome of Parnevik, Garcia and Olazábal. It was two from four, in fact, until Bernhard Langer won the TNT Open in Holland in late July, his first victory for four years. That guaranteed his place in the team.

I was having to use one of my two picks on the World No. 4, as Garcia then was. That could not be right. Olazábal, the hero of so many Ryder Cups, had required a wild card on previous occasions. That also could not be right. Those arguing for the world rankings to be used were sounding more and more persuasive, and by the time the system was changed in 2003, I was in complete agreement.

Three generations of the Torrance swing, as demonstrated by my father, Bob (*top*), me (*centre*), and my son Daniel (*bottom*).

Top: The coaching never stops and advice is passed down…
Above: Team Torrance at St Andrews, 2003.
Opposite: With Suzanne, Phoebe and Anouska at Buckingham Palace in 2003. I had just received the OBE.

Above: A great moment during the *BBC Sports Personality of the Year* Awards, December 2002. My good friend and vice-captain Ian Woosnam presented me with the ball that Paul McGinley sank to win the Ryder Cup.
Right: Taking on a couple of mugs in a practice round at the Open for easy money!
Opposite: David Feherty and me together at the Ryder Cup at Kiawah Island in 1991.

Opposite top: With my great friend Ernie Els. We're holding the cup and the jug.
Opposite below: With another great mate, Ian Botham, on the Sunday night after the Ryder Cup.
Above: I promised Daniel I'd have this done if we won the Ryder Cup!
Left: Feherty and me doing what we did most of – drinking and laughing.

Above: Mine, all mine!

Two years earlier, however, I was faced with a dilemma. It was a problem I knew I could not solve. But I asked the question anyway. I went to the Ryder Cup Committee to enquire if my number of picks could be increased from two to three during my term of office and during the counting period. I knew the answer before I put the question. For reasons of equity, not least to the player finishing 10th on the list, we had to stick with the system employed at the start.

I was going to have to make that difficult decision. It looked like I was going to lose out on a great player. As it happened, I did. As it happened, it didn't matter.

Although my original wild card instincts that year had been for Garcia and Parnevik, I was still debating in my own mind my final verdict come the final day of the final tournament. I was in Germany for the BMW International Open and still I had not made up my mind with 100 per cent certainty.

I watched Olazábal hole a 1-iron that week at the very same hole where four years earlier I had played the wrong ball when trying to persuade Seve of my credentials. But it was clear to me that Ollie was still struggling with his game. Garcia, as I said, was a shoe-in. Parnevik had won in the USA at the beginning of the year and was still playing well. Nervously, he rang me several times that day, trying to find out if he had made the team. Eventually, I called him up with the good news and told him while he was warming up on a practice ground ahead of his final round.

I also called several players with the bad news. I made contact with as many as eight people that day to tell them they had missed out. Some I rang, others I was able to speak to in person as they were in Germany. I found myself almost in tears telling Brookline team member Andrew Coltart that he had failed to make the team, even though his form had been such that the news came as no surprise to him. Paul Casey had made a late run, having won at Gleneagles. Some people were surprised that I made special mention of him having been in contention. But I thought he was the kind of attacking young player who would have done well at the De Vere Belfry. He just missed out. He understood that his time would come soon enough. Casey and Justin Rose are virtual certainties for the next match.

Of course, telling Olazábal was just awful. Frankly, I did not know if I was making the right decision. I know of no man on this planet who had given more for his team, and would again, given the chance. But he wasn't playing well enough. His driving was too untrustworthy for the demands of The Belfry. Parnevik was the choice. Ironically, Olazábal turned his game right round and started winning again, albeit not for a sustained period right up to the match. Meanwhile, Jesper went completely off the boil and arrived at the Belfry a year later with his game in pieces.

To say Ollie reacted badly to my decision would be an understatement. I found myself following him like a little puppy dog from the scorer's tent to the locker room to tell him the bad news. He was totally distressed, which you can imagine and understand. Here was a great man with so much heart and passion for the Ryder Cup being told he was being left out of the team. It was hard for him take. I said very little; he said even less. Later, he complained to the press that I had not spoken to him enough over the final months, not given him enough encouragement. I did not really understand his beef.

My team was complete. We had less than a month to make any last-minute preparations to the course that would suit our players. We had just a few weeks to foster a team spirit. Or at least, we thought we had. I liked the look of my 12, despite the fact that some critics focused on the so-called weaker players at the bottom. But I had played in enough Ryder Cups and appreciated enough of Ryder Cup history to know that some of the least likely players produce the most significant performances. 'Out of the shadows come heroes,' as I said after victory.

I was particularly happy that half of the team had been involved in the defeat at Brookline. They felt robbed and the victims of an injustice. They wanted revenge. No one more so than Colin Montgomerie, who had suffered such abuse in 1999. Monty was always going to be my rock. I didn't care what his game was like coming into the event because I knew the Ryder Cup would bring out the best in him. There was an injury scare concerning his back a few weeks prior to the match. The press painted a bleak picture. But I had telephoned him within minutes of hearing the news and received a personal assurance that he would be fine.

I had always held Monty in the highest regard, even when I was winding him up. I remember once Malcolm Mason, my caddie, had this credit card thing that made the noise of a mobile phone. That represented too good an opportunity for me to miss. Every time Monty reached the top of his swing during a practice round money match, I pressed the button. He became increasingly agitated as he tried to find out who in the gallery was using a phone.

Monty and I played a lot of Dunhill Cups and World Cups together. He was a great team man, great on the course and great with fellow players and caddies. Everyone liked him. You could see him improving with every Ryder Cup, assuming more and more importance as he became a senior figure. Monty became the strong man, inheriting the role Seve provided for Tony Jacklin and, initially, Bernard Gallacher.

Monty was my Seve. He loved being consulted and asked for his opinion. He was a natural leader, the obvious man to put out first in singles. He is totally different off the course from on it, a charming, intelligent person and a good dinner companion. He's been his own worst enemy on the golf course over the years and he knows it. That has been his flaw. He has had the game to beat anyone, anywhere, and win several major championships.

Sergio Garcia was simply one of the most exciting young players in the world, someone who obviously revelled in matchplay, in the cut and thrust of head-to-head confrontation, whether with a partner or on his own. In that respect, he reminded me very much of the young Seve.

Garcia is a tumultuous young man, exuberant, never still, always up to something. He had intended bringing tennis star Martina Hingis as his partner but the relationship ended. As it transpired, he came with his lovely mum, Consuella, and spent the week chasing Bernhard Langer's daughter. If Monty was my rock, Sergio was always going to be a hard place for any opponent.

I called Darren Clarke 'Big D'. I had known Darren a long time, dating right back to when he was an amateur in Northern Ireland. He was my partner in a pro-am at a time when he was deciding between staying an amateur until the Walker Cup or turning professional. He asked my advice.

'Darren,' I said, 'you are swinging well, your game is great. Get out there, boy. Just get out there and play. That is what you want to do. Just get out there and do it.' And he did.

I have always loved his game. He is just a beautiful golfer. Like Woosnam, he's a great striker of the ball. He is very impressive and intimidating when in full sail.

He had become an old hand at the Ryder Cup. He knew what it meant, how it felt and how much you can raise your game. Like most of the boys, he called me Mr Captain.

'Big D,' I would say, greeting him in the morning.

'Mr Captain,' he would reply with that big smile of his.

Bernhard Langer was, for obvious reasons, Fritz. I knew he would be great for me. He had been a tremendous competitor throughout a distinguished career, a tough man to beat and one who had a point to prove. He was bitterly disappointed not to have made the team at Brookline and wanted to show everyone the folly of his omission.

He also brought his vast experience to bear in various situations, from course preparation to tactical awareness. Bernhard was to make a great call as the final match of the second day went down the last, a very important one for us in the context of what had gone before and what was to follow. Paul McGinley and Darren Clarke were playing Scott Hoch and Jim Furyk. The match was all square going down the 18th. With Darren furthest away after the tee shot in the right rough, the spectating Langer approached me.

'Sam, maybe we should get Paul to play first because there's less pressure on his shot and by playing before Furyk and Hoch he could apply some pressure to the Americans,' Bernhard said.

We agreed that it was a great idea. So I wandered over to McGinley and said, 'If you're not uncomfortable at the prospect, we think maybe you should hit first.'

He readily consented and struck a wonderful 4-iron 200 yards to about 20ft from the pin. With both Americans bogeying, McGinley's par tied the match 8–8. We were level going into the singles.

Padraig Harrington was simply a class act, one of my dad's pupils, just the hardest worker on Tour. I knew Paddy – as I called him – would be strong. He had all the qualities, a world-class player who would be winning major championships before long. Like Monty, Harrington was to be one of my floaters, someone who could be paired with anyone. There were certain players you wouldn't put with a scrappy player, certain players who would feel uncomfortable with someone who did not impress them. I had no partner in mind for Padraig at that stage. But he was one I expected playing in all five series.

Thomas Björn was one of my most favourite players in the world. I just loved the way he played golf. He hit the ball beautifully with a lovely wide swing. Thomasina, my affectionate name for him, is a great guy who you would not want to cross. He speaks his mind and does not take any crap from anyone: at 6ft 2½in, a big man in every sense. He was another whom I planned to play all the time. It was not to be. It just shows you the importance of flexibility, something I was to learn during Ryder Cup week.

Lee Westwood was another class act. I told him the old cliché about form being temporary and class being permanent. I knew that I would get a big week from him despite his struggles over the past few years. I call Lee Junior. Many moons ago, I was playing five-a-side football in Largs with John Wilkie when this kid asked for my autograph. It was a nine-year-old Lee Westwood.

He's a great guy. I love him to death. I loved how his demeanour did not change during his slump. He carries himself proudly, as if still winning five tournaments a year. I am so glad he returned to form in 2003.

I did not have a nickname for Pierre Fulke, so he became Mr Fulke. He is always tenacious. He hits the ball with a big hook, but that's his way and he does it very efficiently. I thought him a perfect foursomes player, very straight, always putting the ball in play and, crucially, with a fantastic short game to compensate for a partner missing the green. He is rightly regarded as one of the best putters on our Tour. The Swede made the team early and, worryingly, had not done much recently when the team was selected.

Niclas Fasth was the team member with whom I was least familiar. I had played with him a few times, and all the talk from fellow pros was of someone seriously good. Pros always know. I did watch him finish second at the Open Championship at Royal Lytham in 2001, David Duval's year, and he was unlucky, bloody unlucky. I thought this kid could really play. I was very impressed with the way he kept his nerve coming down the stretch. If he could do that in a major championship, then he would be fine for me. He was a big, strong, powerful lad with a good swing. You never get two Swedes the same. They are all mad, but great. Niclas turned out to be the quiet man of the team, though not in a bad way.

Jesper Parnevik was the third Swede, the craziest of them all. A great man and a great team man, as it proved. Ironically, I had chosen him ahead of Olazábal because the Spaniard could not find the fairway from the tee. By the time we reached The Belfry in 2002, Jasper, as I called him, was having terrible problems with his driving. But his attitude remained tremendous throughout. My first conversation with him that week was typical of the man.

'I'm struggling,' he said. 'I will not mind at all if you don't play me until the singles. Whatever is best for the team.'

I was so pleased that he managed to find some form as the week progressed and that he was able to contribute to the cause. All the Swedes did. It had been suggested to me early on that I should get a Continental as a vice-captain. I resented the idea and told officials where to go in pretty blunt terms. As I said previously, I had friends all over the Continent and I needed as lieutenants people whom I liked and trusted, not examples of tokenism and political correctness.

However, a year on and with three Swedish players in the team, I decided to enlist the help of Joakim Haeggman. He was a real laugh who had made a fantastic contribution to the 1993 Ryder Cup team. He was perfect for the job.

Paul McGinley was another player whose game I liked (McGinty to me, though anything but a goat). He was very solid, a good putter. Like Fulke, I had recognised a tenacity in his make-up. Here was someone who would give everything for the cause on the course and be an important, bubbly figure in the team room. He was one of the rookies who were to feature so large in victory.

The excellent atmosphere in the team room all week was a reflection of the stuff we would do during the 12-month postponement. Every time the members of the team met at a tournament, they would have a word for each other. They knew they had something special between them; they knew that they would be sharing something. I could see the team gelling as time went by.

Phillip Price, former Pontypridd Man of the Year and, little did anyone know, legend in the making. I knew him very well, enough to know that inside he was tougher than he appeared. His game was very similar to Fulke's. They both hit the ball about the same distance and they both putted very well. His wife Sandra turned out to be a real laugh, one of a great bunch who blended in well. It is not easy for newcomers, even more intimidating for the wife than the rookie. Wives, partners and girlfriends play a huge part in helping produce the right atmosphere and, at the risk of sounding chauvinistic, keeping the players happy. Golfers can be a temperamental bunch, more so than in many sports because of the individualistic nature of the game.

The team was picked and I was as ready as I ever would be, and certainly a lot more as a result of being vice-captain to Mark. One of the things I was to tell the Ryder Cup Committee in my debrief was how the greatest asset to my captaincy was my vice-captaincy. I learnt more under Mark than I did in eight matches as a player because it's a totally different job.

As a player you're cosseted and pampered. You're led here, you're led there. Everything is taken care of. All you have to do is hit the ball. Which, of course, is the hardest thing to do. But a captain has responsibility for everything else.

I am not advocating that a captain picks the next captain. But future captains would be much better equipped for the task in hand after a match as an assistant.

There was just a three-week interval between the announcement of the team and the day we were due to meet at the De Vere Belfry. But it was to be one year and 18 days before a ball was struck in earnest.

16

September 11

To those who had never visited the United States of America, or even to those who had, but happily never needed to summon police, ambulance or fire brigade, 9/11 meant nothing. To those weaned on Hollywood movies and television detectives, 9/11 was, of course, the American version of 999.

But since 11 September 2001 (the ninth month and the 11th day) 9/11 became shorthand for the worst terrorist act in history, the day two aeroplanes were deliberately flown into the Twin Towers of the World Trade Center in New York. A where-were-you-at-the-time situation on the lines of the JFK assassination or the Cuban Missile crisis, though on a much vaster scale.

I had just arrived at Sunningdale and was parking my car when Blaize Craven, a friend, told me the news. We went into the clubhouse to find out what was happening. Like most people throughout the world with access to a television, I sat in front of the screen to watch the most horrific scenes unfold, a disaster movie played out in real life. All that day and the next I sat glued to the television, both fascinated and horrified. The world would never be the same again. That was a mantra repeated over and over.

Honestly, and to the disbelief of those I have told, I never once in that period gave a single thought to the Ryder Cup. I may have thought about the Ryder Cup every day of my life for about 21 months previously, but for two or three days it never crossed my mind.

'How is this going to affect the Ryder Cup?' someone at Sunningdale asked later that week.

'Christ, the Ryder Cup!' was my reflex response. 'I don't have a clue. I have no idea.'

The telephone started ringing at about the same time. It was as if all normal activity had been suspended and gradually resumed as the smoke began to clear. There must have been officials from both sides of the Atlantic talking about the ramifications for hours if not days. But those discussions, subsequent deliberations and the eventual decision were made and taken at a level above that of the captains.

My initial instinct on realising that this would impact on the Ryder Cup was that the match could not possibly go ahead. I never wavered in that belief, despite perfectly reasonable arguments from those who thought life – and sport – must go on in order not to give in to terrorism. I just never thought that anyone – especially the Americans – would have the stomach for a contest, the very essence of which combines hard but fair confrontation. I thought that factor more relevant to whatever decision was made than the security aspect.

My first feeling was that the match should be cancelled rather than postponed. Only later did the idea of the same teams coming together 12 months on offer an appeal. There was even a suggestion that we could split the two teams up and have a friendly match – six from America and six from Europe against the other six from America and the other six from Europe. It sounded feasible but for the fact that the Americans would still have had to travel. And most were understandably reluctant to do so.

I spoke to Curtis Strange, my opposite number, three times on the telephone between then and the announcement of the postponement, twice during his 16-hour drive home to Tulsa from the cancelled American Express Championship in Ohio. There were no aeroplanes flying over the skies of America that week, forcing long journeys by car for those wanting to return to their families from wherever they had been doing business.

The conversations were brief and to the point, expressing our mutual shock and agreeing on the relative unimportance of golf at such a time. I knew even then that there was no appetite among the American players to come over in a couple of weeks for the match. In truth, there was little appetite among the European players either. It was just a question of letting everything settle as the various logistical nightmares were dealt with one by one. Despite bullish noises from some of their officials in the early days, it really became a question of waiting until the PGA of America said they were not prepared to come. It was their call.

That call came on Sunday 16 September. Late that afternoon, around 4.45pm, I began telephoning all 12 members of the team to tell them personally that the Ryder Cup had been postponed, a momentous thing for any captain to have to do. There were two for whom I had to leave messages on their answer machines, but eventually I spoke to all of them. They were delighted the matches were going to be played but pleased, too, that they had been postponed. I had spoken to several during the previous week. It was very difficult to make a proper assessment at that stage. There was a general feeling of impotence, a numbness and an inability to function. I think millions of ordinary people all around the world felt like that in the aftermath of 9/11.

A press conference followed on the Monday at which, quite rightly, the practicalities of the postponement were aired. I tried to impress upon the journalists that the decisions taken were way out of my hands and that it would be a continuing honour to be captain for another year. There were questions about the respective

strengths of the teams in a year's time, about whether I
wanted my wild-card picks again and whether I thought
Tiger Woods would stop playing outside the USA.
I dispatched that last one to the boundary.

There was no need to be negative, so I looked for
the positive. 'We have a much younger side than the
Americans, so maybe it will be in our favour a year down
the line,' I said. 'With a two-year qualification process as
opposed to ours of one year, they'll actually be three
years down the line from the start of their qualification.'

But it was almost as if we should not be thinking
about such things at a time like that. Golf had become an
irrelevance. People thought about their families growing
up in a different world. They walked about like zombies,
absorbed in matters of global concern and how it might
impact on their lives. It was a case of seeing the big picture,
not focusing on one small frame called the Ryder Cup.

'I don't think cancelling or postponing is giving in to
terrorism,' I told the press conference. 'I think it is re-
flecting the enormity of the horrors we have seen. It is
not giving in, it is just showing the world that we understand this is the worst thing that probably has ever
happened. We have to sort it out. Golf is nothing, nothing.'

I never thought I would ever say those words. Golf
had been my whole life. And the Ryder Cup had been a
great part of my whole life. And for almost two years I
had thought about nothing else.

It was time at least to step back for a while. The
team had been picked, the clothing was done, the
bookings were made, everything as far as I was concerned was in place. So we just kind of switched off for
a couple of months. I told my players not to think about
the match. It was going to be played in a year.

But I began to realise that this 12-month period
offered a unique opportunity for the team to get to know

each other and bond more tightly than any previous team. A year of knowing exactly the complement of the team served as a huge opportunity. I don't know what Curtis did with the Americans – and it was very much a philosophy of mine never to bother about what they were up to, not to try to second-guess them – but we used the time to foster the strongest possible team spirit and to ensure that the course was precisely set up to our advantage.

Normally, you have only three weeks between the team being announced and practice starting. I used the year to get to know everyone as best as I could. We had four dinners together and one whole day at the De Vere Belfry when we played matches on the course, then did some serious socialising with partners in the evening.

Jesper and Sergio could not come because they were playing a tournament in the States. 'Jesse' James and Joakim Haeggman took their places so that we had a team of 12. They played fourballs, with the perhaps unlikely combination of Pierre Fulke and Phillip Price cleaning up with a score of 10 under par.

I had deliberately pulled Pierre aside prior to the competition to tell him my thinking about pairing the two rookies and placing them in a foursome with James and Haeggman, four of my eyes and four of my ears.

'You two are playing together for a reason,' I said. 'I want to see a marked improvement. You are a valuable member of my team but you have to get the finger out a bit.'

I knew Fulke would not like that. He was tough, a hard worker with a lot of pride. I hoped it would have the desired effect.

A few weeks later, he approached me on the subject, saying, 'You really got to me when you said that I needed to buck up.'

'Yes,' I replied. 'It was intentional. I didn't say the same thing to Phillip. I only told you. I didn't think it would be right for Phillip.'

Price was much more timid, much quieter. To demand more of him in that blunt way might have had the opposite effect. It might have forced him into his shell even more. I was confident that he would find his own way and work everything out by himself. I think you can say that a singles victory over Phil Mickelson, then the No. 2 ranked player in the world, was a case of his having worked things out.

Their performance together was also an indication that they might be a pairing, which, of course, they turned out to be.

I also used that gathering to get an idea about how each member of the team saw the pairings forming for foursomes and fourballs. I gave them all a piece of paper and asked them to write down with complete confidentiality and anonymity who should play with whom in foursomes and fourballs. I reasoned that some, maybe all, would feel inhibited if I asked them in a team room in front of their colleagues. They would be more likely to say what they thought the captain wanted to hear when speaking in an open forum.

A tip for future captains here: don't give golfers pens and paper. You should have seen some of the attempts at spelling the names of the most famous golfers in Europe. Some players were even omitted from lists. Some names were written down twice. It was a shambles, one of my least rewarding ideas.

My efforts to create a course that would suit our players proved much more successful. John Paramor and David Garland, from the European Tour, were a great help to me throughout the year as we tried to fashion a course that would conceal our weaknesses and not play into the hands of the Americans. They accompanied me on my regular trips to The De Vere Belfry. I went as many as half a dozen times. Bevin Tattersall, the excellent Belfry greenkeeper, carried out the structural alterations and conditioning after consultation with Dave Thomas, the original designer.

There were a few bunkers I thought a bit too severe, for example the one in front of the green at the 9th. That was made a bit fairer by removing the riveted sheer face and replacing it with a more sloping one. That took away the possibility of having to play out sideways as had sometimes been the case. The idea was to make a course that suited the Europeans. They do it there; we do it here. It is no different from the Aussies preparing wickets to suit their cricket team at home and England doing the same when the Ashes are in this country. It strikes me as obvious that Wimbledon should do what it can to help Tim Henman or Greg Rusedski win here.

The general principle was to penalise the longer hitters. Although some of our players, most notably Darren Clarke, were long, the Americans possessed a bunch of players who were great carriers of the ball – Woods, of course, Mickelson, Love and Duval, just to name the obvious ones. This was not so much a case of Tiger-proofing but American-proofing. Anything up to 280 yards was made easier, anything over that distance harder.

Most of the bunkers at the De Vere Belfry were obsolete to the big hitters. So we added a deep pot bunker over the right-hand bunker on the 11th, for example, and the shape was changed to allow an easier escape from the front bunker than the back one. In fact, you could reach the green from the first and only chip out from the second. We tried to grow the rough thicker from about 280 yards to 320 yards from the tee, though our main weapon against the longer hitters was narrowing the fairways in that area. We did manage to make it a little thicker at that point. I was really trying to take the driver out of the hands of the leading Americans. Some of my guys were long and it might harm them a little bit but not as much. They knew what was going on and they knew why it was happening.

There was another shot I wanted to take away from the opposition – the chip from deep rough around the greens. Americans such as Mickelson and Woods are brilliant at that, not least because they face rough around the greens at almost every tournament. Again, some of our boys have become very proficient at the flop shot by playing more tournaments in the USA. But I thought this a part of the game where we could nullify their expertise. The result was four bands of short rough around the greens, leaving straightforward chips.

The greens themselves offered another opportunity for us to create something we were used to. The Americans had always provided fast greens when they hosted the Ryder Cup, as a reflection of the pace they are accustomed to every week on the US Tour; our preference was for greens on the slowish side. The Americans did not like the De Vere Belfry putting surfaces.

To paraphrase Duval, Robert not David, 'I love the sound of Americans moaning in the morning.'

Everyone had an opinion on the 10th. I was strong and, I hope, persuasive on this issue. I wanted the tee back. I didn't want it the way it was at the Benson & Hedges when the players were knocking the ball onto the green with as little as a 2-iron. That to me was not the way the hole had been designed. If you attempted to drive the green at the short par 4, it had to be a bloody tough shot, not a formality. And that was exactly how it played. More whining from the Yanks.

I remember being on the 10th tee during the first day when, in a stage whisper clearly aimed at me, Scott Hoch said, 'Great hole for your stats this!' From the back tee, the hole was playing a short iron into the middle of the fairway in front of the water, then a wedge as an approach. Good for your driving statistics and equally for the greens in regulation category.

As it happened, we were to gain a bit of a psychological edge when Sergio Garcia and Lee Westwood knocked their balls onto the green and Tiger Woods and his partner eschewed the chance to match them. Ironically, I had been dead against that tactic.

Nothing would be viewed as too much trouble in preparing the course exactly to our specifications. When a 20-ft chestnut tree was removed to accommodate a scoreboard, it was crane lifted and replanted to the right of the 3rd fairway, again in a position to inhibit the long drivers. Bevin Tattersall, the greenkeeper, maintains that the course played in 2002 was very much easier than the one the players would have confronted in 2001.

Alterations were being made right up to the final days before the start of the event. We held a minor summit meeting at the 3rd hole on the Monday afternoon with the likes of Monty and Langer present. There was a general feeling that the De Vere Belfry was in danger of being a little like a US Open course, and we all knew how badly the Europeans had performed at the US Open over the years. The decision was taken to cut the rough, a mammoth operation at that stage. It was reduced from 4 inches to 3½ inches. It may not sound a lot but it is significant to the professional golfer.

Bernhard Langer came up with another suggestion that was carried out. He noticed that the rough just beyond a bunker to the left of the 15th fairway was very deep. This was a danger to the shorter hitter. He wanted it cut back so that a ball landing there would shoot forward onto the fairway and be in perfect position.

Everyone had an equal say and was treated equally. That was the central piece of advice given to me by Sir Alex Ferguson. I had met the Manchester United manager briefly on several occasions over the years, for example when taking my son Daniel, a Reds fan, to Old Trafford. Sir Alex was an acquaintance, not a friend, someone whom I liked and obviously admired. He is a great man and, more pertinent to my own role, a great manager. Managing a team was something I knew nothing about; managing a team was his area of supreme expertise.

Why don't I just telephone him, I thought? On the basis that I was determined to leave no stone unturned, I gave him a ring. He knew who I was, what I was doing and precisely what I wanted. We talked a couple of times, once for maybe as much as 20 minutes. I listened and took notes. A notepad was never too far away from me during my captaincy as I jotted down thoughts that came into my head. A notepad and pencil lay on my bedside table so that I could write down any nocturnal ideas. That happened a few times, though I could never read what I wrote the next day.

Sir Alex had one basic message that was to prove invaluable to me throughout Ryder Cup week. 'There must be no superstars in your team, Sam,' he said. 'Treat everyone as if they are the most important person in your team but treat everyone the same. Each and every one is special in their own way and they are all part of the team. Get them to work as a unit and not just as 12 individuals.'

I am pretty sure that would have my instinctive way of dealing with the players. But his certainty on this issue crystallised my own thinking. It was to prove particularly beneficial in relation to the rookies who relished being seen to be as important as the senior players and who became significant contributors to the cause, not only in terms of points won but the whole atmosphere of the team.

By chance, I was to draw on the advice of the other high-profile manager in English football. I found myself sitting next to Sven Goran Eriksson, the England manager, on a flight to Spain. I was going to play in a tournament while he was heading for a football match. We chatted as fellow passengers more than anything else, but I did take the opportunity to quiz him a little on the art of being a team manager.

Chatting to people was one thing, speaking in public quite another.

Making speeches terrified me. Like many people without an education, and many with university degrees, I found speaking in public a daunting prospect. I could tell jokes and share anecdotes in company but the thought of standing in front of an audience and giving a speech filled me with dread. Nothing else about the captaincy worried me in the slightest. In fact, I was desperate to do all aspects of the job, from picking the team preparing the players, shaping the course, putting the pairings together and so on.

I would have died if I had dried up, whether at the gala dinner in front of hundreds of guests and sponsors, or at the opening and closing ceremonies in front of a television audience of hundreds of millions around the world.

'You'll only be speaking in front of 300 million,' Queenie would tease me, knowing my fear of speaking in public.

Even as early as my appointment, I began to worry about how a boy who left school at 13 would cope with the ordeal. Would I freeze? Would I let out a swear word? Would I say something inappropriate? I knew there were officials who privately wondered if I would be able to handle that side of the role.

As early as March 2000, just a few months into my captaincy, a possible solution presented itself to me. The centenary dinner of Sunningdale Golf Club, in London's celebrated Claridge's Hotel, was a glittering affair, a sufficiently high-profile event with a sufficiently high-powered guest list to unnerve the best after-dinner speaker.

That was where I came across Professor David Purdie of the Centre for Metabolic Bone Disease at Hull Royal Infirmary, a fellow Scot, like me, a future Sunningdale member and, it transpired, one of the most magnificent speakers I had ever heard. He was articulate, he was funny and he was spot on with both his content and delivery. I sought him out as soon as the formal part of proceedings had finished.

'Sam Torrance,' I said introducing myself. 'Can you help me? I need you for the Ryder Cup.' I was about as incoherent as I feared I might be when called upon to make a speech.

'Sorry, I'm an amateur,' he replied.

We established that I required him not as a player but as a speaking coach. We sat in the corner for a long time that night, talking about my fears and about how I might overcome them. It was a genuine phobia, not just something I thought I might find difficult. At that stage – and even after much preparation and practice – the idea of making a speech filled me with the same horror that would face a vertigo sufferer if asked to stand on top of a tall building.

Actually, any time I had previously been required to speak in public, it had gone all right. But it still petrified me. I could not risk embarrassing myself or my family or my country or the position of captaincy. I could not risk making a mistake. That was what I tried to explain to the Prof that night at Claridges.

'Torrance,' he would say. He addressed me like a public school master would a pupil. 'Torrance, you have to have a beginning, a middle and an end. You have to have a structure. You must take your time, speaking slowly and carefully, deliberately even. You must write your speech on cards and learn it.'

He suggested that I visit him at his home in Hull to go through in greater detail the times when I had to speak and what I wanted to say on each occasion. A car and a driver met me from the station. I was taken to a lovely house in the country.

'Torrance, we're going out for dinner tonight,' he said on my arrival. 'You'll hear something magnificent.'

And I did. We attended a dinner in a large Chinese restaurant. John Prescott was there. So, too, was Tony Blair. The Prof introduced me to both of them. The Prime Minister made a speech that evening. It was, as promised, magnificent, the performance of a tremendous orator. This was not so much about picking up tips as just watching a master at work.

Professor Purdie and I had talked for a couple of hours prior to dinner, and we sat chatting for several hours afterwards back at his home. He was trying to put my mind on paper, finding out what I wanted to say and making it eloquent. Later, he would e-mail or fax with suggestions and I would reply with comments. We went through all my speeches that way, trying to find a voice that was genuinely me.

The end product was me in that it conveyed what I wanted to say, but some of the words were his. I told him what I wanted and he would present it to me in proper form. I would then go through it, marking bits I liked, bits I was not sure about and bits I rejected as not being me. There was a lot of trial and even more error until we agreed on the final content.

Eventually, I memorised all my speeches. I memorised them so well that I could repeat them now. I will probably be able to repeat them word for word in 20 years. I read them over and over and over again, learning them word for word, repeating them into a little tape recorder.

The extra year helped me in this area too. In the last week prior to the event, at David's suggestion, we arranged for the actual Ryder Cup podium – the one that would be used for the opening and closing ceremonies – to be installed in my garage at home. I spent much of the final week in there, trying to perfect my speeches. I was out there three hours a day, standing in front of the podium, making my speech over and over again. Recording it, repeating it, sometimes alone, often in front of Suzanne. Well, not actually in front of Suzanne. She had to stand behind me because the sight of her put me off in the same kind of emotional way that any mention of my family produces floods of tears. She was also prone to interrupting.

The door was shut. It was just me, my speeches and the podium. I learned what I had to say and I learned to say it properly, at the proper tempo with spacing marked and words underlined to indicate emphasis. I did it 50, maybe 100 times. I felt the improvement but I needed the Professor's blessing.

He came down from Hull that week and became a one-man audience in my garage.

'Very good, Torrance,' was all he said.

That was the only time he heard my various speeches. He was travelling at the time of the match, headed for Australia and one of the many conferences he attends as one of the most eminent experts in his field. If anyone remembers seeing a Scotsman blubbing away in Singapore on 29 September, it was Professor David Purdie on hearing the result of the Ryder Cup.

His input had been enormous. If someone could have replayed my speeches to me prior to meeting Professor Purdie, I would have said that wasn't me. I would have asked who the speaker was. It is not for me to say how well or how badly I did in that department, but at least I made no mistakes. I did not hesitate. I did not dry up. I did not fill up. I did not swear. I could have done the lot and would have, but for the help I received and all the hours of preparation.

Hard work was the key. My father might well smile and say, 'I told you so,' at that admission: maybe he was right all these years; maybe I should have worked harder at my golf.

David Purdie had introduced one other element to the mix.

'Get this right and you are a point up,' he said. 'Look at it as a wee competition between you and Curtis. Make sure you're better than him at every stage. Never show him any sign of weakness.'

Curtis was to amaze me at the welcome dinner, the first set-piece function of the week and the first at which the captains had to speak. I had read my speech over a hundred times, learned it and recorded it. And there was Curtis sitting at the table writing his speech! We were sitting having dinner and he was writing his goddam speech. I could not believe it. It did not matter how well he did it, I felt as if Europe were 1 up. I was 1 up.

David also thought it a good idea to find a word or a phrase for the week. Something that I could repeat from time to time, something that would resonate with the players, something they could draw upon for inspiration.

Trans World International had prepared a motivational video for the team, clips of past victories, of great shots, of famous deeds, all woven together against a background of some inspiring music. I showed it to David. The final image was of the Ryder Cup itself, that lovely little trophy, and underneath the Latin motto *Carpe diem*. Seize the day!

The Professor nearly had a heart attack. He jumped out of his seat and exclaimed, 'That's it! That's your phrase. *Carpe diem*. You've already got it. You don't need another one. Seize the day. *Carpe diem*!'

Now, there were not too many Latin scholars in the European team. But for a week they went around shouting '*Carpe diem*' to each other.

I like to think that David might read those words every time he heads out onto the Old Course at Sunningdale or his home club at Old Prestwick for a game of golf. They are to be found around the bottom of the bag (and full set of clubs and covers) I gave him by way of thanks for all his help and guidance. The tournament bag has his name on the front along with a title – Captain's Coach.

Gifts were very important to Suzanne and me. We put a lot of thought and effort into selecting presents for the players and caddies. I had always been impressed how Tony Jacklin had transformed the Ryder Cup with the notion that everything should be first class. My slant on that was simple: I wanted to make my players feel very, very special, each one as special as the other. For example, they were all billeted in great, identical suites. And every night when they sat down for a meal there was a gift at their table placing – some champagne flutes, a pair of silver golf shoes, leather passport holder, wallet and yardage book. I designed that myself, though it took me half a dozen goes to get it right with all the different compartments. The caddies received one too.

The main gift to the players of both teams was a beautiful oak-chested canteen of cutlery with tartan lining and the signatures of the 24 players and captains on individual pieces. It was my idea, one of which I was very proud. I felt it my pièce de résistance. Suzanne and I travelled to Sheffield to look at some samples, but ended up going to Harrods and buying the best they had in the Knightsbridge shop. It was magnificent and, to the horror of the finance department of the European Tour, it cost a fortune. But it created the desired open-mouthed effect. One of the boxes was on show at the welcome dinner; the rest were delivered to each player at home.

I received many letters from players and officials from both sides of the Atlantic after that match and most, if not all, mentioned the cutlery. I remember two Americans saying to me they had been involved in 20 Ryder Cups and had never seen a gift to compare.

It's the thought that counts, they say, and we thought a great deal about the presents. We thought a lot about every aspect of the match.

It had long since become my full-time job. I knew that my golf would suffer, though initially not to the extent that it did. But I had prepared myself for that eventuality. It still came as a shock and disappointment that in 2001 I failed to retain my card for the first time in 30 years. My exemptions meant that I could continue to play and in 2002 I re-entered the top 100, albeit still much lower than I would have liked.

17

Langer's neck

Ryder Cup week started with a couple of pops and a
bang. Champagne corks flew then the earth moved...
though not for me.

My good friend and sometime driver Chris Rudge
drove Suzanne, Daniel and me to the De Vere Belfry on the
Sunday, an occasion for a couple of bottles of bubbly in
the back of the car. We laughed throughout the journey,
probably as much a reflection of our nervous anticipation
as the happiness and relief that we had arrived at where we
had been aiming for almost three years. It had been the
longest, slowest build-up in Ryder Cup history.

One of the best parts of the whole week was having
my son at my side. He was pretty much joined to the hip
with me throughout practice and during the match, a
team member with the complete team uniform. We had
so many special moments together. I remember, for
example, standing with him on the 10th fairway, just
short of the water, watching players putt out.

'Wait a minute,' I said to him. 'Let them get off the
green and come with me.'

We walked onto the green towards the 11th tee and
the crowd went potty, chanting my name and cheering for
Europe. Daniel's reaction was like 'Wow!' It was like that
everywhere we went. The spectators were unbelievable.

Daniel was with me going up the par 5 3rd when we
noticed Curtis had a rather special guest with him in his
buggy. George Bush Snr, the former president of the
United States of America, or rather Mr President, as I
was informed.

'Just for etiquette's sake, Sam,' Roger Maltbie, a friend and an American television commentator told me, 'just in case you don't know, he's Mr President, he's always Mr President.'

I appreciated being told. The introductions were made and we chatted for a while. Then we went our separate ways. Except that Daniel had not been introduced and that began to bother me a little.

'Daniel, we're going back,' I said.

So I drove back in the direction of Curtis and Mr President and reaching there I said, 'Excuse me, Mr President, but can I introduce my son, Daniel?'

'Hey, Daniel, great to see you,' Mr President replied. And we all had another little chat.

We were heading off in our own directions again when Mr President called Daniel back. He gave him a presidential golf ball, complete with United States insignia and his own stamp. But he's a teenager and within a few months he was chipping with it in the back garden. One day, if it is not lost in the shrubbery, he will come to regard it as more than just a golf ball. Or maybe he won't.

Only on the first day did I have to act the heavy parent. Monday morning arrived and I was up early, like every day, without the aid of a call or an alarm clock. It did not matter how late I stayed up or how many drinks I consumed, I had no trouble sleeping and even less difficulty getting up in the morning. I went through to his bedroom in our suite and found him still lying in his scratcher.

'What the hell's going on?' I bellowed. 'This is the friggin' Ryder Cup. Get out of your bed this instant.'

I marched out of the room, leaving him rubbing his eyes like any bewildered adolescent first thing in the morning. Within minutes, he was dressed and right behind me. That's where he stayed.

The earth had already moved. I had heard nothing of the earthquake that night. The largest in England for ten years, as it transpired. It measured 4.8 on the Richter scale and had its epicentre in that great beer-brewing town of Dudley, just 20 miles from the golf course. The news was full of it the next morning.

I had heard nothing, but Jesper Parnevik had. Jesper had been in New York on the morning of September 11. He heard the explosions, he saw the smoke and he breathed in the acrid air that was to hang over the Big Apple for days, weeks and even months. As a resident of the USA and as someone who played on the USPGA Tour, he was more directly affected by 9/11 than anyone else in our team.

He attended a ceremony in Texas when the tour resumed. 'I have never felt more American in my life,' he told an emotional audience

So when the Dudley tremors shook him out of his sleep during the early hours of that morning, Parnevik thought part of the hotel had been blown up. He told us the next morning that he had run stark naked out onto his balcony thinking there had been an explosion and wondering if there had been a terrorist attack.

'Having been in Manhattan on September 11, I still have very paranoid thoughts,' Parnevik told the media. 'It was a very big bang. My bedroom table just kept smacking into the window and the bed was all over the place. I have never been in an earthquake before. It was very scary.'

He had been at the De Vere Belfry for a couple of days. Sergio Garcia was another early arrival. And I had joined Paul McGinley and Lee Westwood for a round the previous week as they enjoyed an early recce while the rest of the two teams competed in the Amex Championship in Ireland.

Otherwise, people were told to arrive Sunday or Monday and be ready to start practice on Tuesday. If anyone wanted to play a few holes or even a round before Tuesday, that was fine. Although the condition of the course and the set-up was well received by my players, the feedback quickly poured in: rough too thick here, too thin there, chop that down, etc. It was not to everyone's taste, of course. There were a couple of requests concerning the 8th hole, the suggestion being that the trees on the left be shaved so that an errant shot there would go into the water. We fixed it also that you could not knock the ball onto the green from there.

Jesper was my biggest problem in terms of being the guy struggling most with his game. He was hitting it sideways, according to the terminology of the professional game, and he was juggling about with as many as six putters. But he had been working really hard and his attitude was tremendous. We had a chat at the start of the week.

'Look Sam,' he said, 'I know how badly I am playing. I will not mind if you don't play me until the singles on Sunday. I will understand. My game is not right. But I'll play any time you ask me to. I will be there for the team.'

That was exactly the kind of attitude I was looking for from the players. Parnevik worked tirelessly all week on his game and I could sense that he was getting close. The other players and the caddies were all reporting back on his steady improvement.

Parnevik had behaved in exactly the way I had urged when I gathered the team together in our room on the Monday night. I have always regarded the team room as sacrosanct, a place where what goes on in there stays there. Just the 12 players, vice-captain, the back-room staff and captain and that's about it. It's a wonderful room to be a part of. You should feel totally privileged to be in there. It's just a great room to walk into. It's almost like walking through a void and coming into a very, very private sanctuary. I made a speech that night, though not the sort of one I had been rehearsing. There was nothing written down and nothing needing the services of Professor Purdie. It was just me being me in the company of fellow golfers over a few beers. I have a PhD in that.

I told them I wanted complete honesty. 'I don't want anything bottled up or kept secret,' I said. 'If something's bothering you, bloody tell me. If there is something you do not like, let me, Woosie, Joakim or Jesse know. If you've got a problem or you're not happy with something, don't keep it to yourself. If you don't tell me, there's nothing I can do.

'If you don't want to play with someone or you have a bad back or you don't want the pin there or you want less rough or you want more rough, tell me.'

And, with one exception, which made for an anxious few hours on the eve of the start of the match, they all complied with my request for honesty and bluntness.

I could hardly complain when the feedback threatened to drive the poor greenkeeper to throw himself in front of one of his tractors. We ended up chopping and changing the rough from Monday to Thursday. Too much rough there, too little rough here. 'Sorry, boys,' I said, 'we cannot actually grow the rough to order.' Too long, not long enough, shave some trees, put up some trees. Think of a request and we received it. The course was never going to please everyone but, once a few alterations had been made during the week itself, the team accepted that it was set up to the advantage of the Europeans.

While some played a few holes on the Monday, Suzanne and I headed for Birmingham Airport to meet the American plane. Just standing there on the tarmac at the bottom of the steps waiting for the US team to appear was very special. Curtis was first down, of course, carrying the Ryder Cup.

'Is this what you want?' he quipped.

It was at last time to put into practice what I had been theorising for more than a year. Who would play with whom and when.

I had a plan that, with hindsight, was perhaps not my brightest. I thought of the uncertainty I had felt as a player and came to the conclusion that it would greatly assist players in their preparations if they knew when they would be playing and with whom and when they would be resting. I reasoned that, free from worries about impressing the captain, they would be able to concentrate on their practice and make sure they were ready for when they were needed.

I threw the idea off my vice-captain and back-room boys. It is fair to say they were not impressed. And, as it turned out, practically none of the pairings I had in my head came to fruition. Some of the players I thought certain of participating in all five series never did, as they became tired or lost form. The need for flexibility became obvious. It has always been obvious.

Of one thing I had been certain for a long time. The Clarke/Westwood partnership, which had done so well in the past, would have to be broken. They were good friends from the same management team, who had been successful at Brookline. But I did not see that working out from a long way off because of Lee's form. If Lee had been playing well and had been his normal self, then Clarke and Westwood would have been pretty much a certainty. However, partnerships do not always repeat their success. I don't know whether the continuing brilliance of the Ballesteros/Olazábal pairing or the example of Faldo and Woosnam is the norm. Faldo and Woosnam were terrific, virtually unbeatable at Muirfield Village, yet they could not win a match back at the Belfry.

Because of how well Clarke and Westwood had performed in the past, I felt that there would be far too much pressure on Westwood's game if he was expected to produce the goods in a settled pairing. If I put him with someone completely different, it was a whole new ball game. That was the basis for splitting up Clarke and Westwood, though I must admit that the idea of Westwood and Garcia could not have been further from my mind at the start of the week.

The core of my team was made up of what I called 'floaters'. I reckoned on being able to play the likes of Monty, Clarke, Harrington, Langer and probably Garcia with just about anyone. I could pair them with anyone and they would work because they were all great players with experience.

Another starting point was a desire to play everyone prior to the singles. It is one thing wanting to – as Mark James had in 1999 – and another actually finding yourself in the position to do so. Mark felt unable to play Jean Van de Velde, Andrew Coltart and Jarmo Sandelin until the Sunday and established a tremendous four-point lead for the singles in the process.

The Americans have done it quite differently in recent matches. Their philosophy seems to be, where possible, field all 12 team members on the first day. They did it in '95 and '97 and played everyone except Steve Pate on the Friday in '99. I disagreed fundamentally with that approach. Day one for me was getting points on the board by using your best team; day two was the time to try to give everyone a match prior to the singles.

I was trying to find a formula for four series, two fourballs and two foursomes. I wanted to put my big guns out first and find a way to play everyone. Those were my parameters. Darren Clarke and Thomas Björn seemèd to me a natural combination right from the start of the week. They were very good mates, both aggressive, a great fourball team. I liked the sound and feel of them and, of course, they turned out to be my first pairing on the first morning.

At that stage Garcia and Harrington seemed great for fourballs, players both with the ability to grab a lot of birdies. But I wasn't 100 per cent sure on the personality side of that pairing. I was trying Monty with Westwood and it seemed quite good. In fact, they practised together on both Tuesday and Wednesday. Suddenly, Monty and Langer sounded great. They respected each other and would go well together. I thought Price and Fulke, who hit the ball similar lengths, kept the ball in play and were fine putters, seemed an obvious alternate shot combination.

The week was young, but old enough for me to have a run-in with my dad. He had asked for a buggy to go out with Harrington and McGinley, two of his pupils. A precious commodity in Ryder Cup week but I was able to find him one. Off he went as happy as a guru with a camcorder, while I finished breakfast and did some thinking.

When I ventured onto the course, I saw him and the buggy in the middle of the fairway, parked about 5 yards behind McGinley. This was a steam-rising rather than gasket-blowing situation.

'Dad, come here,' I said as I approached him. 'You can't park that on the fairway.'

'Come here,' he said.

'What?'

'Come here.' He repeated. I wandered closer to him.

'Fuck off,' he whispered. 'I've waited 40 years for this moment.'

'Okay, Dad, carry on,' I said.

That day Bob Torrance drove where he wanted.

The first drama of the week came that evening as I was preparing to make my first speech. Suzanne, who had lived with my phobia about public speaking for three years, was spoiling me. She ran a bath and poured a glass of champagne for me to have in between the evening press conference and the welcome dinner. She was getting her hair done.

It was about 6.30pm. I had been soaking and sipping for two minutes when the telephone rang.

'Hi Sam, it's Pierre here,' a Swedish accent said.

'Hi Pierre, what's up?'

'I've got a problem.'

'Yeah, what's wrong?'

'I can't tell you on the phone. It's the biggest problem of the week. I need to see you right away.'

'Okay, come on round,' I said.

As it happened, he was in the room next to us and was at the door in 20 seconds. So I jumped out of the bath, put a towel round me and answered the knock at the door. There he was, looking a bit ashen-faced.

'What the hell is wrong?' I asked.

Whereupon, he brought his tie from behind his back and said, 'I can't do my tie.'

For a second, I could have killed him. But this was fantastic. Here was a rookie with the confidence to wind up the captain. This was what I was looking for. I went to the welcome dinner that night confident that the atmosphere within the team was just right. I was delighted.

The welcome dinner was fine and the speech went well. There were perhaps 80 to 100 people in a room at the De Vere Belfry, both teams and all the officials. The players from both teams were mixed up, two each to a table. Suzanne and I were with Curtis and his wife Sarah.

We got on famously. There was an underlying feeling that we had got to get this right. I could sense that from both teams, especially from theirs. It had taken a fraction of a second to ensure there would be no repeat of Brookline when Curtis and I first spoke.

The Americans were a pretty friendly bunch. Paul Azinger has always been a great buddy, Mark Calcavecchia too. I have always liked Phil Mickelson. David Duval is one of my all-time favourites. The same goes for Davis Love. I hadn't known Scott Verplank very well until I played with him in the USA. He was a really tremendous guy, probably the nicest in their team. I had not met David Toms before. He was great. There was no ill feeling, no animosity at all. The only legacy of Brookline was in the determination of the European players to gain revenge.

I have always regarded Tiger Woods as very much the real deal. To be so nice and so friendly and to have the game that he has and be so dominant, yet still be just one of the boys is tremendous. He is a great, great man.

The row about Tiger practising on his own early on Thursday morning was completely overblown and no harm did it do us at all. Anything that suggested disharmony among their ranks – even when it did not exist – was obviously going to work in our favour. And bad publicity for them tended to reflect well on us. In truth, though, my philosophy was to pay no attention at all to what the Americans were doing. I didn't bother about their team because there was nothing I could do about it. I certainly wasn't going to belittle them. We knew they were tough and we knew they were going to be tough, and that was it.

I doubt if I could imagine a situation where any of the European players would ask to practise outside the normal tee-off times on his own. But I would accede to the request. The week is about doing everything to make each player feel comfortable.

I understood perfectly Tiger's position and I didn't see a huge problem. Curtis had told his players to prepare as if playing in a major championship, so Tiger adopted his Open procedure of teeing off at dawn. Although it wasn't very fair to the spectators to arrive and find the World No. 1 had already left the course, I sympathised with his position. The man doesn't have a life. He cannot walk anywhere without being bothered. For him to get out there at six o'clock in the morning, as he did on Thursday, and have the freedom of just playing the course on his own, without getting pestered all the way round, must have been bliss.

The gala dinner was held at Birmingham's NEC. It could have been the middle of Dublin. In fact, I think I said to the guests, 'Welcome to Dublin.' Everything was green and very Irish. The teams were cordoned off with the guests – sponsors, patrons, etc. – at tables all around the vast arena.

The evening was sponsored by the Irish Tourist Board to celebrate the Ryder Cup being held at the K Club in Ireland in 2006. The wonderful Ronan Keating gave a magnificent performance, and the Riverdance cast, er, danced. Superbly. They were not the only ones to dance, though I cannot testify to the quality. The players were up for a bop and the American team quickly followed suit. The atmosphere was amazing, what with Ronan shouting, 'Come on, Europe!' and coming down off the stage to shake my hand. He may not have realised it, but he gave the European team a real lift that night.

There was to be no speech, just each captain introducing his players. I did not need to rehearse that. Except I spotted Curtis at a nearby table scribbling away. I was up and straight over to him in a flash.

'What are you doing?' I askd him.

'I'm writing my speech,' he replied.

'I thought we weren't going to speak.'

'Well, I've not been told that.'

'What are you going to say then? I'm going to look a right idiot. I mean I've been told only to announce the names of my players and I'm not going to make something up now.'

'Okay, I won't say anything,' Curtis said.

I returned to my seat and when it came to the time Curtis made a speech, of course. The bugger. I was now thinking that I was going to look bad. I was thinking that he had got it back to all square. When I was a player I always looked to the captain for inspiration, always felt buoyed up if he was doing a good job in things like public speaking.

We were all square except that when he introduced his team he didn't mention the wives. I had always intended to introduce everyone as a couple, whether husband or wife, player and girlfriend or, in the case of Sergio, player and mother. If anything now, I was 2 up. Get the wives on your side and you've cracked it. But I did something else in relation to our team that I suppose Curtis never needed to. The European team in 2002 contained nine nationalities, if you split up the home nations, plus Ireland, into five. There were Swedes, a German, a Spaniard and a Dane as well. I learned how to pronounce everyone's name in precisely the manner it would be said in their own language. It was just a little touch but I know it went down well.

By Thursday, the pairings were taking shape. Clarke and Björn were concrete. Monty and Langer were definites. A decision had to be made about who would play with Garcia and who would play with Harrington, both of whom were certainties for my fourball line-up on the first morning. Niclas Fasth, too, had practised so well that he was guaranteed a position in the starting eight.

I loved Paul McGinley's golf and his attitude. But his game to me was foursomes rather than fourballs. It was much easier for Lee to play fourball than to play foursomes, which would put more pressure on his game. So he was in, and the identity of the four I was leaving out of the first series was settled: Price, McGinley, Fulke and Parnevik. That was where Garcia and Westwood came from. It was a shock. They had not even practised together. But Westwood is as friendly as they come, and I thought Garcia and him might hit it off. If you don't want Garcia on your side, there's something wrong; the guy's a great golfer.

He was now no longer the high-spirited, exciting foil to Parnevik, no longer the kid with unbelievable talent; he was a senior member of my team, the highest-ranked player in the world and someone of whom I expected a great deal. I took him aside at the beginning of the week to tell him just that.

'You are our top-ranked player,' I told Sergio. 'You are, therefore, one of my senior men, someone from whom I am looking for a great deal. I want you to be a leader this week, not a rookie looking to be led. I want you to take charge out there.'

He seemed to relish the role on the course and was free to chase women off the course.

My final pairing was Harrington and Fasth, the only one of my four rookies to be picked for the first morning. He had made a lot of birdies throughout the year and quite a few that week. And he had a good birdie-making partner in Padraig. Those were my eight best players as of 2pm on Thursday when the pairings had to be submitted.

I had never given a thought to what the American pairings might be or to where Tiger would be played. But the press latched on to the fact that he was lining up against Clarke and Björn, both of whom had enjoyed success against Woods. Clarke had beaten him in the 36-hole final of the Accenture Consulting Match Play Championship in 2000, while Björn won the Dubai Classic in 2002, having played all four rounds with Tiger.

'Thanks for reminding me,' I told the press conference. 'I'll remember that for the team meeting tonight. Thank you. That might be my best point tonight.'

First, I had to negotiate the opening ceremony and the speech I had dreaded since being appointed almost three years earlier. Speaking at the welcome dinner was tough but okay. I knew what I had to say and I was reading it off cards. But this was the biggie, this was the one with a television audience of 1.5 billion.

David had said to me that ten minutes before leaving the hotel I should have one drink. Anything I wanted. One drink, throw it down, so it was a large Scotch. I'm not a whisky drinker but I knew it would hit me more than anything else and have the desired effect. So, just before we had to walk down to the stage, I got the hotel barman to pour me a large Scotch. I threw it down and I think it really helped me. I guess it did because I was pretty relaxed. The walk down was amazing, just amazing, full of anticipation, though nothing compared to the screaming on the Sunday night.

All I had in my mind was what I had to do up there. Everything else was peripheral. I was not really able to take it all in because of thinking about the speech, which I had gone over hundreds, maybe thousands of times. But I was okay, feeling fine, pretty sure I would be able to handle it. You never know, though, until the moment comes.

So now I was on the stage and looking out I spotted Suzanne and all the wives and the PGA officials and the ex-Ryder Cup players and all my friends and the huge grandstands full of people. People everywhere, and television cameras. I was just sitting there waiting...forever it seemed, as Renton Laidlaw, who probably covered every stroke of my career, spoke.

Something helped me then as it had helped me during all the months of anticipation. My great friend and mucker John O'Leary had spoken at Brookline in a similar situation at the opening ceremony. I clung onto this thought: if O'Leary can do it, I'm bloody sure I can.

David had also told me to pick out people and look at them rather than stare vacantly out into the sea of faces. I couldn't look at Suzanne, of course. I could not even look at her when standing on the podium in my garage at home with no one else around. But I did catch a glimpse of her and I was wanting her to look away in case I started blubbing.

As I said before, I can go easily and at the least thing. I had choked and nearly started crying at the press conference that afternoon when a Scottish journalist asked a fairly innocuous question.

'I know you've got your army of family and friends,' he said. 'Is it possible for you to say how many are here because of you and what it means to you?'

The answer was a real struggle as I fought back the tears. 'Well, it means everything to me,' I replied. 'I just got real sentimental, so we'll leave that.'

At last it was time. Curtis had spoken. It was my turn.

'Thank you, Renton,' I said, as I read the most prepared and rehearsed speech in the history of the Ryder Cup.

'Curtis, members of the US Ryder Cup Team, ladies and gentlemen, it is quite simply the proudest moment of my golf career, standing here before you as captain of the 2001 European Ryder Cup Team.

'I pledge that I and the team will at all times uphold the traditions of the Ryder Cup and of the game which we all serve. As Curtis and I have stated in the spectators' guide, it is only our nationalities that divide us. Join with us in showing that golf at the highest level can be a spectacle of which we can all be proud to be a part.

'Curtis, old friend, I bid you welcome to Europe, to England and to The Belfry. You are our invited guests and our worthy opponents and, as the old Scottish saying goes, "Oor hoose is your hoose and you're mair than welcome here." Ladies and gentlemen, let me now introduce to you the 2001 European Ryder Cup Team...'

They rose in turn to accept the applause of the spectators: from Denmark, Thomas Björn; from Northern Ireland, Darren Clarke; from Sweden, Niclas Fasth; from Sweden, Pierre Fulke; from Spain, Sergio Garcia; from Ireland, Padraig Harrington; from Germany, Bernhard Langer; from Ireland, Paul McGinley; from Scotland, Colin Montgomerie; from Sweden, Jesper Parnevik; from Wales, Phillip Price; from England, Lee Westwood.'

I also introduced my back-room team, Mark James and Joakim Haeggman, and 'last but by no means least', as I said, my vice-captain, Ian Woosnam.

'Ladies and gentlemen, it would be remiss of me to see all those great faces down here: if not for you guys, we would not be here, thank you.

'Curtis, have a great week; boys, may the best team win. Thank you very much.'

The relief felt unbelievable. I did not put a foot wrong. Suzanne's smile was all the confirmation I needed. From there, it was downhill. The press conferences and the television interviews never bothered me. And if I mucked up the closing ceremony, so what? The match would be over by then.

By Thursday evening the last of the good luck messages were coming in. We had received hundreds, maybe even thousands, both from friends and from golf supporters all over the world, by e-mail, by letter and by telephone: people we knew well and people we did not know at all, those who love golf and love the Ryder Cup, in particular.

Often people rang the hotel and found me or Suzanne otherwise occupied. The staff took telephone messages from the likes of Paul Lawrie and Jean Van de Velde, who had played at Brookline, and friends from others sports like snooker's Dennis Taylor, the one and only Ian Botham and fellow Scot, Ally McCoist.

There were thoughtful written messages from Ronnie Corbett, with whom I played when I shot 58 at Bathgate, Brian Huggett, Ken and Dawn Brown, Peter Alliss, Roger Chapman and 007 himself, Sean Connery. A message was received from the Czech Republic signed by José Maria Olazábal, Miguel Angel Jimenez, Alex Cejka and Costantino Rocca. I think they were playing an exhibition match.

I liked the card from Kenny Dalglish, my team Celtic's greatest ever player and such an enthusiastic golfer. He wrote: 'You have been very dignified and respectful over the past year, now let's hope we can go and kick ass. A good event is a winning one. Hope Fergie gave you good advice.' The last sentence was a reference to my seeking help in managing a team from Sir Alex Ferguson.

A letter from Europe's greatest ever Ryder Cup inspiration, Seve Ballesteros, demonstrated what the competition meant to him and offered an insight into his, shall we say, cool relationship with American golf.

'Dear Sam,' he wrote. 'To you, Sam, and your team. Play well, enjoy the matches and good luck this week. I know they think they are the last Coca-Cola in the desert but you have a better team, a better captain, so go and get them. I will be watching on TV.'

Worrying about the speech had clearly exhausted me. We went to bed early that night, around 10pm. I was knackered. They were showing a re-run on television of the opening ceremony. It seemed that the German flag had just been raised when the phone rang and a familiar voice was speaking.

'Hello, Sam, it's Bernhard here,' the voice said.

'Oh, hi, are you watching the opening ceremony?' I replied.

'No.'

'Cos you're on.'

'No, Sam, I've got this problem. It's my neck. It's stuck a bit. I've only got 90 per cent movement.'

'When did this happen, Bernhard?'

'This morning,' he replied.

'What!' I exclaimed.

How on earth could he let me put my teams in and not tell me he had got a problem? This was Bernhard Langer, one of the top men in our team, a veteran of ten matches, a stalwart, a world superstar. Should I give him a bollocking or not? I did not.

'Don't you think you should have told me?' I asked.

'Well, I thought it would go away, Sam.'

'I'll see you in the team room in five minutes.'

I started phoning around with the message to meet in the team room. Mark McDiarmid, who was my Mr Fixit throughout my captaincy, Jesse and Woosie. Except when I telephoned Woosie I spoke to his wife, Glendryth.

'I'm sorry, Sam, he's sound asleep. He took a sleeping pill,' she said.

Woosie could sleep. I knew I would get very little sleep that night. We met in the team room and decided

Bernhard needed some physiotherapy. Mark McDiarmid was entrusted with the task of tracking down the Australian physiotherapist Dale Richardson, who was staying off-site in digs somewhere. Mark, the Director of Special Projects at the European Tour, was a huge help to me throughout my captaincy. Whenever I wanted something, he arranged it. Finding the physio was a good example of his perseverance, mixed with a little luck. Having drawn a blank at the Irish party and at all the hotels in the area, he started going through a huge alphabetical list of the B&Bs. His second call struck gold.

A car was sent to pick Dale up but it was close to midnight by the time he arrived and administered some treatment. While he went to Bernhard's room to give him some physio, Suzanne, Jesse and I discussed what we would do about a possible replacement should he be unfit in the morning.

It was agreed that Pierre Fulke would take Bernhard's place and partner Monty if the worst came to the worst. But should we tell Fulke so that he could prepare mentally, risking that he lose sleep, or should we wait and surprise him in the morning, when there would be little time to get ready? Suzanne remembered that he was in the next room to us.

So there she was at midnight, with a glass against our bedroom wall trying to listen to what was happening in Fulke's room. Nothing, as it happened. No noise at all. No telly, no talking and certainly none of that. He was presumably asleep. We decided to let a sleeping Ryder Cup player lie.

Of course, by the morning Bernhard was fine and he played great. But it was a huge scare at the time. Jesse and Mark went to bed, the physio was found a room in the hotel and Suzanne and I looked at each other. Neither of us had the remotest chance of sleeping after such a drama. We looked at each other, opened a bottle of champagne and a couple of hours later fell into a somewhat tipsy sleep.

Despite the Langer problem, I was a contented captain. Already, all 12 players had knitted into a tight team. Your superstars were humble and helpful; your rookies were keen and eager, desperate to learn, desperate to be there, desperate to win. The senior players could not have behaved better. They did not behave like prima donnas; they behaved like team-mates, like friends.

I could not wait for the morning.

18

One Tiger and 12 lions

'Fore!' the most common shout in golf, announced the start of the 34th Ryder Cup.

But this was no normal 'fore', no solitary cry from a player warning a fellow golfer of an errant shot heading his way.

'Have you ever heard 15,000 people yell "fore" at the same time?' Curtis Strange asked later that day. 'I had to smile. I really did. I had to laugh. It was something I've never heard before.'

It penetrated his senses at 8am on the rather gloomy morning of 27 September 2002, as the thousands who were gathered around the first tee and on the giant stand at the back of the 9th green greeted Paul Azinger's opening tee shot, a huge slice over the spectators, by yelling as one.

'Fore!'

I had been amazed that Azinger took the opening shot. He has always been a tough customer but his partner was Tiger Woods, the World No. 1 and arguably the greatest player that ever lived. If I were Tiger Woods, I would have wanted to have the honour as a statement of my intentions as the best player among the Americans and leader of the team. If I were Curtis Strange, I would have hoped for precisely that from my ace.

Of course, Paul might well have requested to go first. Some people try to combat the nerves that way; others relish the responsibility. Surely it would have been Woods' decision as the senior in terms of achievements rather than age. He wasn't going to hit a bad shot, was he? Well, as it happened, he did, finding a fairway bunker at the start of a day that was to bring him two defeats.

The failure of the World No. 1 to earn even half a point inevitably dominated the first day's headlines, particularly since there had been such a storm about him practising at dawn on Thursday and being perceived as not a team player. I would dispute that view, though that kind of publicity deflected any criticism of Europe and put more pressure on the Americans.

'Tiger's a King of the Bungle', ran one headline. Another declared: 'Tiger Trapped'. The broadsheet take was similar, though less punchy and not terribly accurate: 'Woods's game falls apart as his cup demons reappear'. In fact, Woods and his partner managed nine birdies in the opening fourballs, yet still lost on the final green to the brilliance of Darren Clarke and Thomas Björn.

My response to the inevitable question at the press conference was designed to give my side a boost while not being disrespectful to Woods.

'Psychologically, I guess it would be good for the rookies to see the No. 1 player in the world has been beaten twice,' I said. 'It will lift them up. I'm sure he'll be back, though.'

Not only did Azinger hit the first blow in the Ryder Cup, but he changed club as he was about to play. His name had been announced, his ball had been teed up, he was ready to play...and he changed his club. From an iron to a 3-wood, if I remember correctly. The crowd went berserk.

'Thank you,' I thought to myself. What better way to relax my players than to watch Woods stand back, see Azinger show indecision and then belt the ball in the general direction of the practice range. Woods hit his opening shot into sand, to be followed into the same bunker by Darren. While Woods found another bunker with his approach, Darren struck the most glorious 8-iron to about 8ft from the flag and holed the putt for a winning birdie.

We had won the first hole. I reflected on how many occasions in my years as a player that Europe had lost the opening hole.

By that time, I had gone around all the American players individually to wish them well and checked that my second pairing of Westwood and Garcia were in good shape. I walked down from the practice green to the first tee with every match, a procedure I was to follow on Sunday for the singles. You could see it in the eyes of the European players that they were relaxed. They were ready. They were focused.

As I said, I paid no attention to what the Americans were doing in practice. I never went near them and I didn't want to know anything about them. So much so-called intelligence turns out to be complete and utter bullshit. You hear a rumour about someone and you think 'Great,' and the next thing you know the guy's shooting a 64. It is almost better knowing nothing of the opposition and concentrating on your own team.

There is, of course, great interest when the draw comes out. The players want to know who they are against, and the captain, his back-room staff, the caddies and the spectators – everyone really – pore over the line-up to see where points are likely to come from.

My only surprise at the American pairings that first morning was the presence of David Duval. I knew he was not playing well at all. That said, he performed admirably at the weekend, gaining a half point from Darren Clarke in the singles. But I fancied Westwood and Garcia to beat Duval and Love in the fourballs. In fact, they hammered them 4 and 3.

It was noticeable during this match that while

Westwood and Garcia were chatting all the time, laughing and joking, consulting each other on club selection, etc., Duval and Love said very little. Even if it was not the case, our boys looked more of a team, as if they were playing for each other rather than themselves.

The pairings were all dispatched in the same way. An escort to the first tee and a pat on the back after their tee shots with an accompanying word of encouragement, like 'kill'.

It was fairly late in the day that I changed the running order to fourballs, then foursomes, as Seve Ballesteros had done at Valderrama in 1997. Ben Crenshaw had reverted to foursomes, then fourballs at Brookline in '99. But I made another alteration, one that I never knew possible. For the second day I wanted it foursomes then fourballs. I couldn't believe I was allowed to do that. My reasoning was that fourballs on the first morning would help the team relax as it is always easier to play your own ball. I don't care who you are, it is intimidating to begin with foursomes. I viewed that as unnecessary pressure. Saturday was different. I wanted them to finish with fourball, finish in a relaxed frame of mind ahead of the singles. That was my thinking. I know Curtis thought I was trying to pull a fast one.

Monty and Langer were third out. A right pair of invalids. Bernhard had reported fit in the morning – as deep down I knew he would, despite all the drama of the previous evening – after receiving another session of physiotherapy on his neck. Monty had been receiving physio treatment on his back virtually every day for months. A massage bed was installed in his room at The Belfry so that his man could work on him before and after matches. He was my 'rock', as I said throughout, but both he and I lived with the possibility that my rock could shatter, that his back could seize up at any time.

A combination built on mutual respect, Langer and Montgomerie were never behind in beating Scott Hoch and Jim Furyk 4 and 3. Then again, they were never actually behind all week, as they claimed 2½ points in three series.

Once Padraig Harrington and Niclas Fasth were on their way, against America's strongest pairing of Phil Mickelson and David Toms, I retired to the team room for a bacon roll and a cup of coffee. I was starving. With such an early start, I had skipped breakfast. No one was going to miss me for ten or 15 minutes, though I could imagine some wondering as to the whereabouts of the captain. It was just not my style to buzz around everywhere like some captains. Jacket back on and I was off, to where I had no idea. It was a question of going to whatever pairing might need a bit of encouragement. There is really nothing you can do in the circumstances except be seen and be available should anyone need anything. I returned to the course to find us ahead in the first three matches and behind in the fourth, exactly how the morning was to end.

The next task was to submit my pairings for the afternoon foursomes. The difficulty is always in the timing in that they have to be handed in while the first series is still unfolding. Captains in the past have dropped players who went on to win and, conversely, stuck with guys whose form shaded over the closing holes.

Mine was a pretty straightforward job that morning, one that needed little debate with Ian Woosnam, Mark James and Joakim Haeggman. Parnevik was not quite ready and the Price/Fulke partnership had been primed to go as the first foursome on Saturday morning. I had planned bringing in Paul McGinley to partner fellow Irishman Padraig Harrington in the Friday afternoon foursomes. It was a pairing that had done well in the Seve trophy and, as a result, was widely predicted. That meant standing down Fasth, the only rookie who had taken part in the opening series. I saw no reason to change tack, as well as Fasth had played. So Clarke and Bjorn, Monty and Langer, Garcia and Westwood were all going out again in the afternoon.

We ended the morning with a lead of 3–1. It might easily have been 3½–½ with Harrington's beautifully struck 20-footer on the last green looking in until it horseshoed the hole and stayed out. But there was no point being greedy. Bjorn had holed a similar length birdie putt on the same green to clinch a win, adding to the other two victories secured on the 15th green.

There's never any time for anything other than a quick snack at lunch and your feet up for a few minutes. If you get half an hour break, you are doing well. So there was no time for any fancy speech or great tactical input.

'Great performance, boys, well done, good stuff, get going, do it again.' If I managed anything more than that I would be astonished. To be honest, I don't remember. The week can easily become a blur.

So it's back to the first tee with Clarke and Björn again – they sound like an Abba tribute band – this time against Hal Sutton and Scott Verplank. At one stage in the afternoon we were ahead in three matches and down in one, looking at a possible scoreline of 6–2 at the end of the first day.

But we ended up winning just one, losing two and halving the other for a 1-point lead. It had been going almost too well. It was looking fantastic. But things change. They always do in the Ryder Cup. Matches change, things happen. There is nothing you can do as it unfolds in front of you. You can cheer them on and try to instil some confidence in them. However, you cannot change what is happening on the golf course. All you can do is believe in your team and have faith that they'll turn it round. Both teams will enjoy their good runs.

It was their turn. Thomas and Darren, having been two up with six holes remaining, fell apart; Harrington and McGinley struggled on the back nine; and Monty and Langer, tiring a little at the end of a long day, lost three of the last four holes for a halved match with Mickelson and Toms. Sergio and Lee finished Friday with two wins out of two, beating Woods and Calcavecchia 2 and 1 in the foursomes. The score was 4½ to 3½ in Europe's favour.

'If we get the last two days rained out, we've won,' I told the press conference, to much laughter. I meant it. 'I have not seen one drunk yet. There may well be a couple later, and I might be one of them after today.'

There was a serious message in my flippancy. Crowd behaviour had been a worry since Brookline, especially when fuelled by alcohol. I am one to talk about having a bevvy, but lots of measures were taken to ensure that any drunkenness did not get out of hand. I knew the galleries would be loud, partisan and entirely fair.

'They were fantastic,' Curtis said. 'They were great. They rooted for their team and they were fair to the American players. It was very, very nice.'

Once again, there was a selection to be made. The first of the departing cars had not crawled to the M42 by the time the pairings for Saturday had to be deposited with the referee. There was no way I was going to go back on my promise to Fulke and Price that they would open the batting the next day. But I never thought at the start of the week that I would be leaving out Harrington, one of my 'definite' five-match players. The Irishman turned out to be not the only team member in that particular boat.

Omitting Harrington was tough, even though he asked to be rested in order to sort out his game. A player like Harrington can turn it on anytime. But his game wasn't right and he needed a morning to sort himself out. In fact, he was out on the range with my dad until darkness while his team-mates unwound in the team room with dinner and the usual banter.

Once the match has begun, everyone is too tired for anything other than a bite to eat and a quiet chat. We just sat around, talking as golfers on an outing would do in the clubhouse.

'Can you believe he holed that?'

'You should have seen the one I holed.'

'The bastard chipped in.'

Stuff like that. Just discussing the day's events as if it were the captain's prize not the captain's life.

In leaving out Padraig and keeping back Parnevik for the fourballs, which would put less pressure on his game, I needed loads of experience to set alongside the inexperience of rookies Fulke and Price. It was, therefore, a 'no brainer', as Curtis liked saying, for me to stick with the tried, tested and successful.

For the third time, the three pairings of Monty and Langer, Westwood and Garcia, and Clarke and Björn were handed to officials. All I had to make sure was that the last out in the morning was not going to be first out in the afternoon. Tiny little logistical things like that were easy to overlook.

I knew at this stage that Bernhard would sit out in the afternoon. He was always going to be playing in four matches at most, a desire he indicated to me at the beginning of the week. It could not have worked out better. He was to give me three great matches with Monty, then rest for the singles on Sunday. By Friday evening I was contemplating a new partner for Monty on

Saturday afternoon, little knowing that a second of those players I identified as playing in every match would need to be replaced.

For the moment, however, we could reflect on a day that might have yielded more but still gave us an advantage. I was more convinced than ever that the atmosphere within the team could not have been better. As soon as someone's match was over on Friday, they would be in touch asking where I wanted them to go, which pairing I wanted them to support. Not a single player needed to be asked, let alone told.

I informed the press conference of what I was looking for on Saturday. 'I'd like to be more ahead tomorrow night,' I said. 'I don't think we *have* to be more ahead tomorrow night, but it would be nice.' I remained incredibly relaxed, 'As calm as a cucumber', I said, slightly mixing my metaphors.

I have always enjoyed a great relationship with the press, even though I have never been a fan of tabloid journalism. I had been bitten pretty hard by the tabloids on one occasion and remained shy of their pursuit of certain kinds of stories ever since. But I never had a problem with them throughout my captaincy, and during the week of the match itself they were fantastic.

There were places they could have gone, stuff they could have raked over. They didn't go there. Some of their more predatory editors might not approve, but they were really supportive, true custodians of the integrity of the Ryder Cup. There was nothing untoward. There was not one single occasion when we walked into the team room, looked at the newspapers and thought, 'Christ, what the hell is this?' They looked after us and it helped our cause. It was greatly appreciated. So much so that the players applauded the media at the closing press conference on Sunday. An interesting precedent.

The pairing of Fulke and Price, who had both struggled to find their form during the year, was seen as a gamble, of course. I thought it would have been more of a risk throwing them into the singles without having had a match. They lost on Saturday morning but they took America's top pairing of Phil Mickelson and David Toms to the 17th and, I think, showed the benefit of the outing in their performances in the singles.

Fulke and Price were actually 1 up after ten holes and had shortish putts at both the 11th and 12th to increase their advantage. The Americans raised their game sufficiently, however, to move 2 ahead with three to play. Whereupon, Mickelson, the master of the recovery shot, played what was, even for him, a stroke of real genius. It was as good a bunker shot as I had seen in my life. From a really badly plugged lie under the lip of a greenside bunker, he splashed out to about 3ft for a half.

There followed one of the few moments of the week – perhaps the only one – when I thought of intervening but decided against it. Price was about to attempt a 5-wood shot from a fairway bunker at the 17th that needed to be perfection to achieve the desired effect. A very good shot would not have been sufficient. Anything less than 100 per cent would end up still in the bunker, thick rough or water. The odds were too stacked against what he was attempting.

The right play – the experienced play – was to move the ball down the fairway and make the Americans win the hole and the match. Just don't give them victory. All this was racing through my mind as I contemplated stepping in with some advice. I was right there on the spot. But I was not quick enough and decisive enough. I think I made an error in saying nothing.

In actual fact, he nailed the shot but unluckily the ball ended up in the water. That shows how difficult it was.

The morning progressed with no clear indication that we would hold on to our advantage, never mind build on it. My most successful pairing of Westwood and Garcia eventually defeated Stewart Cink and Jim Furyk 2 and 1, while Montgomerie and Langer edged out Verplank and Hoch on the final green. But the gathering at the side of the 17th fairway late that morning, including Woosie, Jesse, Joakim and Derrick Cooper, another of my back-room boys, was not looking at a crystal ball. All we knew as we discussed the fourball selection was that Clarke and Björn were struggling. Thomas, in particular, was fighting with his game.

That was when I took the decision to leave Björn out of the afternoon series. I had already rested Harrington, a definite for five matches at the start of the week. Now I was planning the same for Björn, another I expected to play every series. I walked a bit with Clarke and Björn that morning. I could see that the Dane was unsettled and getting mad with himself. I thought it would be best to give him a rest and let him get ready for the singles. He didn't need another five hours out here banging his head against a brick wall.

This is where instinct comes into captaincy. You do what you believe is right and do it as it happens and, of course, you cannot always plan it. That meeting was quite a lengthy one with plenty of debate and discussion rather than argument. We had the envelope and we had the list and we were running out of time. It amounted to a last chance to establish a lead before the singles. I was not thinking about the singles and I was not thinking about winning the Ryder Cup. All I was thinking about was getting a lead by the end of play. There were important decisions to be made.

Do I play Parnevik? I very much wanted to, though it was tight and his form really made it something of a gamble. He could not have played on Friday.

'I think he is ready,' I told the assembled company. 'He is playing a lot better, he has been working hard all week and he has been very honest with me. I think he deserves his chance.' I had told Jesper at the beginning of the week to forget his form. 'You were selected for this team. You're in this team because you deserve to be in this team.'

Niclas Fasth was a good partner, a fellow Swede, someone who had been strong all week. Jesper had experience. Fourballs was the right format. They were in. It was agreed. They would go first, giving the others more time to rest. Garcia and Westwood would go a fourth time, Monty and Clarke too, though with different partners. I liked the sound of Harrington and Monty and McGinley and Clarke. Perfect.

Or so I thought.

The envelope had just been sealed and dispatched when I spotted Monty walking up the 15th. 'Just to let you know, you're playing with Harrington this afternoon,' I said as he was handing his club back to caddie Andy Prodger. He turned round to look at me and said, 'Can I play with McGinley?'

'No, you can't, you're playing with Harrington,' I replied. 'He's perfect for you. Go out there and win.' Nothing further was said.

I have no idea what that was about to this day. He was not averse to playing with Harrington. In fact, I thought he was his preference. Perhaps he thought he would be partnering McGinley. Maybe I had suggested that. Maybe it was just the fog of the conflict.

McGinley was to give me my second major scare of the week that afternoon, albeit not on a par with the telephone call on Thursday night from Bernhard Langer. As it happened, McGinley and I played together in the first round of the 2003 Benson & Hedges International at the De Vere Belfry, no doubt a draw designed to reflect the fact that we both holed putts to win the Ryder Cup on the 18th green there.

'This was where I got the biggest fright of my life,' I said to Paul as we walked onto the 8th tee.

He gave me that impish look of his. 'You got a fright!' he exclaimed. 'How do you think I felt?'

We had held on to our 1-point lead after the foursomes, despite Clarke and Björn losing 4 and 3 to Woods and Love. It seemed that Woods was not such a duffer after all! The afternoon fourballs were always going to be tight, and so it proved, with three matches going to the 18th and the fourth decided on the 17th. Nerves were jangling, I suppose, when McGinty, as I called him, came over as I leaned against the advertising hoarding behind the 8th tee. He had just ripped an absolute snorter right down the middle.

'I'm sorry, Sam, but what rules are we playing under?' he asks.

'What do you mean?' I ask in return.

'Sam, I'm using an R driver.'

I knew exactly what he was on about. The R driver was banned in America and legal in Europe. But were we playing under European rules because the match was in Europe or were we playing under American rules because the United States were our opponents?

'You're fine,' I said, 'you're absolutely fine. It has to be European. I'll check. But you're fine.' And with that he was off down the fairway to catch up Darren.

He might have been fine; I was anything but. I started running, though I did not really know where I was running to. I just ran. If any spectator is wondering what I was doing running up the 5th fairway around 3.30pm on Saturday, then I can tell them now. I was panicking.

'How's it going, Sam?' People would ask from behind the ropes and I ignored them. At last, I thought to contact Jesse on the walkie-talkie. He was my rules man. He would know.

'Jesse, come in Jesse, I need you,' I shouted. 'This is fucking major. Come in now.'

I swear the walkie-talkie crackled, like it would do in a movie.

'I can't hear you,' he said.

He was on the 10th. Westwood and Garcia had both just driven the green against Woods, who laid up, and it was mayhem. The crowd were going nuts. Eventually the noise abated.

'I need to see you now behind the 5th green. Don't say anything. Just get down there.'

I explained to him that McGinley was using an R driver. I asked him what rules we were playing under. He said it would have to be European rules or they would have said something at the rules meeting. Just to make sure, however, we contacted John Paramor, the chief referee. He was 20 yards away from us on his buggy when I shouted at him, 'What rules are we playing under?'

'European Tour rules,' he replied.

The driver was legal. I had been worried on two counts: not just whether it was legal but what the penalty would have been if it had been illegal. We could not have afforded the loss of a match.

'You lose only the hole you are on,' the rules guru declared.

The fourballs continued. The best we could be at the end of the day was 5 points ahead; the worst we could be was 3 behind. I never actually thought that way. Those were simply the facts.

Fasth and Parnevik were unlucky to lose on the last green in the sense that they ran into a bit of a hurricane on the inward half. Mark Calcavecchia, in particular, played phenomenally well as he and Duval made seven birdies on that stretch. Monty and Harrington were magnificent, beating Mickelson and Toms 2 and 1, the Americans to whom Monty had dropped half a point the previous day.

The Garcia and Westwood v Woods and Love match was one of those classic Ryder Cup encounters and a travesty of justice. The Europeans should never have lost. They had won three out of three and were within sniffing distance of a fourth when 'shit happened'. When you have played golf professionally for the best part of 30 years you know that anything can happen on a golf course at any time.

Garcia and Westwood were 1 up playing the 17th. Garcia blasted an enormous drive down the fairway and reached the green at the par 5 in two. Woods, meanwhile, found the rough from the tee, but such were his powers of recovery that he was left with a 3-ft putt for a birdie. For good measure, Love chipped in for the birdie 4. That left Garcia with a putt for the match and two putts to preserve the slender advantage going down the 18th. He three-putted.

He three-putted the 18th as well. So did Lee, missing his second putt from 4ft. The boys had committed the cardinal sin of losing a hole to a par. Not only a hole but the match. The disappointment was etched on their faces and audible in the groans of the galleries. The Europeans had played fantastically well for two days and been denied what would have been a famous 100 per cent record as a partnership by putting lapses, no doubt brought on by the incredible pressure of the Ryder Cup. Sergio had missed out on a moment of glory against Woods, theirs being a rivalry with enough wattage to light up a small town.

I also felt for Lee, who indeed demonstrated that week what I had told him at our get-together months earlier: that form was temporary, class permanent.

It was Sergio, however, who reacted like the firebrand he is. He threw his ball into the water and started kicking his bag in a show of temper. I could hardly blame him, and I didn't when asked about the incident at the press conference.

'It's his bag,' I said in that teasing way I employed to defuse any controversy. 'He can bloody well do what he likes with it. He didn't hurt anyone, did he? I'm sure he didn't upset anyone. You've got to understand the guy's a superstar and he's just lost a match he felt he should have won. He kicked his bag. It is a good thing I wasn't there; he probably would have kicked me.'

The defeat was unbelievable to me, and if we had lost the last match as well, we would have been in big trouble. It had turned very smelly towards the end of the afternoon, so Clarke and McGinley winning the 18th to secure a half point was fantastic. Instead of feeling deflated about the pendulum swinging towards the Americans, we were given a real lift.

As in the match ahead, Europe lost the 17th when they had looked like winning it. That put Clarke and McGinley 1 down playing the last. That was when, with the light fading as fast as the tension was mounting, Bernhard made his inspired suggestion of Paul taking his second shot before Darren in order to exert pressure on their opponents. It worked to perfection. Paul struck a glorious 4-iron 200 yards to about 20ft from the hole.

There are few arenas in the world that can match the 18th at The Belfry during the Ryder Cup. That giant scoreboard seemingly perched in the middle of the lake gives the scene a special uniqueness. What drama it has witnessed then reflected in its colouring, blue for Europe, red for the United States.

It was looking at its most ghostly as the last four players on the course that Saturday evening walked onto the green. Would we salvage an 8–8 scoreline going into the singles or would we be behind 8½–7½?

Paul beckoned me across.

'Find Padraig and ask him if this was the putt we were talking about,' he whispered. Harrington was somewhere back down the 18th fairway, but if I was quick I had time to get there and back.

'Yes,' Padraig replied, 'it is the putt we were talking about in practice.' I relayed the message back to Paul.

Apparently, it swung more than one would expect and it was faster. Great care was needed. McGinley struck a lovely putt stone dead, leaving Scott Hoch a putt from about 12ft to halve the hole, win the match and give America an overnight lead. He missed.

The last event of the day often determines the mood of the team that evening. For Clarke and McGinley to win the final hole of the day definitely raised our spirits. Yet half an hour earlier we looked as if we would be taking a lead into the singles, a lead we needed according to the commentators and critics. There was, therefore, some sense of disappointment in the ranks, which, of course, I concealed from the media.

In any case, there would shortly be genuine buoyancy in the camp when we saw the draw for the singles and, more significantly, saw the reaction of the Americans.

My immediate task was to portray the bravest, most optimistic face. 'Tremendous,' I told the assembled scribes. 'It was a great note to finish on, to win that last hole and to get to 8–8. We are not behind, so the morale will be quite high.'

All week I had been relaxed. I really don't know why. I was as relaxed as I had ever been on a golf course, from the Monday right through. The speeches made me nervous, of course. Once the opening ceremony had gone, the nerves disappeared. It was just so exciting, such a great week, such a magnificent occasion. I felt in total control of my emotions. I don't know about destiny, but I believe what's for you will not go by you.

'They've got one Tiger, I've got 12 lions,' I said.

19

Out of the shadows

'They've got one Tiger,' I had said, but where was he?

While my 12 lions were in the order I had planned 18 months earlier, you had to look right down the American list to the 12th and last singles to see the name of Tiger Woods, the greatest golfer in the world. The match might well be over before he could make his class tell.

I returned to the team room from my own media grilling to find a mixture of laughter and astonishment from the assembled company as they watched the American captain struggling with the simplest questions.

He had seen the same draw we had and it seemed as if he had come to the same conclusion we had. It looked great for Europe.

Suzanne took hundreds of photographs during the week, some black and white, some in colour and all very good. Her photographs from the European team room around that time show European players and wives standing open-mouthed in front of television sets watching a most uncomfortable American captain.

Curtis had been great all week. But you could see he just wasn't himself. He was flustered, definitely flustered. We could see that the draw had got to him and, presumably, to the American players. He was not happy; therefore, in all probability his players were not happy. It gave us a huge lift.

'If you could follow one match, only one, which would you pick?' a journalist asked. It seemed a pretty innocuous question.

'Give me a second here,' Curtis replied. 'I'd have to go early because it is important what happens early. I don't know. I am thinking about this. I won't do that, but – are you asking me as a spectator or as a captain?'

'One match is all you could see?' the questioner persisted.

You could see from his body language that Curtis was unhappy. He kept looking at the list and, for all I knew, he kept seeing blue. Maybe, like me, he could not see where America's first point was coming from. He had mentioned the importance of what happened early. Precisely my thinking.

'Meaning one match might be very important,' Curtis mumbled. 'Honestly, I don't know. Let me back up. Let me go beyond early. Let me go back where it might be a swing match, seven, eight, nine and ten could possibly be. See, I think we are going to win the last number – I don't know. You've got me. You've got me there. I am not sure.'

Later, it was put to Curtis that just the previous week Europe's best player in the Solheim Cup, Carin Koch, had been out last in the singles and, as the interrogator put it, 'the match did not matter'.

Curtis talked about everyone being comfortable with the order, then admitted, 'You're right, it could happen.' It seemed a strange concession in the circumstances.

It appeared that Curtis had tried to second-guess me, something I tried never to do in respect of him. My plan, my order, the one I had in my head since the beginning of 2001, deliberately took no account of how the Americans would line up. But the Americans had expected me to put Montgomerie and Garcia where they positioned Mickelson and Woods, at 11 and 12.

'If they somehow were to win the first five matches or so...' Curtis said. 'Momentum as we know is incredible in the Ryder Cup matches, generating enthusiasm which would maybe carry over to the rest of the boys.' It was as if he were articulating his fears and my hopes.

Finally, he was asked, 'Now that you've seen the pairings, do you like them?'

The European team room knew the answer, though we did not expect him even to allude to his own reservations.

'You know, I'm not sure what to think. I've never seen somebody front-load like this. So I don't know how – I don't know what to think. I know exactly what Sam has tried to do. I know what we have tried to do. We'll have to wait and see. I'm confident, obviously. You just never know.'

He did not sound confident to us. We interpreted the whole press conference as a sign of weakness. The draw had been a lift. Now we had received a further lift. The buzz in the European team room that evening was incredible.

Jesper Parnevik subsequently pointed out how differently the 1999 and 2002 singles draws were viewed. 'Saturday night at Brookline, when the draw came up, Monty and I looked at each other, exactly at the same time, and we looked into each other's eyes and said, "Where are we going to get the points tomorrow?" But it was like 180 degrees the opposite this time round. We felt good about the draw. We could not have picked a draw that was better for us today. Sam is probably a lot smarter than he looks.'

Europe had needed just 4 points on the final day to retain the Ryder Cup and didn't get them; we required 6½ points at the De Vere Belfry.

I looked down the list. It looked fantastic. As a gambling man, I was well aware of the odds. The United

States were odds-on at that stage for the match, while we were 3–1 against. Yet we were favourites in at least eight of the 12 individually priced matches. I could not understand the bookmakers. Unusually, I never had a bet. Hopefully, though, lots of punters were on Europe. I thought we were a great price.

I never tired of looking at the list that evening.

Colin Montgomerie v Scott Hoch, Sergio Garcia v David Toms, Darren Clarke v David Duval, Bernhard Langer v Hal Sutton, Padraig Harrington v Mark Calcavecchia, Thomas Björn v Stewart Cink, Lee Westwood v Scott Verplank, Niclas Fasth v Paul Azinger, Paul McGinley v Jim Furyk, Pierre Fulke v Davis Love III, Phillip Price v Phil Mickelson, Jesper Parnevik v Tiger Woods.

Monty against Hoch: that looked perfect. Hoch is one tough mother, but if you could have hand-picked an opponent for Hoch, it would have been Monty. Monty knew him and he had his case, having been denied victory over him at Valderrama when captain Ballesteros conceded the American a half at the end of the match. Monty had also beaten him on the opening morning at the De Vere Belfry. That match looked great to me.

David Toms had probably been America's best player throughout the week, while Garcia had been fantastic for Europe. That was a good match, which I was convinced we would win.

Duval had not been playing very well. He was struggling from the tee in particular. Darren Clarke has always been a great matchplay competitor. I thought that clash perfect for us.

Langer against Sutton: I thought we were a certainty there, a nailed-on certainty that would have demanded a substantial bet had I not been otherwise occupied. Harrington and Calcavecchia: I would take Harrington every time there, a world-class player who is going to win a lot of big tournaments over the rest of his career.

Björn against Cink: that was another where I would select Thomas every time. Cink is a fine player but Thomas has real potential for greatness. I think he is a great player. Halfway down the list and I could not see a loser, though, of course, it was never going to work out exactly like that. Ryder Cup singles are littered with shock losers and shock winners. That was always part of my argument. Points come from unexpected sources.

Westwood v Verplank looked like one of those ties that could go either way. Lee had found his game and was playing great. But Verplank, too, looked in good form. His straightness from the tee made him hard to beat. I thought that match would be close. I regarded Fasth v Azinger as the first real toughie for us, merely because of Azinger's reputation. He just never knew when he was beaten, as he was to demonstrate on the 18th green. That was match No. 8.

The rest looked difficult. You could never make McGinley, Fulke, Price and Parnevik favourites to beat Furyk, Love, Mickelson and Woods respectively. But 18-hole matchplay has thrown up many a surprise over the years, and a phrase was already forming in my head: 'Out of the shadows come heroes.'

The idea for my singles order had come from the same Sunningdale centenary dinner where I had met Professor David Purdie. I had sat next to David Holland, 'Bugsy' to his friends, who had had what I came to regard as an interesting view of how I might make my selections for the singles. We had no idea of who would make the team at that time, other than, of course, definites like Monty, Clarke and Garcia.

'You could do worse than put your players out in order of best to worst,' he had said.

I preferred to think of it as best to least best, an

order based not just on current form but on previous form and general standing in golf that year. I suppose it was a reflection of how I would rank my team at 6pm or whatever on Saturday 28 September. The idea was simple, uncomplicated and it took no account of the tactics of the opposition. I wanted momentum on my side. I wanted points on the board. I wanted that giant scoreboard over the lake at the 18th to turn blue. I wanted the later players to be inspired and the spectators to be excited.

It was time to put the plan into action. To that end I went around as many of the players I could find in that short period between the fourballs finishing and the deadline for the names to be submitted. Most were in the team room. I asked them all the same question.

'Do you have a preference where you want to play?' I asked without giving them the chance to reply.

'I've got a plan. I just need to know if you prefer to play anywhere particular in the order.'

The reply was the same in each case, even if the exact wording might have differed.

'No, not a problem, wherever you want to put me,' each replied in turn. They all said the same. That was great. This was my last plan and probably the only one that survived time and events.

Was it the gambler in me and was this the biggest gamble in my life? It would probably provide the neatest circle to this story if I said that the boy standing by the dyke at Routenburn Golf Club waiting to gamble with the priests was now the man gambling with Europe's chance of winning the Ryder Cup.

Too neat really. Although many did, I never regarded my singles order a gamble. There was an element of risk all right, the risk being not saving one or more of my bankers to the last three or four matches in case points were needed late in proceedings. That was the gamble, according to the commentators.

I didn't think I was taking a gamble at all. Matches eight to 12 on singles day at the Ryder Cup can defy form and reputation. Anything can happen. I don't care who you are, you can be affected by the pressure of the occasion. A god can fall and a rookie can soar.

'Out of the shadows come heroes.'

I knew before I wrote down the names on a piece of paper that the players at the bottom of the draw were ready. I knew the rookies would not let Europe down even before I saw them together round the breakfast table on the Sunday morning. They looked like the Three Musketeers, not three rookies, as they sat together almost as a statement of intent. All for one and one for all.

I spotted them and left them alone. That's fine, I thought. They obviously have something to talk about. There was no point my interfering at that stage. To my mind, they were bonding, preparing themselves for the distinct possibility that one or more of their number would be needed to secure victory for Europe. I saw real determination in the eyes of Messrs McGinley, Fulke and Price as they drank their orange juice and ate their croissants that morning.

I read later how they had decided to have a 'wee chat'.

'Myself, Pierre Fulke and Phillip Price talked about it at breakfast,' McGinley said. 'One of us is going to finish it. It was unlikely that the first six matches would all be won.'

'This could come down to one of us, boys,' was their text for the day.

Unlike Raymond Floyd at Brookline in 1999, I did not feel 'something in the trees'. Unlike captain Ben Crenshaw that same year, there was no sense of destiny.

Crenshaw had finished his Saturday evening press conference with the words: 'I'm a big believer in fate. I have a good feeling about this. That's all I am going to tell you.'

For three years I never allowed myself the pleasure of thinking that we were going to win. I always thought we could win. That was always prominent in my mind. I also never thought we were going to lose. But I was determined not to tempt fate.

Nor did I seek any help from outside with some inspirational words on the eve of the singles. Crenshaw had brought in the then Governor George W. Bush to read Col. William B. Travis's letter from the Alamo to the American team. Maybe I should have asked Tony Blair to read Henry V's Agincourt speech. That was not my style. Actually, Sir Alex Ferguson was going to bring a few of his Manchester United team down for dinner that week, but it never happened due to other commitments. I would have loved to have met David Beckham.

We restricted ourselves to a quiet dinner and a screening of our motivational video, which showed each player hitting some great shots and ended with the words *Carpe diem*. 'Seize the day' was as good a message as any when talking about the Ryder Cup singles. There were no speeches, no particular words of inspiration from anyone, no readings from the scriptures or from the songs of Bob Dylan. Just a tremendous buzz around the team room from players who loved the draw and seemed both determined and ready to win.

Suzanne and I were last to go to bed, like a naval captain and his missus on the bridge. But this was no sinking ship.

Sunday is different from any other day at the Ryder Cup because of the later start and the fact that there is a two-hour difference between the tee-off times of the first and last matches. It is not as if you walk into the breakfast room and they're all there. They're not all there. Those playing late are unlikely to see the early players and vice versa. So I did not get to see everyone prior to the practice putting green, where I spent most of the morning counting them out.

Apologies for the militaristic metaphor, but the job of a Ryder Cup captain on the final morning is to count his team out and then count them back and, of course, count the points on the board. We needed 6½ points out of a possible 12 to bring the trophy back to Europe.

Again there were no emotional speeches, no need to stoke up the fires of desire any more than they already burned. There would be time enough for tears.

Daniel and I had driven down to the practice ground that morning to be greeted by the biggest roar I had ever heard on a golf course. They saw us coming and cheered us all the way to the range. I had missed Monty's light-hearted banter with one of the spectators, whom he had invited from the stands to hit some shots. It was a sign of how relaxed he was feeling and an indication that his back was fine. My 'rock' looked solid.

My plan was to meet all of the European players individually on the putting green in front of the ivy-covered hotel and to escort them the 30 yards or so down the slope, through a gauntlet of supporters and onto the 1st tee. My message was exactly the same to each player.

'You were born for this,' I said. 'This is what you practise for, what you live for. This is your day. You will remember it for the rest of your life. Go and enjoy it.'

First Monty, then Sergio and Darren. The words may have varied slightly but the tone was always upbeat, the message always the same.

No one present will forget the 300-yard-plus opening tee shot Monty smote with his 3-wood, or the

35-ft putt he holed for a winning birdie 3. The cheers seemed to sweep back down the fairway to the 1st tee like flames shooting along a corridor. Only Clarke of the other 11 players won the opening hole for Europe. The more significant statistic showed that Europe took the lead initially in eight of the 12 matches.

Blue for Monty and, before long, blue for most of the rest of the boys. The momentum was beginning to build.

David Feherty was standing beside the putting green drinking a pint of Guinness. Not his first of the day, apparently. He offered me a slug. I did not need to be a genius to imagine a scenario where Europe loses and the next day a newspaper prints a photograph of the captain drinking on the job before midday. I turned him down, though only for the moment. Later, I popped through a hotel door and drained a pint in a oner before you could say Phil Mickelson.

Speaking of whom... He was on the putting green, standing next to Tiger Woods, looking at a leader board that showed Europe ahead in most of the matches. Their body language made it unnecessary to hear their conversation. It seemed to be very much a case of 'What the hell are we doing here?' One and two in the world; 12 and 11 in the singles.

Fulke had just driven off, Price was hitting a last practice putt and Monty was leaving the 9th green, 3 up against Hoch. Remembering Hoch's catty remark about the 10th being a 'great hole for your stats', I ran towards the 10th tee and leaped two crash barriers to form a one-man welcoming committee. His remark had not rattled me; it had lifted me. Anything I did within the rules and spirit of the game and that upset the Americans I considered great for Europe. But I remembered his comment and I wanted just to be standing on the 10th tee when he arrived.

I got there just in time to see them walking up the avenue leading from green to tee. Monty, who possesses perhaps the most revealing body language in golf, was striding ahead, taking giant steps for Europe. He barely gave me a glance but I could see he was so into the match and the occasion. He was so focused. I made Hoch aware of my presence but never opened my mouth. Nothing needed to be said.

I ran all the way back across the putting green, reaching Price just in time to walk him down to the 1st tee. Another roar was heard from out on the course. I looked up to the top of the grandstand, where I had built up a great rapport with the spectators. Using sign language, they were telling me everything that was going on. Phillip Price was one of the most interesting characters in my team. He is a lot tougher than you would give him credit for if you had just met him. If you sat down to dinner with him, you would think him very quiet, very nice, neither outspoken nor outgoing. However, he has a lot of fire in his belly. I had played with him enough over the years to have detected an inner strength. I knew he was capable of digging in and finding extra.

Everything was flowing from Monty and through the likes of Darren. They both enjoyed slightly dubious reputations of being temperamental and combustible. But they were both magnificent all week, on and off the course. They proved great team men who were great in the team room. Garcia, too, seemed to respond well to my little chat in which I stressed he was a leader, not the rookie kid waiting to be led.

All the matches were now on the course. Instead of trying to dart here and there, Daniel and I took up position behind the 9th green, where we must have sat for the best part of two hours. From there we were able to see everyone through the 9th and view all the action on the huge screen, just like the spectators in the grandstand or the millions in their armchairs at home. I could not be everywhere, so I thought there was no point trying. I was in constant communication with my vice-captain and back-room boys, who were going round with different matches. If a problem arose, I could react.

From start to finish that day, however, victory never looked in doubt. We were always in the ascendancy, always miles ahead to be brutally honest. A run down the list illustrated how well the day went: Monty – won the first hole and always ahead; Clarke – won the first and second hole; Langer – never behind; Harrington – won the 3rd and never behind; Björn – won the 5th and never behind; Fasth – won the 2nd and ahead until the final hole; Price – won the 5th and never behind.

Just before 2pm, Colin Montgomerie gave Europe its first point of the day, completing a crushing 5 and 4 defeat of Scott Hoch. 9–8. It was nearly 50 minutes later when Padraig Harrington achieved a victory over Marc Calcavecchia by the same convincing scoreline. 10–8. Within ten minutes Bernhard Langer had completed a 4 and 3 win over Hal Sutton. 11–8. We needed just 3½ from the remaining nine matches.

Sergio Garcia losing to David Toms on the last green was a blow. Then David Duval holed a 15-footer on the final green to steal a half point from Darren Clarke. 11½–9½. Thomas Björn restored our 3-point advantage with a 2 and 1 defeat of Stewart Cink. 12½–9 ½. But Scott Verplank proved too steady for Lee Westwood, who had enjoyed a tremendous week, despite losing 2 and 1. 12½–10½. We now required 2 points from five remaining singles.

'Out of the shadows come heroes.'

I was with Niclas Fasth and Azinger on the 17th. Niclas hit the biggest drive I have ever seen at that hole.

He finished up right down by the stream, in the rough and blocked by a tree. Although forced to chip out backwards onto the fairway, he was still left with just a 6-iron to the green. The Swede missed his 12-footer to win the hole and the match, whereupon Azinger holed from 8ft to stay alive. We knew that Price was 2 up with three holes to play against Mickelson. Suzanne was by my side.

'Right, you drop back and bring McGinley in,' I said to Suzanne. 'He is immediately behind on the 17th. I'll go up the 18th with Niclas.' I was not thinking that it would finish here. I was just where I felt I needed to be. We were a large group of players and wives. I wanted some to stay behind for McGinley and Price.

What a superb drive Fasth struck down the last hole. It was a wonderful feeling to stand there and watch one of your players execute a shot like that under the most intense pressure. Inspiring to see how he handled the situation. We were halfway down the fairway when we heard a tremendous roar from the direction of the 16th green. It could only be Price. Was it a birdie or had he hit his approach close? We didn't know. We knew he had not won. The radio told me he had birdied. Another roar was followed by more sustained cheering and the realisation that he had beaten Mickelson. Price, ranked 119 in the world, had defeated the World No. 2. 13½–10½.

With Fasth 1 up playing the 18th, it became clear that the Swede just needed to halve the hole for Europe to regain the Ryder Cup. The worst we could do was tie. Azinger dumped his approach into a greenside bunker, while Fasth located the correct second tier of the green, leaving a nasty long downhill putt.

And I spoke without engaging my brain.

'We've won.'

The tall, erect, straight-backed figure standing next to me shot me a glance that would have withered an evergreen.

'We ain't won anything yet,' Thomas Bjorn snapped, pointing a warning finger at me. For three years I had not afforded myself the luxury of thinking we would win, and here I was on the 18th fairway committing the cardinal sin of any captain in declaring victory before it had been secured. Here I was not so much tempting fate as offering it a human sacrifice.

The moment of victory was getting closer, though, and I was starting to crack up for the first time in the week. I crossed the bridge to the right of the 18th fairway and moved forward to just short of the green.

'Where's Suzanne?' I asked to no one in particular. 'Suzanne has to be here.' I tried the radio.

'Get Suzanne here, now,' I barked.

It could not be done right away. There were too many people in the buggy. I had to try to overcome my disappointment. Azinger was in the bunker, Fasth was on the green and I was just standing there looking lost. An arm went round my shoulders.

'Nice spot,' David Duval said. 'Nice spot.' He, like me, must have thought it was over and he was just telling me I was in a good place to see the conclusion. It was such a touching thing to say and do. He could see that I was completely in bits. I was crying, unable to look at either of the cameras that were following me about.

And then it happened. Azinger holed his bunker shot. Niclas, who had played so well, was shattered. His putt had been really difficult; now it was impossible. He missed his long putt and all eyes looked down the fairway to the waiting figure of Paul McGinley. 14–11. We now needed just half a point.

'Out of the shadows come heroes.'

His words at the rookie breakfast chat that morning had been only slightly different. 'One of us could be a hero,' he had said to Price and Fulke.

At least Azinger had given Suzanne time to be at my side. We had moved higher up the right-hand side of the green by the time McGinley and Furyk played their second shots. Furyk found the left bunker, while Paul drew his further left, wide of the sand. I left Suzanne and went down to the bridge to bring Paul across. I had not a clue what I was going to say to him.

In the end, I think I blurted out, 'Do it for me, okay?'

He played his difficult pitch almost to perfection, though instead of the ball releasing properly and rolling down the slope to the hole, it stopped about 10ft short. Whereupon, Furyk almost did an Azinger by holing his bunker shot. The ball lipped out after giving me my worst moment of the week.

The best moment swiftly followed, as McGinley held his nerve to become 'the man who holed the putt that won the Ryder Cup'. Now where had I heard that phrase before?

My initial reaction was not to jump into the air with joy or run to McGinley but to remain head bowed in a state of semi-paralysis. I mumbled something about having won the Ryder Cup, while three years of self-control drained from my body as if sucked up by the roots of the mighty English oak tree to the right of the 18th green. My green.

I'll never forget it. I couldn't move. I might still have been there now had Willie Aitcheson, my caddie when turning pro in 1970, not grabbed me. He was the first. Lee Westwood was the second to wrap his arms around me before Suzanne and I could embrace. Somehow we managed a special moment together in the middle of the mayhem.

There were some very special moments in the minutes that followed. A hug from a proud mum, my greatest fan, and another from Daniel. I'm his greatest fan. There was, too, an emotional clinch with my dad, a rare instance of physical contact between two Scots who grew up in the west of Scotland working-class culture, where men were allowed to embrace only when drunk or at Hogmanay.

After my initial overwhelmed reaction, I had joined in the general euphoria, hugging, and being hugged, by everyone who moved. Paul was engulfed by people, just as I had been in 1985. It was his moment, just as it had been mine. Eventually, we saw each other and we embraced, as Tony Jacklin and I had done 17 years earlier.

The celebrations had begun with two matches still on the course. It became 15–12 when Fulke and Love agreed a half on the 18th fairway, not least because there were people on the green. They thought it was all over, and it was. That was the difference between the De Vere Belfry and Brookline.

Parnevik and Woods, meanwhile, played up the 17th and back down the 18th. These situations are always highly unsatisfactory. Some serious consideration should be given to finding a way whereby, when the match is over, the results of the remaining singles are declared as of that moment. I know there are the records of individuals at stake and thousands of pounds of bets on final scorelines, etc., but no one wants to be out there in such circumstances. Members of the winning team want to rejoice with their colleagues, while losers just want to commiserate with their team-mates. When it is over, it should be over.

Parnevik and Woods apparently asked to stop, only to be told by their referee to continue. This is why I found myself crouching at the back of the 18th green trying desperately to hold onto a magnum of champagne while Tiger was preparing to putt. To my horror, the cork popped and flew into the air. I was waiting for it to land on Tiger's head to complete my embarrassment. Fortunately, it landed safely elsewhere.

Tiger and Jesper were still finishing off when a Spanish press guy handed me a mobile telephone with Seve Ballesteros on the other end.

'Fantastic, San,' he said in that special way. 'You did a great job. Fantastic.' I so wanted to hold the phone up to the spectators and tell them that the great Seve Ballesteros was on the line.

Björn emptied an entire bottle on my head so that I was as wet as McGinley, who by then had dived into the lake. I did not know whether to laugh or cry, so I did both. I chased him but managed to soak Furyk instead. I apologised to the American. He did not need a drenching to add to the disappointment of defeat. Jim was fine about it.

At the height of the madness, I suggested to Suzanne that we slip back to the hotel. Maybe I was getting too old for this; maybe I wanted the players to enjoy their moment; maybe I felt suddenly exhausted with the whole draining emotion of the occasion; maybe it was a combination of everything. I don't really know. But we held hands and walked through the stands, across the putting green, right round the side of the hotel, followed by a camera the whole way. The atmosphere was just incredible.

Back in our room, I removed my champagne-soaked clothes and went under the shower. People in sport talk a lot about great achievements not sinking in until later. My 'sinking in' moment came under that shower as I thought about the last three years, my professional career, my whole life and my family. Always a dangerous thing to do for a serial blubber like me. I was as happy as I could be standing under that shower.

Only the closing ceremony remained. The job was not quite done. We dressed as quickly as we could and headed back to the team room, pausing only to arrange a replacement shirt for Paul McGinley, who somehow had got his wet. The team room was buzzing as we stood at the open window and responded to the cheering of the fans below.

I remembered the advice of Professor Purdie. A large whisky ten minutes before the speech. Only this time it was ten minutes before, nine minutes before and eight minutes before. One was never going to be enough.

I had a devil of a job getting everyone organised to head for the closing ceremony. There was plenty of time to celebrate and laugh and relax. This was a time for honouring the opposition, a time to remain respectful and not to gloat. I did not want to keep them waiting. In the event, we were ready before the Americans.

The long walk down to the stage was incredible, Curtis and I at the front behind a pipe band playing 'Campbletown Loch, I wish you were whisky' and other Scottish tunes. Paul Azinger put his arm round my neck as we chatted about another extraordinary Ryder Cup day. The noise of the spectators was deafening.

A band played on but their notes were drowned out by the crowd singing 'One Sammy Torrance, there's only one Sammy Torrance.' Sammy was what Lee Trevino always called me. But I have only ever been Sam. I suppose Sammy fitted the music better.

Tony Jacklin was there, shaking my hand and saying, 'I love you.'

I just looked at him and replied, 'I learned all of this from you, all of it from you.' I was right too. He was the best Ryder Cup captain there has ever been.

Curtis made an excellent speech in which he referred to the spectators as the 'toughest and fairest' 13th man he had ever confronted. 'We got a European butt-whipping today,' he said, to the delight of the massed stands.

He did me a huge favour by mentioning my mother and father. 'Congratulations to Bob and June Torrance,' he said as they stood up to acknowledge the applause. 'I know it means so much to you. Your son did it, damn him,' he added.

I could not have gone there. When I was writing the speeches or even rehearsing them in the garage, there were places I could not go. I knew if I had mentioned Mum and Dad I would have slipped over the edge. I have always been an emotional wreck when it comes to my parents. His incredibly kind and thoughtful words meant I could decently stay away from that cliff.

'Curtis, I accept the Ryder Cup into our safe keeping,' I began. 'And I accept it from an outstanding captain of a fine US team. We will cherish it for two years until we meet again.

'On behalf of the European team and myself, I thank Curtis and his men for the way the Ryder Cup has been contested – with passion and intensity but also with the tradition and courtesy and sportsmanship which are the bedrock of our great game.'

I thanked Suzanne and my family – 'Thanks for putting up with me for the last three years' – and I thanked the spectators, our '13th man', as Curtis put it.

I had waited three long years for my last thank you, a thank you that accompanied the victory I hoped for and dreamed of. I looked along the line of players, from Thomas Björn on my immediate right to Lee Westwood at the far end. I gathered myself.

'My last thank you is very special and it is to the

winning team,' I added, as I urged them to take a bow. 'This is very special for me. I have got to say that only the birth of my children and my marriage to my wife have been more special. I will remember this forever. Thank you very much.'

The voice trembled only at the very end. Every single word was planned and rehearsed. I could not have done it any other way.

The press conference was the time for ad libbing, as Sergio Garcia demonstrated.

'It was absolutely amazing,' Garcia said when it came to his turn to speak. 'Only the birth of my child and the marriage...'

Even now, the captain was being teased. I like to think that it was done affectionately and that a great deal of our strength was our ability to laugh with and at each other.

A great deal of laughter lay ahead as the celebrations began in earnest.

20

'Your captain here'

Samuel Ryder would surely have approved that the contest he gave his name to was used to patch up a row that night.

His closest surviving relative, Mrs Mary Moore, certainly nodded in the direction of events at the De Vere Belfry. I received a charming letter from her in the days following our success. She wrote: 'May I offer my warmest congratulations on your triumph at the Ryder Cup. What bold scheming and what great players to carry it out. As Sam Ryder's grand-daughter, I was particularly moved by your thoughtful words before the matches, reminding everyone of his original aim and ideals. Thank you for keeping them so strongly in mind. I believe they were amply upheld.'

The above row had simmered for years and boiled over at Brookline. It had upset me no little that David Feherty, my dearest friend, and Colin Montgomerie, a mate, a fellow countryman and, frankly, a hero, had never really cleared the air in a dispute that reached its height three years earlier.

Monty, who blamed Feherty for introducing to the American public the – more affectionate than he realises – nickname Mrs Doubtfire, had insisted on the removal of Feherty from the team room in Boston, the culmination of several run-ins involving the pair. I knew that Feherty truly admired Monty, that, in fact, Feherty had been wrongly accused and that the lingering bad blood hurt him a great deal. Colin was a dear friend; David was my best friend. I had to get it sorted.

I sought out Monty. I found him outside the team room having a kiss and cuddle with Eimear. Far be it from me to interrupt a couple in a passionate clinch, but my mind was set on doing my United Nations bit.

'Come with me,' I said to Monty, apologising to his wife before taking him by the hand into the room. 'I have a friend of mine I need you to speak to.' A winning captain could demand anything that night.

Feherty was talking to Tiger.

'Sorry, Tiger, but this is important,' I said, interrupting.

I held on to Monty with one hand, grabbed Feherty with the other and pulled them face to face. 'You two need to get this fucking sorted now,' I said. This was an occasion for strong language.

They did it for me, just as McGinley had done on the 18th green. They put their arms around each other and hugged. It was a perfect moment, which I know meant a great deal to Feherty.

'It was one of the greatest moments of my career and I get goose-bumps every time I think about it,' he later told me. 'It was huge for me.'

David might not have realised it, but it was pretty big for Monty as well.

Only subsequently did I discover quite how much that week meant to Monty, when Suzanne and I received a brief note from Eimear among the hundreds of letters of congratulation written by friends and golf enthusiasts.

'Darling Sam and Suzanne,' she wrote. 'What can we say??!! Feet are still not touching the ground. Happiest week of Colin's career. Think the world of both of you. It was worth all the hard work. Loved all the pressies. Fantastic. Play it again, Sam. Eimear and Colin.'

There was not the slightest chance of my deciding to 'play it again', though to a man my team-mates urged me that night to consider another term of office. I wanted to be me again. Many of my closest friends were to say that the secret of my success in the role was that I had been myself. That was true in so far as I changed nothing about how I interacted with players.

Feherty thought that would be the strength of my captaincy, and he wrote as much in his always witty column in *Golf* magazine. For all that he was a faithful friend, it takes courage to nail yourself so firmly to a mast that could have crashed down onto the crew.

I would like to reproduce two sections from the article, not out of bumptiousness, but because I think he captures the essence of what I am. He wrote in August 2002:

> Given the serious nature of recent Ryder Cup
> competition, it goes without saying that the job
> vacancy for captain of the European team needs
> to be filled by an upright man of solid reputation,
> given to neither frivolity nor mischief. As the master
> of the great ocean-going steamer which carried Sir
> Samuel Ryder and his little golden trophy across
> the Atlantic might have told you, a captain must
> never gamble, and show no tendency toward
> strong liquor.
>
> Bearing all this in mind, one could be forgiven
> for asking, why the hell would anyone pick Sam
> Torrance? Maybe it's because the competition itself
> has changed over the years since Sir Samuel got used
> to steaming back across the Atlantic, empty-handed.
> For so many years, the Great Britain and Ireland
> team was hindered by the great British and Irish
> tradition of losing with an almost institutionalised

grace, accompanied by 12 quivering, but stiff upper lips. Thank you, sir. May I please have another?

Still, the men of those teams fell in love with the Ryder Cup, because it was about playing the game, and nothing else. The Ryder Cup is the last bastion of pure professional sport on the planet.

After describing his playing experiences at Kiawah in 1991, Feherty returned to his theme:

During that week, Sam made me feel bigger and better and more important than I ever had. He, Bernard Gallacher and the veterans on the team gave me and the other rookies, including David Gilford, Paul Broadhurst and Steven Richardson, a sense that we were part of a special club, a brotherhood if you like. It's a feeling that lasts a lifetime, and one upon which Sam has thrived for more than two decades.

Some of the greatest armies in history were filled with men who were willing to die for their leader, and in order to earn such devotion, those leaders spent a lot of time with their men.

Sam has not lectured his team, unless you consider a lecture to be telling dirty jokes over cold beers in smoky bars, or playing cards in a hotel room. Over cold beers. He has gambled on the golf course, and probably robbed them, but more than anything else, he has made them feel special, because now, numbered among their friends, is Sam Torrance.

Sam has given the media short shrift, at least in press conferences, because he has no time for anyone who wants to make a story out of anything but the golf. He cares little for speeches, or ceremony. Like a fighter, he just wants the bell to ring and to get it on. It's killing him that he isn't playing, but he knows he has a great team that has a great chance.

Win, lose, or draw, you can be certain of one thing, there will be no stiff upper lip, largely because no one has seen Sam's upper lip for years. For the best part of three decades, the European golfing public has known exactly how Sam Torrance has felt. The Belfry holds special memories, tears of joy and a red V-neck, a broken toe and bitter disappointment. For the record, he tackled a yucca, and no, he hadn't been drinking. (If he had, he probably would have beaten the crap out of the cactus as well.)

I think Sam will be the greatest captain the Ryder Cup has ever seen, but then again, I'm a little biased. Like the rest of the European team, and many of the Americans, I love the man. I know him so well, but then, if you're a golf fan, so do you.

Not everyone knew that sometimes during my captaincy I felt as if I were wading through concrete. I wanted my life back. I wanted to be able to let myself go and not have to worry about the consequences. I wanted to be able to relax completely and not feel inhibited.

All inhibitions disappeared on Sunday night when, just like in the match itself, I led them to the water... 'and they drank copiously', the phrase I used during the post-match press conference. Actually, they went by themselves and it wasn't water that they drank.

The main bar in the De Vere Belfry was turned into part football match, part last night of the proms, with singing and cheering and flag waving and just unrestrained jubilation. Suzanne and I had been taken there from the cocktail party by Lee and Laurae Westwood, a lovely natural couple who know how to have a good time.

Lee was emceeing proceedings like a cross between a wrestling announcer and Leonard Sachs from *The Good Old Days*. 'Ladies and gentlemen, I bring you the man from Spain…Sergio "El Niño" Garcia.' That sort of thing. The player in question would climb onto the arm of a couch to be greeted with singing and chanting from the hordes of supporters.

'We love you, Monty, oh yes we do,' echoed around the room to indicate the arrival of Colin Montgomerie.

'Ladies and gentlemen, I bring you the man who has visited every planet in the solar system… Jesper Parnevik.'

'We love you, Jesper,' filled the air. And so on.

'Olé, olé, olé, olé', the unofficial Irish football anthem, welcomed McGinley and Harrington. There seemed like a million people in the room. Westwood would announce players in turn and lift them onto the arm of a couch in the lounge.

'One Sammy Torrance, there's only one Sammy Torrance,' got a few airings. At last, it was Phillip Price's turn. Westwood was doing the introduction while being punched on the bottom by a Welshman repeating the words: 'Tell them who I beat, tell them who I beat.' That was definitely his moment. He said it so often that it has become the phrase most associated with Price. 'Tell them who I beat' is how he has been greeted by teammates ever since.

He beat Phil Mickelson. That's who, as I have relished reminding him every time we meet.

'Your captain here,' I said when leaving a message on his mobile answering machine the following day. 'Christ, how well did YOU play against Mickelson?!' He picked it up 24 hours later, having slept for the best part of a day.

Westwood was magnificent as master of ceremonies, a role he was to repeat at the Jigger Inn in St
Andrews that week as we all descended on the home of
golf for the Dunhill Links Championship.

Eventually, we repaired to the team room for a very
well-organised celebration, with entertainment provided
by two Swedish friends of Jesper Parnevik. Davis Love
and his wife popped in, as did the Suttons, Hal and
Ashley. Curtis stayed for a while; his sons for much
longer. The two boys, Thomas and David, had a fantastic
time. We sent them back to their rooms steaming. But
David Duval stayed into the 'wee sma' 'oors'. He was
terrific fun, confirming my view of him as one of the good
guys. I remembered how one year the late Payne Stewart
put his head in the European team room, saw 'Jesse'
James and me singing away at the bar and disappeared,
only to return five minutes later. He came back with a
plastic bag full of harmonicas and stayed till dawn.

I would not have insulted the American team by
asking them to come round for a drink. The door was
open and they knew that. But it is never everyone's idea
of spending the hours of your greatest disappointment
with the victorious opposition. I have lost and gone to
the American room and been the only one. I could hardly
criticise the Americans for not appearing in the European
room.

Curtis and I had worked for more harmony and we
could be grateful for what went on during the match.
Our plan had been to reinstitute the dinner for both
teams on the Sunday night. But some of the American
players were dead against it. Fair enough.

The night was epic and the drinking of bacchanalian
proportions. But we were on so much of a high that there
was no hangover to spoil the euphoria I felt when waking
up on Monday morning after just a few hours' sleep.

Suzanne and I woke up with smiles on our faces and ear-to-ear grins that never left us for days. We read the newspapers in bed and I burst into tears. Everything was fresh in my mind but to read it in black and white merely brought home to me how special everything had been. I felt very humble about how much of the coverage revolved around my contribution. I had only led them to the water...

As the man who holed the winning putt, Paul McGinley was the focus of much attention. I knew that feeling. Monty, too, received due praise and recognition for a huge contribution of 4½ points out of 5. But the accolades for me were very humbling and very satisfying. At times, I felt I would never get through the ordeal. There had been the row over Mark James; there was, of course, the extra year brought on by the tragic events in New York; and I had slipped up at a PGA dinner when my network of European Tour 'minders' broke down. Eventually, Suzanne and I threw on some casual clothing and headed for the team room. We wanted to see everyone again before they left. We wanted to thank everyone before they went their own ways. Although there was talk of reunions and getting together again as a team in the future, it does not work out like that. Golf is a very individual sport normally, with each individual following their own schedule. The miracle of the Ryder Cup in the case of Europe is that so many nationalities come together for a week and they bond together as a genuine team, as the Manchester United of golf, if you like. Somehow I knew that, despite all the promises and fine plans, there would be few occasions when this very special team came together again. If ever.

So the atmosphere that morning was as much that of an end of an era as the end of a successful week. Some of the players would make future Ryder Cup teams but the 2001 team – the 2001 team that played in 2002 – would never take to the field again. The captain was not going to be around again.

I became certain of one thing during my term of captaincy. Any future captains would have to be still in their playing career and still very much involved with the members of the team on a week-to-week basis. I don't care who you are, you have to be there, you have to be in their pockets. You have to get them to love you, get them to trust you and get them to win for you.

I was 50 in August 2003, time to move away from a European Tour that had been my home for 30 wonderful years. Time to make the swift and potentially lucrative switch to Seniors' golf. My durability should not be a problem. I expect to be playing well and scoring low numbers into my dotage. But with so many great players turning 50 over the next few years, and with the nature of the beast, the window of opportunity to make a financial killing is a relatively short one. It stands to reason that, unlike when turning professional, you are likely to be at your most effective in the first couple of seasons.

I would have liked my golf game to have been in better shape at the start of 2003, but three years of captaincy took its toll in that my focus, sometimes only subconsciously, was elsewhere. And when the big five-zero approached I was looking ahead rather than concentrating on the events in which I was playing.

I also underwent surgery on a troublesome knee, which forced me to withdraw from the Scottish Open and Open Championship final qualifying. But I was there at Sandwich as a member of the BBC golf commentary team. I had dabbled in commentating on several other occasions, though something seemed to click during the final round of the Volvo PGA at Wentworth in May.

It was an absolute delight to work on big golfing occasions with Peter Alliss, the master of his profession. I hope to do a lot more television work when I eventually stop competing.

Ironically, Professor Purdie had done such a good job teaching me how to talk in public that I joined the celebrity after-dinner speaking circuit and began to look forward to – rather than dread – engagements. This was part of a gradual process of making sure the family was financially secure when I stopped earning on the course. A long way off, I hope.

Champagne flowed in the team room that Monday morning for those who could face it and those not needing to drive. We had a beautiful breakfast with all the papers spread over the tables and people coming and going. We seemed to be there for hours, which was the time it took the Westwoods to pack their car. We all laughed at the carry-on involved in trying to pack their gear into the car. You leave with a great deal more than you arrive with, not least the memories.

One final meeting with the press, a few photographs at the 10th where I hit a ball or two at the green, and it was time to head south. We said our goodbyes to Mike Maloney and his staff at the hotel, who had been tremendous in catering for our every whim. The champagne continued to flow on the journey home, a trip broken only by the need to satisfy the hunger pangs of father and son. So it was into the nearest motorway service station to load up with goodies from Kentucky Fried Chicken. No one can accuse me of lacking style. Ryder Cup in one hand, KFC in the other.

The reception from the public at the motorway services place was unbelievable. There was clapping and cheering and countless requests for autographs. It seemed as if the entire nation had been captivated by

Europe's victory. I have continued to receive a fabulous reception from people ever since. Everywhere I go, people want to shake my hand. Of course, it has been particularly fantastic in Scotland. I was in Helensburgh the following July with Daniel, who was competing in the Scottish Boys Strokeplay Championship. Everyone was still as enthusiastic as they could be about the Ryder Cup victory. The reception I receive in Scotland has always brought out the emotions in me.

Although I took the Scottish Professional Championship title five times, I would have loved to have won a Scottish Open or a big European Tour event in my native Scotland.

It was not until driving home on the Monday afternoon that I turned on my mobile telephone. 'You have 56 new messages,' the voice declared.

Each one – from friends and fellow players – was better than the previous one. Each one a tear-jerker, it seemed to me. The emotions could flow now that the match was over. I had been so much in control of myself during the match itself, strong for the team as I felt I had to be. I was allowed to crack up in the aftermath.

We sat and listened to messages for much of the drive home. There was one from Darren Clarke, which got to me more than the others. 'Hi to the bestest, winningest captain ever,' he began. Just hearing his voice with that simple greeting really affected me. Messages poured in for days and weeks to come, of course. From all over the world and from all manner of people. From the famous to the ordinary golf fan, from friends to strangers inspired to put pen to paper because of our victory.

Some were unexpected, to say the least, and at least one vindicated European feelings about the so-called Battle of Brookline. It came from Mark O'Meara, who had played in the winning US team in 1999.

'You and Curtis should be commended for getting the Ryder Cup back on track,' Mark wrote. 'Let's hope the same spirit carries over to Detroit in two years' time.'

Ben Crenshaw, the victorious captain, also mentioned spirit, though without conceding that Sam Ryder's train had been derailed. 'What a lifetime in golf you have had! I know you and Curtis tried so hard to remind people of the Ryder Cup spirit, which on all accounts was successful. Wonderful work, Sam – enjoy. Sincerely, Ben.'

Brian Huggett referred to the 'dark days of Boston', while Gary Player was very kind in suggesting that my 'inspiration and direction were clearly evident'. There were letters from Jack McConnell, Scotland's first minister, and Richard Caborn, the Westminster minister of sport. Lord MacLaurin of Knebworth managed to watch the final day's play on Sri Lankan television, despite attending an International Cricket Council meeting in Colombo. 'You have done a fantastic job for European golf and this weekend was a huge triumph for you personally,' he wrote.

We arrived home in time to pick up the girls from their school, the Marist Convent at Sunninghill. We had promised to take the Ryder Cup in. No sooner had we got through the door than Phoebe grabbed the trophy and ran to her friends in her classroom. There she was, belting along the corridor holding the Ryder Cup, with Anouska chasing after her. It was great. We promised the headmistress that we would be back some days later for a photograph with all the children.

Little did I know that my Ryder Cup press conferences had not ended when I left the De Vere Belfry. We returned to the school to discover two stools on a stage in the assembly hall with the entire junior school seated in readiness. Suzanne and I were given the most thorough examination, fielding more imaginative and probing questions than we had ever had to face. It was just terrific.

The Dunhill Links Championship is a great event, much loved by the participating professionals, celebrities and amateurs who visit St Andrews every October, come rain, hail or shine. The last thing I needed was to have to head to the east of Scotland within 48 hours of our glorious victory. However, it did offer an opportunity for yet another celebration, more accurately just a continuation of what had been going on since McGinley holed that putt.

An arrangement had been made by some of the team to meet that evening at the Jigger Inn, a one-time legendary watering-hole for caddies, and nowadays an appendage of the Old Course Hotel, still popular with everyone who loves golf. I checked into the St Andrews Bay Hotel and headed to town. The pub was strangely silent as I walked in. Only for a second, though. Suddenly everyone was singing my song. 'One Sam Torrance, there's only one Sam Torrance...' And so on. Westwood had apparently spotted me coming and ordered silence. The night continued 'wi' sangs and clatter', to quote from Rabbie Burns, with Westwood again leading proceedings. I made a speech, though God only knows what I said. No doubt I wept and no doubt all the players threw paper napkins at me. At least they should have.

We drank for hour after hour, moving eventually up to the top bar in the Old Course Hotel. I found myself very drunk, sitting next to Boris Becker, an absolute hero, telling him the biggest load of tosh. Then it was on to the St Andrews Bay, more drink and some pizza.

I woke up in the morning at 6.30am feeling about as bad it is possible to feel without being declared clinically dead. I thought to myself, what on earth am I doing here? I wanted to be in the bosom of my family. I love Scotland and, hopefully, Scotland loves me. But I could not have survived a week of what I went through on the Tuesday night. I would have been an alcoholic by the end of the week.

So I telephoned Johan Rupert, the head man at Dunhill, a passionate lover of links golf, a South African and a good friend of Ernie Els. I apologised profusely and told him I could not play in his event. He understood perfectly and was really decent about the whole thing. So too was *Miami Vice*'s Don 'short-sleeved-jacketed' Johnson, who I was supposed to play with. He said something very nice to the media.

I had occasion to telephone Johan the following year to ask another favour. It had been an ambition of mine to play a tournament with my son. The time was ripe. Daniel, who had just tied first in the Gold Medal at Sunningdale, was now good enough and old enough at 15 to cope. There was another side to the equation. Pretty soon I would be too old and maybe not good enough.

'Any chance of getting Daniel in?' I enquired of the man who has received such unwarranted criticism for his event.

'We have a waiting list a mile long,' he replied, 'but we will see what can be done.'

Iain Banner, his right-hand man, was put on the case. He recognised the publicity potential of the Ryder Cup captain and his son competing in front of a Scottish crowd.

'We will put you to the top of the list, but you will have to pay,' Iain told me.

I had no problem with having to fork out an entry fee of £5,000. I knew that Ernie Els, for example, though a close friend of Johan, always insisted on paying for his father.

I texted Daniel at his boarding school on the Monday of the week preceding the tournament. 'TRYING TO GET U IN DUNHILL,' I wrote.

'WHAT R THE CHANCES?' came the reply.

'80%.'

Within five minutes, as it happened, I received an e-mail from Dunhill confirming our participation.

'SORRY, NOT 80%, U R IN,' was my next text to Daniel.

I waited for a return message. Nothing. I tried again. 'HAVE U PICKED URSELF OFF FLOOR YET?'

Eventually, two buzzes signalled a response. 'NO HE HASN'T. THIS IS DANIEL'S MATHS TEACHER.'

I sent another text, apologising profusely for interrupting his lesson. I heard nothing more until Daniel telephoned me later in the day in a very excited state.

'Oh, by the way,' he said, 'the bit about the maths teacher. It was me. I was just winding you up.' I knew then he would handle the occasion.

Little did I know how well.

Our victory in the Dunhill Links Championship Pro-Am with a better ball score of 251, 37 under par, was one of the highlights of my career. It was every bit as special in its own way as the 1985 and 2002 Ryder Cups or any of my tournament victories. The whole week was a blast.

I do not know who was the more excited, father or son, as we headed north and checked into the St Andrews Bay Hotel. There was time for a quick nine holes over the Old Course, always a thrill for any golfer, professional or amateur, young or old. Tuesday saw Sam and Daniel take on Lee and Thomas, namely Westwood and Björn, two of my other boys from the Ryder Cup. With Daniel receiving five strokes, we beat them.

One of Daniel's shots – an 80-yard pitch from a divot over a hazard, which landed just beside the pin –

prompted Thomas to put his arm round the lad as they walked down the final fairway.

'You will make your dad's record look like shit,' the big Dane said in that endearingly blunt Scandinavian manner of his. Words like those were a tremendous boost and, occasionally, a good balance to my sometimes critical approach.

'You are too hard on him,' Nicky Price said the next day at Carnoustie as we played a practice round. Not as hard as my dad was on me, I thought. But we do have our ups and downs, just like 'faither' and me. The truth of the matter is that, like most fathers, I am tremendously proud of my son. I am also very ambitious for him. I will not hold him back. If he is good enough, I will do everything I can to help him become a successful professional golfer. He has wanted to do nothing else for a number of years. His performance that week proved he has the potential and he has the temperament. He is certainly a natural at television interviews. As he replied with ease and no little humour to questions at the end of the week, I thought back to the interview he did with American television in front of The De Vere Belfry Hotel on the morning of the Ryder Cup singles. Yes, and the eyes moistened yet again.

'I never really felt nervous at any time, Dad,' Daniel insisted.

For the record, Daniel posted rounds of 73, 70, 68 and 67 over, respectively, Carnoustie, St Andrews, Kingsbarns and St Andrews again. Although playing from the amateur tees, which were only marginally forward of ours, his 10 under par total of 278 would have given him 29th position in the professional event. He beat me by one stroke. His driving was the strongest part of his game all week.

'Bloody hell, is that 'is drive?' Mark Roe exclaimed

as he looked down the 5th fairway at the Old Course after one of Daniel's longest. We measured it at around 350 yards, leaving him only an 8-iron to the green at the par 5. To play the first three days with Roe and his partner Gary Lineker helped put Daniel at ease. Gary is a family friend and a fellow Sunningdale member.

Although we entered with the intention of winning, it was not until our third-round better ball 59 that we focused our thoughts on the possibility of victory. That night, on the eve of the final round, we checked on the Internet to see our position. We looked at the names of the main contenders and calculated what we might have to score. Ironically, I had been 'eliminated' from the professional competition. I could not believe, when missing a short putt on the 54th green, that my three-round score of 4 under par would not be good enough. The cut proved to be 5 under. I got into the last day because of my amateur partner!

By now, what with shooting 59, the media had warmed to the story. Everyone seemed to know what was going on. We were finishing practising prior to our last round when the great Samuel L. Jackson spotted us.

'Hey, great play,' he called to Daniel, as cool as any of the dudes he plays on the silver screen.

Darren Clarke took time out to give Daniel a bunker lesson. He taught him how to get spin on the ball by pointing the back of the left hand to the sky during the back swing. It works. The ball flies straight into the sky and bites on landing. Not that Daniel needed to try it out. One of his greatest thrills was playing 36 holes at the Old Course without going into a single bunker. Just as Tiger Woods had done when winning the 2000 Open Championship.

The Scottish galleries had been fantastic to us all week, never more so than on that final day at St

Andrews. We started at the 10th, so our march to victory was out towards the River Eden estuary and not, as usual, back towards the famous skyline of the Auld Grey Toon. But a large crowd gathered and grew as we played our last nine holes from the 1st to the 9th. A television crew joined us with five holes to play when it became apparent that victory was within our grasp.

The sight of 'Torrance and Torrance' at the top of the leader board made me choke. When Daniel sank a 25-footer for a birdie on the 6th, I knew we would win. I could hardly speak with emotion. The 9th was pure theatre. I struck what I thought was a great drive straight into the bunker, the only protection afforded to a green easily drivable by even modest hitters. I probably should have played safe with a 4-iron, though our advantage was such that there was really no need to take the cautious approach.

'A 6-iron is the shot,' I said to Daniel as he prepared to tee off. It was merely a suggestion. He has his own mind; he plays his own game.

'My only thought was driver or 3-wood,' Daniel told me later. His driver would have been too much club. He took his 3-wood and fired the ball onto the green to about 25ft from the hole at the par 4. Two putts for another birdie and victory was ours, ahead of another father and son team Neels and Ernie Els. We hugged as I fought back the emotion that always grabs me at such times. It was precisely a year to the day since Europe had won the Ryder Cup.

'I had a lot of help from 12 great men at The Belfry,' I told the assembled media. 'Today I had a lot of help from one great young man.'

Daniel seemed as confident and composed as ever. 'As much as I respected Dad before, it's doubled now.

If I can go on to win half as much as he has done, I'll be happy,' he said.

He also said he wanted to turn professional right away. His mother would have loved that! Naturally there has been some discussion on the subject. As 2004 proceeds, Daniel is still at school, studying for GCSE examinations. Only after that would we consider taking him out of school and allowing him to concentrate on golf. And if he has progressed and looks like fulfilling his great potential, only then, probably by the age of 17, will he turn professional. As I say to him all the time, 'I'll not hold you back, son.'

Meanwhile, his work with Grandad will intensify. I can play; I can't teach. My father will handle that side of it. It will be a case of Torrance and Torrance and Torrance, as it was that week at St Andrews. The photograph taken on the famous Swilcan Bridge that week of the three generations is already a big favourite, commanding a prominent place in my den.

The following week, another momentous occasion was not allowed to pass without comment.

We were playing the 16th in a fourball match at Sunningdale and Daniel was five foot from the pin in 2.

'Do you know you are two down?' he asked me. I had been concentrating on our match against a couple of friends while he was keeping an eye on Torrance v Torrance.

He eventually won 3 and 2, the first time he had beaten me without receiving strokes and playing from the same tees. Another moment to cherish.

It had been an amazing year. Everywhere I went people mentioned the Ryder Cup. Some wanted autographs, others just to shake my hand. I loved it and I never tire of it. Maybe a couple of times in my whole life have I felt pestered or threatened by people coming up to me like that. I suppose it is a two-way process. My fans have always treated me well because I have treated them the same.

The invitations poured in. I had been made an MBE in 1996 for my services to European golf. It was a terrific honour, a great day I shared with my son Daniel and daughter Phoebe. You are only allowed two children at Buckingham Palace. Her Majesty the Queen performed the ceremony, as she did in 2003 when I received the OBE. This time I took my two beautiful girls, Phoebe and Anouska. The Queen remembered and made a few knowledgeable comments about golf.

We talked again later in the year when I was invited to an intimate lunch for eight at Buckingham Palace, with the Queen and the Duke of Edinburgh. The food and wine were great. Anouska was more thrilled that I would have been allowed to stroke the corgis while sitting at the table. I told the Queen cheekily that my daughter loved dogs and that she wanted me to take the corgis home with me.

The *BBC Sports Personality of the Year* ceremony has always been one of my favourite events. We won team of the year in 2002. When I was called to receive the trophy, though, there was a surprise. Paul McGinley, who was in Mexico representing Ireland in the World Cup, had arranged for the ball he used to hole the winning putt to be presented to me by Ian Woosnam live on television.

Ray Roche, a Dublin jeweller friend of Paul's, prepared a beautiful mahogany base on which the names of all the players in the team were engraved. 'I know it was my ball and my putt,' said Paul, 'but I felt we owed so much to Sam as an inspirational captain. I wanted him to have the ball as a token of how much he meant to the players.'

I was touched by his generosity, deeply moved that Paul should want to give me something associated with one of the greatest achievements of his career. But the reality was that it was his moment. If anyone appreciated that, it was me. I had been there. I made the same putt he had. I knew how special it was. It was for him to keep, not me.

That was brought home to me even more when out of the blue my parents were contacted by a chap in Perth about the Titleist 1 ball I was playing when holing the putt to win the Ryder Cup in 1985. For more than 17 years I never had a clue where it was, if indeed it still existed. There was no thought given at the time to keeping it as a memento or auctioning it for charity, the fate of so much memorabilia these days. It just disappeared in the confusion.

I was to learn all those years later, however, that my caddie, Brian Dunlop, had given it to a woman standing by the green. Barbara Macleod had attended the event with her husband, John, as her son, Nigel, was to reveal. He had inherited the keepsake on her death. The ball had been mounted, along with a copy of my autograph. Then one day in December 2002 he read an article in the newspaper that prompted him to watch the *BBC Sports Personality of the Year* programme on television.

'I had not known what to do with the ball. Now, I knew,' he told my mother.

Considering what the Ryder Cup meant to me, it was like the return of a long-lost brother. Now that it was back in my possession, I knew I could not keep Paul's ball.

The dinner at which I received honorary membership of Sunningdale Golf Club seemed like the perfect opportunity to return it to the rightful owner. Paul practises at Sunningdale, as does Darren Clarke. I knew that both would be at the dinner. Preparations were made and the deed was done.

'It's your ball, Paul,' I said as I presented it back to him. 'I've just got my ball back and I know how special it is.'

As great as the aftermath of the Ryder Cup was, I knew that decisions about my future would eventually have to be made. There was a period in my life when I was really looking forward to putting my feet up, playing a few events, doing some television commentating and some course design. Let life unfold. As I said, I am essentially a lazy bugger, albeit one who can be pretty determined once I put my mind to something.

I never felt any sense of anti-climax throughout 2003, though it is certainly true that I took a while to get going. Refocusing on the next challenge – if there was to be one – took some time. There were also a few fitness problems, principally a knee injury that required surgery. Consequently, I played only nine European Tour events during the year and missed the halfway cut in six of them. I was, therefore, a bit underdone, not as prepared as I would have liked to have been, when I reached 50 and made my debut in Seniors' golf.

My first tournament in August was happily in Scotland. I loved it. They treated me like a king, to be honest. The Duke of Roxburgh, Guy to his many friends in golf, was a magnificent host. My game was anything but magnificent. I would have loved to have been sharper but it was not to be. I did not play at all well, though a second-round 67 over the Roxburgh helped me finish tied for 15th.

My second outing was at Woburn, a happy hunting ground for me throughout my career. I played beautifully and finished fourth without, as they say, holing a thing. I had my chances to win but my putting let me down. It had taken just two weeks for me to fall in love with Seniors' golf. I did not find it any more relaxed. It was still competitive. You are still trying to make a living, still trying to do what you do best, still trying to beat the guys you are playing against.

By the time I left the main Tour I was beginning to feel a little bit of an outsider. I could walk up to 70 per cent of them, say hello and shake their hand. I knew most of them but, other than golf itself, I did not have a great deal in common with many. It was simply a generation thing. I knew 99 per cent of the guys on the Senior Tour from days gone by. It was wonderful to see them and play with them again. It was like a huge school reunion.

Yet already I was looking across the pond. In the United States, the big five-0 has for a long time been viewed as a licence to print money for quality golfers who can sustain their form into middle age and beyond. The 'fat bellies', as Lee Trevino christened senior golfers in the early days, have slimmed down as the purses have grown fatter. The Champions Tour offers prize money I could never have dreamed of when turning professional in 1971.

Tom Watson, the leading player in 2003, won $1.85 million in just 14 events at an average of more than $132,000 per outing. The 2004 schedule declared total prize money of $52.5 million for 30 official events. These represent the kind of figures that are hard to resist for someone whose life has been professional tournament golf.

The situation is different in Europe. Not bad, just different. It is as if Europe is travelling along the same road, only hundreds of miles behind. The Champions Tour in America compares with the European Seniors Tour in exactly the same way as the USPGA Tour compared with the European Tour when I started as a teenager. It takes time. Europe will become bigger and better as the calibre of golfers improves and sponsorship increases. It happened on the main tour, it will happen on the Seniors' tour.

I have always been a home bird, someone happy to support European golf. But there was a financial imperative in trying to play over there. My former mates from the European Tour who were playing in America – people like Roger Davis, Eamonn Darcy and Des Smyth – were all saying the same thing. 'You have got to get yourself here,' they said. They told me with almost child-like enthusiasm about the condition of the courses, the good climate and the great prize money. I noticed that Des won a few dimes short of a million dollars in 2003. My own experience hinted at what was possible. Sponsors' invitations allowed me to play two tournaments in the USA towards the end of the year, the idea being that a victory would make me exempt for 2004.

That would have been too much to hope for. But I performed creditably in finishing tied for fourth place in my US debut at the Constellation Energy Classic in Baltimore. Although I managed only joint 29th at the subsequent event in Texas, I pocketed $100,000 from just two tournaments. The experience was awesome. It was great to have the sun on your back, something you appreciate more at the age of 50. Great too to be able to sit on a buggy and relax between shots. That's my laziness for you. I know a traditionalist like me who grew up playing links golf should frown on the use of buggies, but I confess that I love them. Imagine if I had been able to use them up and down the hills at Routenburn when I was growing up. Now that would have been awesome.

My mind was made up. I was ready to make the biggest bet of my life – $100,000 on myself. A $100,000 gamble to win an amount to be determined.

To explain: I was contracted to play in the UBS Cup,

formerly the Warburg Cup, a 12-a-side match between golfers from the United States and the Rest of the World. There was a guaranteed minimum of $100,000 per team member, with the winners each collecting $150,000. But the event clashed with Qualifying School for the Champions Tour. I was set on trying to gain my card to play in America. By withdrawing from the UBS, I was effectively forsaking at least $100,000.

First I had to get through regional qualifying, a step into the unknown for me. Fortunately, I had never been to Q-school in 32 years as a pro. But I know plenty who say it is the worst experience of any professional golfer's life. You are given six courses to choose from at regional level, with no guarantee of being allocated your first pick. I was lucky in being sent to my first choice.

I had selected Disneyland's Magnolia at Lake Buena Vista, Florida. John O'Leary and I had played a better ball tournament there in the dim and distant past. Dim to the point of total darkness, as it transpired. I never remembered a single hole, not one. But it was a good, tough course.

My biggest concern when nervously teeing off early in the day was simply not knowing how good the other guys were going to be. There were 17 spots available from a field of around 90. I opened with a 71, which looked a lot better as I studied the scoreboard. A 94 caught my eye, then an 89, an 88 and an 86. I felt a lot happier. By the fourth round I could have carded an 87 and still gained one of the places available. As it was, a 73 gave me fourth position.

The week in between regional and final qualifying was spent with my great friend David Feherty at his home in Dallas. I relaxed by attending my first rodeo and an ice hockey match. But I also golfed every day, including some pretty ferocious but highly competitive money matches against Lanny Wadkins at the exclusive Preston Trail Club. Lanny remains one of the toughest guys to beat when a few dollars are at stake.

I stayed in the USA but John, my caddie, went home. Having a friend carrying my bag was just not working. I thought it would and I was wrong. I needed a professional caddie, one who could help me with my yardages and on the greens. As luck would have it, Lance Ten Broeck – 'Last Call Lance' as he is known – had become available after the recent ending of a lengthy association with Jesper Parnevik. We had played together in Asia years ago and, of course, knew each other from the Ryder Cup. As a former pro, he knew the game inside out. As a member of the Eagle Trace Club at Coral Springs, he was also very familiar with the venue for the Qualifying School.

Our first practice round together offered a glimpse of what he could do for me. I watched as he paced off the distance from my pitch mark to the front of the green. He repeated the same procedure every hole for four days so that he could find out, then confirm, how far I hit every club. I had never seen a caddie do that before. I was mightily impressed.

Lance was also great at reading the lines of putts. Only Billy Foster of all my caddies had ever been allowed to do that for me. Just hitting the ball where I was told and not having to worry about the subtle borrows eased some of the pressure I was feeling. There were 110 players fighting for the seven cards that gained entry to every tournament in 2004.

They had taken us to a devil of a course with water on 14 holes and no respite from first to last. I could not remember feeling so nervous. In fact, my hands were shaking quite badly before my opening tee shot. There was very little improvement in that area all day. For the first time in years my hands were wobbling when I swung the putter back. It must have looked as if I had been on the batter. That was not the case. I had prepared thoroughly and drank very little. Alcohol that is. But I was downing about three large bottles of Diet Coke a night in my hotel bedroom, and umpteen coffees throughout the day.

I realised in time what was making me shake. I was overdosing on caffeine. A switch to water and decaff steadied my hands. The nerves remained but I was feeling great. I played really well, as illustrated by one of my stats. By the end of the week I had missed only seven greens in regulation. And I missed a play-off by a single stroke. One more at the end of the 72 holes and I would have been required to go into extra time to gain the seventh and last card. As it was, my rounds of 71, 72, 70, 70 meant that I would be able to cash in my winning betting slip.

It had been a great week for the old stalwarts of the European Tour. Mark McNulty won the Q-school after being chased all the way by my dear friend Mark James. 'Jesse' finished second. I would have no shortage of dining partners throughout 2004.

I hit every fairway and every green during the final round, yet still sweated to the very end. There were no scoreboards and, therefore, no precise information of what was happening. When Vicky Cuming, my hard-working manager, reported to me at the back of the 17th green that I was lying fifth, I worried whether that was before or after the birdie I grabbed there. I knew it was close and that I would have to hold my nerve.

My drive down the last was perfect, while my wedge to about 40-ft behind the hole was a case of safety over bravado.

'We know that putt,' Lance said.

I nodded. I had faced that putt in a couple of money matches during practice. Once again, my preference for playing competitive games for real cash in practice was bearing fruit.

'Good speed,' I shouted to my caddie as the ball was halfway to the hole. It stopped a fraction short and I tapped in for a draining closing 70. The computer revealed that I was tied for sixth and seventh. There were two three-balls still to finish. It turned out that one guy would have to birdie and another hole his second shot at the last for me to fail. But one more stroke would have meant a play-off.

I phoned home to Suzanne and the kids, unable to speak with emotion. I was gone. Yet again in my fortunate life I was as happy as I could be. I had identified the next challenge of my life and I was now in a position to pursue it.

Tournaments offering around $1.6 million every week, three rounds, no cut, 80 players – well, let me loose. It was very exciting, almost like starting all over again; if not another life, then certainly another chapter. I knew I was going to feel homesick and that there would be sacrifices on the family front. But I had resolved to win enough money by the age of 55 so that I would never again have to worry about the prosperity and security of my family.

Using Feherty's house in Dallas as a base to which I could return every Sunday night was going to help. But as I headed out to the USA at the start of February 2004, I had clear targets in my mind. I wanted to be No. 1 – that was what I always wanted to be. I wanted to win a major – that had been my goal when leaving Largs for Sunningdale in what seemed a different world. I wanted to play golf – it has always been what I do.

My plan was to play in America for five years. Who knows, by then there might be a Seniors' Ryder Cup and more crying?

EUROPEAN TOUR VICTORIES

VENUE	DATE	SCORE	MONEY	MARGIN
1976 Piccadilly Medal Coventry GC, Coventry, England	May 12–15	67-72-66-72=277 (-15)	6,000	2
1976 Martini International Ashburnham GC, Pembrey, Wales	June 9–12	69-67-71-73=280 (-8)	2,500	2
1981 Carrolls Irish Open Portmarnock GC, Dublin, Ireland	August 13–16	68-67-69-72=276 (-12)	13,328	5
1982 Benson & Hedges Spanish Open RSHE Club de Campo, Madrid, Spain	Sept 30–Oct 3	71-65-67-70=273 (-15)	8,578	8
1982 Portuguese Open Championship Penina GC, The Algarve, Portugal	November 4–7	71-67-69=207 (-12)	7,000	4
1983 Scandinavian Enterprise Open Sven Tumba G & CC, Ullna, Stockholm, Sweden	June 30–July 3	73-69-68-70=280 (-8)	14,251	1
1983 Portuguese Open Championship Troia GC, Setubal, Portugal	November 3–6	72-73-71-70=286 (-2)	7,500	3
1984 Tunisian Open Championship El Kantaoui GC, Sousse, Tunisia	April 12–15	66-71-75-70=282 (-6)	10,830	1
1984 Benson & Hedges International Open Fulford GC, York, England	August 15–19	63-68-70-69=270 (-18)	20,000	1
1984 Sanyo Open Real Club de Golf, El Prat, Barcelona, Spain	Sept 20–23	71-69-70-71=281 (-7)	16,660	Play-off
1985 Johnnie Walker Monte Carlo Open Mont Agel GC, Monte Carlo, Monaco	June 28–July 1	69-63-62-70=264 (-12)	20,790	1
1987 Lancia Italian Open Monticello GC, Milan, Italy	April 30–May 3	64-68-71-68=271 (-17)	23,507	Play-off

Tournament	Date	Score	Prize	Position
1990 Mercedes German Masters Stuttgarter GC, Stuttgart, Germany	October 4–7	70-65-64-73=272 (-16)	75,000	3
1991 Jersey European Airways Open La Moye GC, Jersey	April 11–14	68-69-69-73=279 (-9)	33,330	1
1993 Kronenbourg Open Gardagolf, Verona, Italy	March 25–28	69-68-73-74=284 (-4)	33,330	1
1993 Heineken Open Catalonia Osona Montanya GC, Barcelona, Spain	April 22–24	71-63-67=201 (-15)	50,000	3
1993 Honda Open Gut Kaden, Hamburg, Germany	June 10–13	68-69-68-73=278 (-10)	83,330	Play-off
1995 Conte of Florence Italian Open Le Rovedine GC, Milan, Italy	May 4–7	69-70-63-67=269 (-19)	61,716	2
1995 Murphy's Irish Open Mount Juliet, Kilkenny, Ireland	July 6–9	68-68-70-71=277 (-11)	111,107	Play-off
1995 Collingtree British Masters Collingtree Park, Northampton, England	Sept 14–17	67-66-68-69=270 (-18)	108,330	1
1998 Peugeot Open de France Le Golf National, Paris, France	June 25–28	64-70-72-70=276 (-12)	83,330	2
2003 Dunhill Links Championship Pro-Am (with Daniel)	September 25–28	Winning score of 251	–	–

WORLDWIDE VICTORIES

1972 Radici Open (Italy), Under-25 Match Play Championship

1975 Zambian Open

1978 Scottish Professional Championship

1979 Colombian Open

1980 Australian PGA Championship; Scottish Professional Championship

1985 Scottish Professional Championship

1991 Scottish Professional Championship

1993 Scottish Professional Championship

TEAMS

Amateur
Scottish Boys' Team 1970

Professional
Ryder Cup 1981, 83, 85 (winners), 87 (winners), 89, 91, 93, 95 (winners), 2002 (Captain)

Alfred Dunhill Cup 1985, 86, 87, 89, 90, 91, 93, 95, (winning team), 99

World Cup 1976, 78, 82, 84, 85, 87, 89, 90, 91, 93, 95

Four Tours World Championship 1985, 91 (Captain, winning team)

Hennessy Cognac Cup 1976 (winners), 78 (winners), 80 (winners), 82 (winners), 84

Double Diamond 1973 (winners), 76, 77

UBS Warburg Cup 2001, 02

Index

Agfa-Gevaert 1971 34
Aitcheson, Willie 85
appearance money 90
Asahi Glass 1991 149
Australia 66–7, 149-50
Australian PGA 1980 66
Azinger, Paul 141, 148; RC 2002
    244, 255, 256, 276, 277,
    285–6, 287, 290

Bagge, Jimmy 43–4
Baker, Stanley 45, 51
Ballesteros, Seve 66, 84–5, 89,
    90, 98, 116, 251-2, 289; RC
    1983 89–90, 96; RC 1985
    108, 109; RC 1989 141; RC
    1991 148; RC 1995 175; RC
    1997 179–80
Bannerman, Harry 23, 50
Barcelona 160
Barnes, Brian 51–2
BBC golf 301
Bean, Andy 117
Beck, Chip 141, 148
Beck, Mary 21
The Belfry 9, 108, 142, 153, 156,
    197, 224–6, 237, 239, 243,
    250, 297
Bell's Scotch Whisky 97
Benson & Hedges 1988 127
Benson & Hedges 2000 157
Benson & Hedges 2003 267
Biggins, Tony 25
Bjorn, Thomas 214; RC 2002
    242, 256, 260, 265; RC 2002

singles 276, 277, 284
Blair, Tony 192, 230
Bognor Regis 40
Brand, Gordon, Jr 114, 117,
    141–2
British Boys semi-final 23
British Caledonian Golfing Lions
    51
British Masters 1996 168
Broadhurst, Paul 149, 296
Brookline 187–91
Brown, Eric 50
Brown, Ken 105
Burrows, Gaylord 62
Bury, Stephen 18
Bush, George, Sen 235–6

caddies 97, 156, 313
Cage, Stuart 167
Calcavecchia, Mark 244, 269,
    276, 284
Callahan, Tom 76
Campbell, Michael 168
Canizares, Jose-Maria 98, 105,
    114
Carnoustie 23, 185
Casey, Paul 210
Champions Tour 315–17
Charles, Bob 132
Chillas, David 23, 61
Cink, Stewart 265, 276, 277, 284
Clark, Howard 91, 105, 107,
    111–12, 114, 167
Clarke, Darren 28, 212–13, 309,
    313; RC 2002 212–13, 240,

241, 242, 246, 248, 250, 256, 257, 258, 260, 262, 265, 266, 270–1; RC 2002 singles 276, 277, 281, 282, 284
Club de Campo 87, 95
Coles, Neil 90
Colombian Open 1979 64
Coltart, Andrew 177, 194, 195, 196, 209
company days 80
Connolly, Billy 128
Conte de Florence Italian Open 1995 166
Corbett, Ronnie 45, 158–9, 251
Cotton, Henry 40, 45, 48, 106
Couples, Freddie 149, 172–5
Craven, Blaise 25
Crenshaw, Ben 89, 118, 185, 188, 191, 279, 302
Cuming, Vicky 319
Currie, Henry 44

Dalglish, Kenny 251
Daly, John 168
Darcy, Eamonn 117–9, 133
Davies, John 78
de Savary, Peter 162–3
DeFoy, Craig 50
Deutsche Bank Open 1996 167
Devetta, Martin 25
Dickson, Bob 50
Double Diamond 1973 50
Dunhill Cup 1985 29, 114–15, 199
Dunhill Cup 1995 177
Dunhill Links Trophy 2001 115, 305–6
Dunhill Links Championship Pro-Am 2003 306–10
Dunlop, Brian 313
Dunlop Masters 1972 40

Duval, David 188, 244, 257, 274, 284, 286, 299

earthquakes 235–7
Elliott, Bill 112
Elliott, Myles 12
Els, Ernie 139
English Open 1989 142–3
Eriksson, Sven Goran 226
European Open 1982 29–30
European Open 1990 137
European Open 1992 29
European Tour 1972 34, 39–45
European Tour 1976 54
European Tour 1982 94
European Tour 1992 157
European Tour 1993 159–60
European Tour 1998 182–4

Faldo, Nick 29, 105, 112, 116, 119; RC 1981 91; RC 1985 105; RC 1989 141, 142; RC 2002 202–5, 206, 241
Fasth, Niclas: RC 2002 196, 215, 259, 260, 266, 268; RC 2002 singles 276, 277, 284, 285–6
Faxon, Brad 172–3
Feherty, David 47, 67–9, 138, 282, 293–5, 317; Asahi Glass Championship 1991 149; English Open 1989 143; RC 1991 146–8
Ferguson, Alex 227
Fitzpatrick, John 25
Floyd, Raymond 76, 89, 98, 105, 107, 114, 140
Fortune, Mrs 27
Foster, Billy 160
France 135, 182–3
Francis, Peter 34

French Open 1998 137, 182–3
French Open 1999 157
Fulke, Pierre: RC 1999 196; RC 2002 214–5, 216, 222, 242, 243, 247, 250, 253, 259, 261, 262, 264; RC 2002 singles 276, 277, 279, 282, 287, 288
Furyk, Jim 259, 265, 287, 289

Gallacher, Bernard 10, 40, 101, 154, 155, 156, 158, 172, 296
Gallacher, Lesley 163–4, 173
Gallagher and Lyle 13
Gallagher's Canyon 34
Garcia, Sergio: RC 2002 105, 208, 209, 212, 226, 237, 241, 242, 246, 250, 257, 260, 261, 262, 265–6, 268, 269–70; RC 2002 singles 274, 276, 281, 283, 284, 292
Gardagolf Golf Club 159
Garland, David 223
Garrido, Antonio 176
Germany 144, 159, 185
Gilder, Bob 98
Gilford, David 155, 296
Ginn, Stewart 81
Goodman, Danny 96
Grade, Michael 35
Gray, Tony 86
Great Britain and Ireland team 1977 86–7
Greater Manchester Open 1977 86, 202
Green, Hubert 105
Gut Kaden 161

Haas, Jay 172, 176
Haegmann, Joakin 193, 216
Harrington, Padraig: RC 2002

214, 241, 242, 246, 250, 259–60, 261–2, 265, 266, 269, 271; RC 2002 singles 276, 284
Hawksworth, John 20
Heineken Open 1993 159
Hennessy 1978 108
Hillside 23
Hoch, Scott 259, 265, 271, 276, 282, 283, 284
Hogan, Ben 47, 179
holes-in-one 94, 121
Holland, David 277
Honda Open 1993 159
Horton, Tommy 53
Huggett, Brian 56, 87, 304
Hughesden, Mike 25, 30
Hunt, Guy 39

In Search of Tiger (Callahan) 76
India 62
International Open 1997 180
Into the Bear Pit (James) 203
Ireland 67, 167, 177
Irish Open 1981 72, 89
Irish Open 1995 167
Irwin, Hale 89
Italy 40, 159, 166

Jacklin, Tony 88, 90, 97, 105, 116–7, 140, 141, 288, 290
Jacobs, John 30, 43, 89–91
Jacobsen, Peter 106, 108
Jaeger, David 63
James, Jane 173–4
James, Mark 96, 143–4, 190, 193, 196, 197, 200, 202–7, 319; RC 1981 90; RC 1993 166; RC 1995 176; RC 1999 184, 190, 217

Jersey European Airways Open 1991 144
Jigger Inn 299, 305
John Player Trophy 1972 40
Jones, Bobby 28–9

Kaunda, Kenneth 54
Kemble, Mike 112, 169
Kennedy, Grace 120
Kenwright, Bill 125
King, Michael 11, 25, 58
Kinsella, Jimmy 40
Kite, Tom 89, 101, 104, 105, 107, 117, 142
Koch, Carin 274
Kronenbourg Open 1993 159

La Manga 63
Laidlaw, Renton 44, 249
Langer, Bernhard 133, 138, 161, 250; RC 1985 105, 107; RC 1987 116, 117; RC 1991 148; RC 2002 208, 212, 226, 241, 242, 246, 252–4, 258, 260, 261; RC 2002 singles 262, 265, 276, 284
Largs 14, 17, 21, 127
Las Vegas 34
Lawrie, Paul 115
Leatham, Trish 27
Lee, Jackie 81
Lees, Arthur 11, 24, 27, 31
Lehman, Tom 175, 187–9
Leonard, Justin 187, 190, 191
Lester, Eric 23
Letters, Jimmy 24, 65
Levy, Laurence 165
Lietzke, Bruce 89
Lilleshall 26
Lineker, Gary 309

Loch Lomond 210
Locke, Bobby 47
London Standard 1987 122
Love, Davis 172, 244, 258, 267, 269, 276, 277, 288
Lu, Mr 42, 118
Lucas, Oliver 78–9
Lyle, Sandy 94–5, 105, 106, 107, 114, 116, 141

Macari, Lou 13
Madrid 63
Madrid Open 1972 40
Maggert, Jeff 172, 176
Maloney, Mike 302
Marr, David 89
Martin, Miguel Angel 85
Martin, Stevie 87
Martini International 1975 55
Mason, Malcolm 156, 160, 167, 211
McAllister, Jim 134
McCleod, Nigel 313
McGinley, Paul 28, 312; RC 2002 196, 213, 216, 237, 242, 247, 259, 261, 266–7, 268, 270; RC 2002 singles 271, 276, 277, 279, 285, 286–7, 290, 300
McKenzie, Angus 33, 34
McKenzie, Gerald 33, 34
McKenzie, Norman 33, 34
McLelland, Doug 40–1, 51, 176
McNulty, Mark 122, 177, 319
medal matchplay 49
Mercedes German Masters 1990 144
Mickelson, Phil 76–7, 223, 224, 244, 259, 261, 264, 269, 274, 276, 282
Miller, Johnny 89
Miller, Mike 160

Mize, Larry 118, 132
Money Lists 90
money matches 78–9
Montgomerie, Colin 29, 47, 55,
    149, 166, 168, 293–4; RC
    1995 171, 172, 177; RC 1999
    189, 197; RC 2002 211–12,
    241, 242, 259, 261, 262, 265,
    266; RC 2002 singles 276,
    281–84, 298
Montgomerie, Eimear 197, 294
Moody, Orville 135
Moore, David 60
Moore, Mary 293
Morecambe, Eric 120
Muirfield Village 115
Murphy's Irish Open 1995 167
Murray, Ewen 23
Muscroft, Hedley 80
My Story (Norman) 58

Nardini, Daniela 13
Nelson, Larry 89
Nicholas, Brother 19
Nicklaus, Jack 42, 47, 52, 56,
    88, 93, 97, 100, 101, 102, 116
Nigeria 60–1
Norman, Greg 30, 58–9, 66, 67,
    80, 199
North, Andy 105, 107, 109–11

Ocona Montanya 160
O'Connor, Christy, Jr 136
O'Connor, Christy, Sr 47, 49
Olazábal, José Maria: RC 1987
    116; RC 1989 141; RC 1991
    147; RC 1995 172; RC 1999
    190–1; RC 2002 208–10
O'Leary, John 44, 63, 69–71,
    80–2

O'Meara, Mark 105, 114, 147,
    191, 304
Oosterhuis, Peter 90, 91
Open Championship 1972 41
Open Championship 1978 185
Open Championship 1981 94–5
Open Championship 1982 134
Open Championship 1996 166
Open Championship 1999 41,
    185
Order of Merit 39; 1976 54;
    1980s 66, 93, 94, 95; 1990s
    29, 157, 166
Osborne, Chris 12

Packenham, Paddy 12
Palmer, Arnold 41, 132
Paramor, John 143, 223, 268
Parnevik, Jesper 237; RC 2002
    208, 209, 210, 215–6, 238,
    259, 262, 265–6, 268, 275;
    RC 2002 singles 276, 277, 288
Pate, Jerry 89, 91
Pate, Steve 155
Pavin, Correy 146
Peete, Calvin 105
Piccadilly Medal 1975 49, 55
Pillage, Derek 51, 80
Pinero, Manuel 53, 105, 107,
    114
Platts, Lionel 80
Platts, Mitchell 191
Player, Gary 29, 47, 304
Poker Million 84
Portmarnock 72, 81
Portuguese Open 1982 95
Portuguese Open 1983 96
press 256, 261, 263
Price, Nick 139
Price, Philip 216, 298; RC 2002
    196, 222–3, 242, 247, 259,

261, 262, 264; RC 2002
singles 276, 277, 279, 282,
283, 284, 285, 287
Price, Sandra 216
pro-am tournaments 44–5
Purdie, David 229–33
putting: broomhandle 132–9,
141, 144–5, 176; practising
135–6;
10-second rule 143; yips 43,
119, 132–3, 138

Radici Open 1972 40
Rafferty, Ronan 149
Rees, Dai 62
Reeves, Vic 77
Rennie, Frank 54
Richardson, Steve 149, 296
Rivero, José 105, 167
Roberts, Loren 175–6
Rocca, Costantino 115, 160,
168, 172
Roe, Mark 309
Rogers, Bill 89, 94
Rose, Justin 210
Rossendale 18
Routenburn Golf Club 11, 152
Royal Calcutta 62
Royal St George's 94
Rudge, Chris 123, 235
Rupert, Johan 306
Russell, DJ 20
Ryder Cup 100–2, 104–5, 139
Ryder Cup 1969 87
Ryder Cup 1979 88
Ryder Cup 1981 89–93
Ryder Cup 1983 97–102
Ryder Cup 1985 10, 65, 103,
104–13, 313
Ryder Cup 1987 115–9
Ryder Cup 1989 139–42

Ryder Cup 1991 146–9, 296
Ryder Cup 1993 85, 151–6
Ryder Cup 1995 171–7
Ryder Cup 1997 179
Ryder Cup 1999 185, 187–98
Ryder Cup 2001 212–17
Ryder Cup 2002 131, 197–8;
captain's picks 207–10;
celebrations 297–9, 305;
closing ceremony 290–2;
congratulatory messages
303–4; disappointments
269–71; Gala Dinner 245–6;
gifts 233–4; good luck
messages 250–1; opening shots
255–7; pairings 246–8,
255–72; the plan 240–1, 258,
274, 277–8; practice 79, 238;
press conferences 248, 249,
256, 261, 263, 270, 273–5;
rules scare 267–8; singles
273–88; spectators 261;
speeches 248–50; the team
210–17, 238–9; Welcome
Dinner 243–4
Ryder, Samuel 293
Ryder, Steve 142

Sandelin, Jarmo 194–5
Sangster, Robert 44
Sant Cugat 95
Sanyo Open 1982 95
Scandinavian Open 1983 96
Schofield, Ken 28, 86, 87, 192,
199
Scotland 306, 314
Scottish Boys team 23
Scottish Open 1995 167
Scottish PGA Championships 48,
64
Senior, Peter 139

September 11 218, 237
Shade, Ronnie 26, 50, 54–5
Skibo Castle 162
Smith, Gary 60
Snead, Sam 47
Snell, David 43
snooker 20–1
Southport 81
Spain 63, 156, 159
Spanish Open 1972 39
Spanish Open 1982 87, 95
Spence, Jamie 150
Sports Personality of the Year 312
Stadler, Craig 96, 105
Stepping Out 124
Steve the Doc 65
Stevenson Institute 20–1
Stewart, Payne 117, 197, 299
Strange, Curtis 105, 114, 117, 141, 142; RC 2002 198, 232, 245–6, 273–5, 291
Sunningdale 11–12, 25–33, 78, 218, 229, 233
Super Mex (Trevino) 76
Sutton, Hal 105, 108, 276, 284, 299
Switzerland 103

Tattersall, Bevin 224, 226
The Taverners 121
Taylor, Dennis 20, 112, 251
Ten Broeck, Lance 318
This is Your Life 34
Thompson, Titanic 75
Thorburn, Cliff 20
Toms, David 244, 259, 269, 276, 284
Top of the Pops 35
Torrance, Anouska (daughter) 128, 164, 304, 312
Torrance, Bob (father) 15, 16, 17, 18, 19, 22, 178, 288, 291, 242–3; as coach 36–7, 134–5; golfing career 17; 'Son's Footsteps' 49
Torrance, Daniel (son) 9, 16–17, 36, 127–30, 149, 288, 303, 312; meets George Bush 235–6; Dunhill Links 306–10
Torrance, June (mother) 14, 16, 18, 24
Torrance, Marion (grandmother) 14, 16
Torrance, Phoebe (daughter) 128, 304, 312
Torrance, Sam: autograph embarrassment 153; best golf 93; Boy International 49; as captain 149, 197–8, 203, 204–6, 228, 295–7; celebrations 112–13, 115–16; character of 9–10; dangerous times 60–1; disqualification 185; drinking 71, 178–9, 181–4, 186; early life 14, 16, 18–19, 20–4; early promise 18; earnings 54, 94, 142, 144, 158, 167, 169; engagement 117, 125; enjoying life 46–8; and family 129–31; fan incident 103–4; French cuisine 70–1; gambling 19–20, 21, 33–4, 72–3, 75–9, 82–5; injuries 151–2, 154–7, 166, 182, 185, 301; James's resignation 206; major championships 145; 'man of God' comment 187, 191–2; marriage 162–5 MBE 312; moustache 93; public speaking 228–32, 248–9, 305; and the

Queen 312; Rookie of the Year Award 1972 40, 45; self-assessment 133–4; Senior's golf 301, 315–20; sleepwalking 151–2; as a spectator 192–3; style 36–8, 46; team golf 49; turns pro 23; unacceptable behaviour 62, 95; as vice-captain 193; weight problems 14

Torrance, Sammy (grandfather) 15–16

Torrance, Suzanne (wife) 117, 120–31, 162–5, 173–4, 181, 273, 280, 285, 286, 287, 289, 291, 294, 297, 300, 305

Townsend, Jay 160

Townsend, Peter 72

Trevino, Lee 15, 41, 64–5, 76–7; RC 1981 89, 91–3, 94; RC 1985 105

Troia 96

Troon 134

Under 25 Match Play 1972 40

Upton, Richard 25

US PGA Tours 57–8

Van de Velde, Jean 193–4, 195–6

Verplank, Scott 244, 260, 265, 276, 284

Virginia Water 11

Volvo Masters 1996 169

Wadkins, Lanny 76, 101, 105, 106, 107, 117–8, 147, 148, 154, 156

Walton Heath 89

Walton, Philip 176

Watson, Tom 89, 101, 132, 138, 140, 141–2, 153–4, 155, 156

Watt, Jimmy 32

Way, Paul 105, 107, 114

Weir, Russell 23

Welsh Open 1980 71

Westwood, Lee 214, 287, 291, 298–9; RC 2002 226, 237, 240–1, 247, 257, 262, 265–6, 268, 269–70; RC 2002 singles 276, 277, 284

Wham, Jimmy 24

Whitehead, Ross 40

Wilkie, Bunny 75, 83

Wilkie, John 75

Wilmslow 86

Windsor, Robert 120

Woods, Tiger 77, 179; RC 2002 244–5, 247, 255–6, 261, 267, 268, 269, 272; RC 2002 singles 273, 274, 275, 276, 282, 288

Woosnam, Ian 20, 114, 116, 138, 144, 200; RC 1983 98–100; RC 1985 105, 107; RC 1987 116, 117; RC 1989 141, 142; RC 1995 172; RC 2002 241, 250

World Cup 1976 52–3

Zambia 53–4, 59–60

Zambian Open 1975 53

Zoeller, Fuzzy 105

Zulu 51